PINK SARI REVOLUTION

'With he̶r̶ ̶usual d̶
expla̶ ̶ ̶a̶
life a g̶o̶ ̶ Hеath Library
of us ca̶ ̶ ̶ne t̶ ̶25 ̶6̶1148
well chang̶ ̶ ̶a̶ the West̶s ̶i̶m̶a̶g̶e̶ ̶o̶ ̶ ̶̶ be
a w̶o̶man in the so̶ ̶called Third World.'
Hanna Rosin, author of *The End of Men: And the Rise of Women*

'Corruption was a fact of life in Uttar Pradesh, and females were too often the victims of the social, political and economic inequalities that defined this Indian "Wild West". But as Fontanella-Khan shows in this lively account, they were not without hope, nor were they without a champion ... As delightful as it is intelligent and important.'
Kirkus Reviews

'This beautifully rendered book is a call to women everywhere to take the world into your hands, to rise and resist.'
Eve Ensler, author of *The Vagina Monologues* and *In the Body of the World*

'A powerful, engrossing portrait of one woman's fight for female empowerment in India. Sampat Pal's extraordinary courage will inspire you, delight you and fill you with hope.'
Sonia Faleiro, author of *Beautiful Thing*

'A maze of political intrigue, personal melodrama and feminist activism unfolds in this account of the Pink Gang ... Fontanella-Khan brings a novelist's pacing to a timely page-turner that is essentially political.'
Publishers Weekly

Pink Sari
Revolution

A Tale of Women and Power in the Badlands of India

AMANA FONTANELLA-KHAN

ONEWORLD

A ONEWORLD BOOK

Published in Great Britain and the Commonwealth
by Oneworld Publications 2013

First published in the United States by W. W. Norton & Company, Inc.,
500 Fifth Avenue, New York, NY 10110

A CIP record for this title is available from the British Library

ISBN: 978-1-78074-312-7
eISBN: 978-1-78074-313-4

Cover design by Christopher Sergio
Interior design by Barbara M. Bachman
Printed and bound in the UK by Page Bros Ltd

Oneworld Publications
10 Bloomsbury Street, London WC1B 3SR, England

Stay up to date with the latest books,
special offers, and exclusive content from
Oneworld with our monthly newsletter

Sign up on our website
www.oneworld-publications.com

For my parents and James, naturally

CONTENTS

. . . .

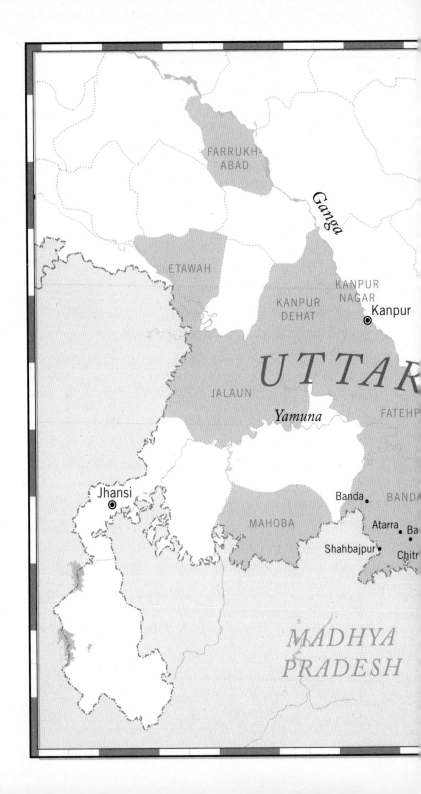

FARRUKH-
ABAD

Ganga

ETAWAH

KANPUR
NAGAR

KANPUR
DEHAT

Kanpur

UTTAR

JALAUN

Yamuna

FATEHP

Jhansi

Banda

BAND

MAHOBA

Atarra   Ba

Shahbajpur   Chitr

MADHYA
PRADESH

AUTHOR'S NOTE AND ACKNOWLEDGEMENTS

. . . .

THIS BOOK IS, FIRST AND FOREMOST, ABOUT SAMPAT PAL AND
her extraordinary group of women. However, a great part
of it also deals with the case involving Purushottam Naresh
Dwivedi and Sheelu Nishad.

The version of events I recount is based on countless
interviews, newspaper articles and press statements related
to the case. That said, it is just one version among many.
Dwivedi staunchly denies any wrongdoing, and there is
much ambiguity about the exact nature of the relationship
between Sheelu Nishad and Rajju Patel.

Much of the dialogue in this book comes from the best
recollections of participants, whom I almost always quote in
verbatim. Unfortunately, it was not always possible to interview both participants in any given dialogue. In those cases,
I relied on their interlocuter's account of what they said
and added a keyword note to attribute the quote. In those
instances in which I was able to obtain transcripts of conversations, I detailed sources in the notes section.

I spent two years (August 2010–August 2012) researching this book, while I still lived in India. One year into my travels to Bundelkhand, I lived with Sampat at her family house in Badausa (in August 2011 and December 2011). I have many happy memories from that time. In those days, we all bathed at the same water hand-pump and I learned by observing others how one washes more or less fully dressed. I spent many evenings with Sampat's daughters and nieces during which we cooked together, cracked jokes, and sang songs around the wood-fire after the power had gone out. Sampat's little nephews were drawn to the accoutrements I had brought with me. They liked to get tangled in my mos- quito net, wear my rubber flip-flops, and were fans of my camping torch (all three of those items are still with them today). I spent much time chatting to Sampat's father-in-law, who loved to eat jalebis first thing in the morning, washed down with a glass of hot chai. Then, of course, there was Sampat, who is one of the most fascinating people I have ever met. Sometimes it felt like she was the one interviewing me. She wanted to know everything from whether there were also rainbows in my country to whether I had a love mar- riage. It was an experience I will always treasure. Mindful of the great trust with which Sampat and her family received me into their lives, I always made a distinction between what was 'on record' (my Dictaphone was blinking red in those moments) and what was not. The primary purpose of my staying with Sampat was not so much to gather concrete anecdotes and quotes that would find their way into the text but, rather, to gain a deeper understanding of Sampat's life – a knowledge that I hoped would inform my interviews and my eventual telling of her story.

Sampat and Jai Prakash Shivare (Babuji) also stayed at my

home in New Delhi for a week (June 2012). Sampat's time in Delhi gave me a glimpse into her growing political clout, reflected in her numerous engagements with party officials when in the capital. Apart from hard work, those days were also filled with good times and, of course, invaluable interviews, for which I am grateful to Sampat.

There is no doubt that, after spending much time with the Pink Gang, I have become sympathetic to Sampat and her women. I also have made financial donations to the Pink Gang, which I hoped would go towards strengthening an organisation that I believed was doing a tremendous job and was in need of financial support. Despite being close to the gang, however, I am very aware of the shortcomings of the organisation and the challenges it faces. I have not hesitated in discussing these frankly in the book. I remain in touch with Sampat and Babuji, who update me on how their work with the gang is progressing.

During my field trips to Bundelkhand, I also spent much time in Shahbajpur visiting Sheelu, who allowed me to use her full name in the book, as well as Santoo and Achchhe. They patiently answered all of my many questions and gave me the access I needed to tell this story. Sheelu and I still speak regularly on the phone too. Ever resilient, Sheelu is moving on with her life with incredible speed.

Here, a note about language should be made too. Over the course of my time in India, I learned enough Hindi to converse on my own with people. Hindi was the language in which all interviews were conducted, except a few with Babuji, whose English is very good. I had several talented interpreters with me during most of my interviews, who are named in the acknowledgements below. Towards the end of my research, however, I was able to go to Bundelkhand and conduct interviews on my own. These interviews, like almost all others, were taped and later translated and transcribed by Cuttingedge Translation Agency, a professional company specialising in that service, for the sake of accuracy.

THERE ARE MANY people without whom this book would never have been possible. First and foremost, I wish to thank Sampat Pal, who gave me so much of herself, and Babuji, for the same reason. I am grateful to everyone I interviewed in Bundelkhand, who shared their life with me and gave me their precious time. I especially want to thank Sheelu Nishad, Achchhe Lal Nishad, Santoo Nishad, Lakhan Upadhyay, Bola Dwivedi, Dr. Khanna, Jai Karan Bhai, Geeta Singh, Deepak Singh, Munni Lal Pal, Munna Pal, Beenu Pal, Nisha Pal, Champa Pal, Prabha Pal, Tirath Pal, Mahima Pal, Seema Pal (Guru-ji), Mitu Devi, and Hemlata Patel. A special thank-you to Amit Tripathi at Hindustan, for providing me with valuable information and his time. Also, I am immensely indebted to Arun Dixit at Sahara Samey TV's Banda bureau for the footage he so generously made available to me.

This book was born out of an article I wrote for *Slate* in 2010. The enthusiasm of Hanna Rosin, the editor of *Slate*'s Double X blog, and her deft editing are largely to thank for the subsequent attention it attracted. I am greatly indebted to Hanna for her expert touch and that she took a chance with me. Were it not for her, it is very likely that this book would never have been written.

I also want to thank the following people for their friendship, advice, and encouragement along the way: Ansie, Maryanna Abdo, Carlo Invernizzi Accetti, Consuelo Accetti, Prashant Agarwal, Helen Alexander, Brendan Allthorpe, Massimiliano Altabella, Sarah Andries, Lucy Archibald, Shyamantha Asokan, Vikas Bajaj, Sheetal Baliga, Paul Beckett, Aadya Bedi, Marina Benedetti, Jessica Bennett, Andre Béteille and the Béteille family, Surya Bhattacharya, Rhys Blakely, Adam Blencowe, Cass Briggs, Emma Broughton, Tom Burgis, Tapas Chakravorty, Chandrahas Choudhury, Antonio Coello, James Crabtree, Elisabetta Cutillo, Giampaolo Cutillo, Matthew Daniels, Siddharth Das, Ruth David, Rodrigo Davies, Will Davies, Xin Chen Davies, Deepali, Augusto Di Giacinto, Friends of Nariman Point, Annette Ekin, Elise Foster Vander Elst, Antonio Fasano, Iona Fergusson, Romano Fontanella and Dolores Fouche, Henry Foy, Arjun Gadkari, Lucy Gadkari, Pia Gadkari, Ratan Gaikwad, Padmaparna Ghosh, Anand Giridharadas, Jeff Glekin, Franka Godina, Michael Edison Hayden, Elliot Hannon, Abhishek Honawar, Andrea Ianetta, Anita Jain, Kaveri Jain, Mehboob Jeelani, Joemon Joseph, Sunitha Joseph, Amy Kazmin, Sid Khanna, Nayantara Kilachand, Erika Kinetz, Sruthijith KK, Shefali Kothari, Priyanka Kripalani and the Kripalani family, Julien Lafleur, Hannah Lambert, Claire Lamont, James Lamont, Joe Leahy, the Le Pain Quotidien staff at Gateway of India, Tanja Lightfoot, Lukhimai Linnebank, Prisca Llagostera, Mr. Lobo, Anand Mahadevan, Krista Mahr, Naresh Kumar Mahrolia, Rakesh Mani, Myles Mayall, Sean McLain, Diah Mehera, Nikhil Mehra, Annalisa Merelli, Susmita Mohanty, Tony Munroe, Neil Munshi, Kishan Negi, Jane Ong, Akshata Pai, Ritesh Pandey, Francesca Parini, Dipesh Pandya, Tom Parker, Akshay Kolse-

Patil, Rohan Patki, Basharat Peer, Dan Pimlott, Snigdha
Poonam, Dino Prevete, Manju Rajan, Prasad Ramamurthy,
Eric Randolph, Anjli Raval, Stéphane Reissfelder, Andrea
Rodrigues, Rosy, Kevin Conroy Scott, David Shaftel, Naina
Shah, Mihir Sharma, Varun Sood, Mehul Srivastava, Mar-
gherita Stancati, Flora Stubbs, Aishwarya Subramanyam,
Priya Tanna, Hannah Thistlethwaite, Ben Thompson,
Heather Timmons, Héloïse Toffaloni, Colin Walker, Aarti
Wig, and Marco Zolli.

When I was out on the field I relied on the help of numerous talented interpreters:

I am deeply indebted to the talented Suresh Panjabi, whose
knowledge of Bundelkhand and rapport with Sampat made
him invaluable to me. Suresh and I spent countless hours
together on the road, visiting small, remote mud villages.
We regularly skipped lunch and returned home after dark –
not ideal in an area known for banditry. Still, Suresh never
complained. He had my back and was fully invested in the
project, knowing that any success in this endeavour would be
his, too. His contributions to this book have been immense,
and I am grateful to him for all of his excellent work.

Unnati Tripathi, a gifted interpreter and researcher, was
also a blessing. She was particularly good at conveying the
nuances of people's speech and was a fountain of insight-
ful observations. Unnati also made numerous astute sugges-
tions about chapters she read and had a thorough, rigorous
approach to work that I admired and benefited from greatly.
I am also grateful to her for throwing herself into the project
so quickly after we met, which was unfortunately only in the
latter stages of research, and for her remarkable ability to hit
the ground running.

Sanghmitra Ghosh, an incredibly talented interpreter and translator, came to my rescue in the final months of my research. Mita turned around audiotapes with incredible speed and efficiency when I went out to Bundelkhand on my own to conduct interviews. Although we never met in person, which I still regret, I always knew I could rely on her, even when the workload was immense. I do not know what I would have done without her.

Towards the end of my reporting, Seema Gurnani, my 'translator in residence', went through hours and hours of audiotapes and video footage from Sahara Samey TV, churning out translations for demanding deadlines. Seema, now a good friend, was indispensable to me, and I am so grateful that she stepped into my life when she did.

Of course, all of this tremendous activity, which drew in so many people, would have been in vain had I not found an editor who believed this story needed to be told. Alane Salierno Mason at W. W. Norton had a compelling vision for the book, and thanks to her it evolved far beyond what I ever expected. I want to thank Alane for her patience, wisdom, and that she granted me the time I needed to complete my writing and research. I am also grateful to Denise Scarfi, an incredibly talented assistant editor at W. W. Norton, who brought sparkle to the manuscript. Also Jessica Purcell, publicity manager at W. W. Norton, for making sure people noticed the fruits of our labour.

There are two superb literary agents who deserve to be thanked. First, Leslie Kaufman, who spotted my story in *Slate* and saw the potential in it. Leslie worked with me in the early months of the proposal before leaving her literary agency for another calling – the medical profession. I remain ever-grateful to her for planting this seed and wish her all the best for her new career. After Leslie's departure I had the good fortune of meeting Sophie Lambert at Conville & Walsh. Sophie is everything an author could want from an agent, and I owe more to her than I can say here. I am particularly grateful for her superb edits of early drafts and her endless ideas and feedback. Her responsiveness over the phone and email kept me sane in what can be a daunting process. At Tibor Jones, my gratitude goes to James Pusey, for his fabulous work on foreign rights, Sophie Hignett, and Kevin Conroy Scott.

Of course, I would not be writing these words right now if it weren't for my exceptional parents, Khalid and Marian Khan. Apart from their love, they placed in my hands one of the greatest gifts of all: a stellar education, without which I would not have been able to embark on this project. As time goes by, my appreciation for their gifts and sacrifices deepens; I hope they are proud of what I chose to do with the opportunities they gave me. My brother and sister, Zahra and Karim, inspired me throughout the time in which I wrote the book. Seeing them pursue their dreams, armed with talents and self-belief, gave me the courage to pursue my own.

And finally, how do I thank my loving husband, James Fontanella-Khan, for all he has done and continues to do? I search for adequate words, but find only one that echoes into time: Anëssuau.

PINK SARI REVOLUTION

NOTHING CAN GO WRONG

SHE ESCAPED TO SAVE HER LIFE.

—Achchhe Lal Nishad

AT DAWN ON AN OTHERWISE QUIET MORNING IN THE TOWN of Atarra, in the back yard of feared liquor don and state legislator Purushottam Naresh Dwivedi, Achchhe Lal Nishad was writhing over the licking tongues of a fire. Two beefy men were dangling the wiry farmer over the flames, one holding him by the arms, the other by the legs. A third man was slapping him around the head and punching him sharply in the ribs.

Achchhe, an illiterate farmer, had not been there long – half an hour at most, though time was hard to measure when you feared being burned alive. He had received the phone call summoning him around four o'clock in the morning on 13 December 2010. The ringing wrenched him out of his fitful, uneasy sleep and caused him to bolt upright in his rope-bed. He knew that bad news awaited him at the other end of the line.

'Wake up, bastard! Your daughter has stolen from the legislator and run away! You come here right now or we'll drag you out of bed ourselves,' the voice on the other end of the line growled. It was one of the politician's men.

The line went dead.

It had been only five days since his daughter, Sheelu, had gone to live at Dwivedi's house – officially the arrangement was that she would be his maid – but Achchhe had felt uneasy about it since the beginning.

After receiving the phone call, Achchhe hastily borrowed a motorcycle from a neighbour, and then with his eldest son, Santoo, the widowed father of four travelled from his mud-hut village of Shahbajpur to the town of Atarra. They bounded down the pot-holed roads for two hours as fast as the motorbike could go; by the time they arrived, dawn was breaking.

Achchhe parked the motorbike on the main road, near the front entrance of the politician's house. A timid man in even the best of times, Achchhe instructed Santoo to wait for him there, and then he proceeded down the dim alleyway that led to the politician's back yard. After what seemed like a long time, Santoo decided to creep around to the back of the house to see what was going on.

When he reached the end of the lane, along the edge of which flowed a stream of sewage, Santoo saw his father. He was being tortured in the centre of the politician's yard, which sat well shielded from prying eyes.

'Your daughter is a *thief*. Is that why you left her at the legislator's house?' one of the musclemen bellowed, as Achchhe squirmed over the flames.

Santoo silently watched his father snivel and plead before the men.

'It wasn't my idea – the *vidhayak* said she should stay here,' Achchhe whimpered, referring to the legislator.

'And it was the *vidhayak*'s idea for her to rob him also?' one of the henchmen shouted back.

'You have a hand in this. You told her to steal!' another one barked, slapping Achchhe around the head.

'No I didn't! Come see my house!' Achchhe cried out desperately.

At this they dropped Achchhe next to the fire with a thud. Kicking him, they said, 'Get up! Go to the car! Now we'll see what you have in your house or not. Don't you tell us lies!'

They dragged Achchhe and Santoo, who had been spotted by the men, into a black Scorpio jeep and retraced the same route father and son had taken in the predawn darkness.

When they arrived at Achchhe's home, the politician's men crashed cooking pots, banged doors, but found nothing. Cursing loudly, they turned Achchhe's house upside down. Some of the other villagers stayed in their houses, while those who were already outside slipped away and out of sight.

'This bastard thinks he can hide his loot from us, but we'll show him!' one of the men shouted. Achchhe and Santoo were bundled into the car once again and delivered to the Atarra police station.

'Lock up these dogs,' the men told the police officers. 'They have dared to steal from us!'

Though they hadn't been charged, Santoo and Achchhe would later claim that they were locked in a cell by obliging police officers. 'We'll slice off your asses,' one of the policemen allegedly hissed through the bars.

Finally, after several long, anguishing hours, the politician's men came to pick them up. 'Okay, you can let them out now,' they ordered the police, who opened the cell door. No documents exist recording their confinement.

The henchmen took father and son back to the politician's house, and there Dwivedi informed them that his men had found Sheelu and were going to take her to the police station. When Achchhe and Santoo asked to see her, the men threatened them with another beating and ordered them to go home.

Achchhe ignored their warnings and went to the police station anyway, but the police turned him away too, as he had feared they would. 'I was not able to talk to the girl. They didn't allow me to meet her. . . . They said that my daughter is as good as dead and that I should just leave now. The inspector said, "I will break your legs if you don't leave right away,"' Achchhe would later say.

Achchhe and Santoo rode back home for the second time that day, sick with fear and at a loss of who could help them. The villagers in their community had not stood up for Achchhe and Santoo when the politician's men were threatening them, but Santoo did not blame the villagers. 'In Shahbajpur, all are poor people, who can help? All of them are farmers who only eat what they get from the earth,' he later said.

As the fragile structures of support and justice that he had relied on crumbled around him, Achchhe considered joining the bandits. Outlaws have historically hidden in the ravines and forests surrounding Achchhe's village, attracting men who have not received justice through the state and have taken up arms instead.

He might well have done so had not, quite unexpectedly, another solution presented itself.

CHAPTER ONE

A ROSE IN THE BADLANDS

EVEN GOD CAN'T CONTROL CRIME IN UTTAR PRADESH

—TIMES OF INDIA *headline*

WINTER MORNINGS IN BUNDELKHAND ARE TEETH-CHATTERING, body-stiffening affairs. In homes that are designed to stay cool in the blistering summer months, even the faintest warmth – such as the kind that resides in a blanket heated by your body overnight – flees in an instant. Getting out of bed is the hardest part. In uninsulated brick houses, an insidious dew-damp chill lingers on the polished concrete floors, clinging to the soles of your bare feet.

Sampat Pal was unflinching in the harsh cold. On the morning of 14 December 2010, like all other mornings, the commander in chief of the Pink Gang rose at dawn and trod from her two-room office to the courtyard in the centre of her landlord's house, to bathe.

She grabbed the cold steel lever of the hand pump and thrust it up and down, causing the metallic, hair-raising sound to echo against the chilled walls. A few seconds later, water gushed forth into an old paint bucket. When it was full to the brim, she dunked a small plastic beaker into the water and poured it over her brown, goose-fleshed body.

Sampat Pal barely noticed the biting cold. Her thoughts, like a tenacious hound, were digging over the details of a suspicious story that had been brought to her attention the day before. One of her district commanders, Geeta Singh, had told Sampat that her brother-in-law, Suraj Singh, had come to ask Geeta for help.

Suraj worked at a small shoe shop located near the house of Purushottam Naresh Dwivedi, a member of the Legislative Assembly in the state of Uttar Pradesh. As a result, Suraj was an acquaintance with the politician's son, Mayank, who had in the past invited Suraj to their home. Suraj had recently heard that a mysterious girl was living there. Shortly afterwards, he saw a girl taken out of Dwive-di's house and shoved into a police van. 'She's stolen from the *vidhayak*'s house,' people told him, but Suraj felt that something fishy was going on, so he alerted Geeta, who in turn informed Sampat.

When Sampat is deep in thought, her eyes, unusually virescent and specked with hints of gold and amber, narrow. Her feathery eyebrows, which curve upwards slightly in the middle when at rest, plunge south. This, coupled with her unconscious tendency to poke the tip of her tongue out when pursuing a thought, caused her, in moments like these, to resemble a child busily working out demanding arithmetic calculations in her head.

'None of this is true!' Sampat said to herself, rinsing the soap bubbles off her body with a beaker of tepid water. 'How could a girl steal from a politician? Who could she be? A maid? A lover?'

Sampat had good reasons for being suspicious. In Uttar Pradesh, India's Wild West, more than a fourth of the elected representatives in the Legislative Assembly had been charged with criminal offenses. Nineteen per cent had serious charges pending against them, including attempted murder, rape, extortion, and kidnapping. Sampat, fired up now, rushed to get out of the house. When short of time, Sampat hastily wraps herself in her sari, and if it is winter, she throws on a knitted cardigan to keep the cold at bay. After dressing, she grabs her comb and rigorously drags it through her shoulder-length black hair, working out the dripping knots and tangles until it is smooth. Most days she gathers her hair in a damp ponytail and, giving it one quick twist, clips it into place with a metal barrette. With that, the precious few moments that Sampat has for herself every day between the toilet and the bucket bath are over. Wiping the sleep from her eyes for the final time, Sampat then marches outside in her webbed toe socks and rubber-soled flip-flops – her usual winter footwear – to face the day.

SAMPAT'S PATIO OVERLOOKS Bisanda Road – so-called because it leads to the nearby town of Bisanda – which is one of the main thoroughfares in Atarra. The haphazardly arranged town, with a population of 10,700, is still largely undeveloped: part rural village, with its pockets of simple mud huts. The traffic on Bisanda Road is composed of trundling, garishly painted trucks, tricycle rickshaws with their steel bells ringing, wandering cows, and people carrying produce in woven palm-leaf baskets carefully balanced on their heads. A low cloud of dust, kicked up by this endless to-and-fro, hovers perpetually over the ground.

On winter mornings, mist often lingers on the far end of the street outside Sampat's office, and the air is scented by the acrid smell of burning plastic waste, garbage bonfires being a means of both rubbish disposal and heat generation during the dreary winter months. The street scene in front of Sampat's office is as bleak as the smell. The boxlike brick homes and family-run stores on Bisanda Road resemble auto workshops, despite the fact that the buildings are painted in a cheery assortment of pastel colours: mint green, powder blue and candy-floss pink. All these crude, windowless struc-tures have metal shutters running down the front of them, adorned with hand-painted advertisements for unglamorous products such as Fevicol, India's largest brand of adhesives. Every morning, these shutters rumble upwards and reveal small shops selling plastic tubes for irrigation, tractor tyres and plywood.

Atarra is enveloped on all sides by unpredictable, drought-prone farmland where gaunt men wearing *dhoti* loincloths and vests are silhouetted by the sun as they bend over to pull weeds by hand or arduously manoeuvre the oxen ploughing the fields. Every year, farmers pray for a good monsoon rain-fall so that masoori rice seedlings, chickpea, split red gram, wheat and yellow-flowering mustard will grow. When rain-fall is particularly low, waves of suicides by indebted farmers sweep the region. Too poor to pay back money owed for expensive insecticide when crops fail, many farmers end up, as a way out, drinking the very chemicals that plunged them into debt. There are some parts of Bundelkhand, the region where Atarra is located, where entire villages are indebted to loan sharks as a result of the droughts.

For all the dreariness of Bisanda Road that morning, Sampat felt a certain pride when she looked at the road, for it did not exist before her arrival here in 2005. Before, a rocky, rutted path made the axles of wooden carts jolt out of their wheels and doubled the journeying time of anyone who took it. 'See this road?' people in Atarra will say. 'It's thanks to Sampat Pal that it got laid.' One day in 2006 she and a group of disgruntled women had convened on the road and, with wooden hoes in their hands, proclaimed loudly, 'This is a road, what? Looks like a field to me! Come on, let's grow vegetables here, at least we can eat them!' They started sowing seeds, tilling the stony dirt road and blocking the traffic. Passersby stopped and stared. People got off their carts, or gearless Atlas bicycles, to get a better look. Sampat had called the district magistrate to show him the state of the roads and made him make a promise in front of the crowds: 'Yes, Sampat-ji. We'll fix the road. Definitely.'

Her gang of women, who wore striking pink sari uniforms and carried pink-painted sticks, had made their first public appearance that day. The local journalists who covered the event christened them the Gulabi Gang, Hindi for the 'Pink Gang'. At the time, they numbered but a few dozen. By 2008, however, there would be about twenty thousand members, making the gang double the size of the Irish army and eight times larger than the estimated number of al-Qaeda operatives in Afghanistan.

'Now I am so *feh-mas*,' Sampat likes to say, using the imported English word in a thick accent and spreading her arms out wide to demonstrate the scale of her notoriety. A friend of Sampat's says that in just a few years she had shot, to use his expression, '*from zeero to heero*'.

SAMPAT'S OFFICE, EFFECTIVELY the headquarters of the Pink Gang, as it has become known in English, is a windowless affair on the ground floor of a two-storey brick house. It is also next to where her son-in-law once had a small doctor's clinic.

Though Sampat calls this her 'office', it is devoid of desks, computers or anything else you would expect to see in a place of work. If it weren't for the loudhailer lying on one of the shelves, a quick look into the clean-swept space wouldn't suggest that anything out of the ordinary happens there.

Sampat's front door opens onto a small roofed patio, which is shaded from the sun and is popular with mosquitos. Most days, it is on this small patch of concrete that Sampat receives a steady trickle of aggrieved parties – men and women – who start arriving shortly after dawn and continue bringing their problems until nightfall. Much like patients in a doctor's waiting room, they sit with hopeful faces on the flimsy plastic chairs and *charpoys*, rope-beds, that are huddled together on the patio. Some clutch badly photocopied documents in their hands – things like police reports, property deeds or marriage certificates (which are useful when men take on a different wife and kick out their previous spouse, denying her any rights). Occasionally, women come directly after their husbands have beaten them, blue bruises burgeoning under their eyes and split lips still throbbing and raw.

Often, Sampat, whose days are filled with visits to the police station, protests outside the courts, and trips with women to the hospital, is out when these people arrive (it is rare for anyone to make an appointment in advance), so they either wait or come back another day – few have nine-to-five jobs, making their movements and plans fluid.

That, in fact, was the reason why Sampat, a woman in her late forties, moved out of her family house in the nearby town of Badausa, where her husband lives with four of her children: her family's domestic life was being upended by the continuous to-and-fro of people with tearful stories.

In a place like Atarra, it is highly unusual for a woman to live apart from her family, but Sampat has a way of making exceptions to all the rules that normally apply. That is also how she gets away with sharing her room with her male colleague, Jai Prakash Shivhare. A former high-school teacher turned social activist, Shivhare is an exceedingly gentle man. He has cropped silver hair that contrasts appealingly with his swarthy skin; heavy eyelids, which always look like they are going to close for a nap; and a soft, sleepy voice. Sampat calls this faithful companion who rarely leaves her side 'Babuji', a respectful appellation reserved for older men and fathers – and a good title to use if you want to deflect gossip.

SAMPAT AND BABUJI moved into her Atarra office in 2005, when they were both small-time social workers. In those days, Sampat and Babuji would wake up at the crack of dawn; eat a meagre breakfast, often just a *chapatti* – the flat, unleavened bread – and a raw onion with some green chilli paste; and cycle to the nearby hamlets located among the vast rice paddies surrounding Atarra. In these hamlets she and Babuji would organise 'self-help groups', a government-sponsored scheme whereby women pool small amounts of money in order to qualify for a government loan. Sampat had worked as a facilitator for the government's program since 2003, when she started an NGO, the Tribal Women Upliftment and Empowerment of Women Organisation, for that purpose. The government believed that self-help groups could bring millions of families above the poverty line. It was over the course of that year that Sampat would transform one of her many self-help groups into what would become a nascent vigilante organisation.

Few parts of the country were as badly in need of justice as desolate Bundelkhand, located in the southwestern frontier of Uttar Pradesh, India's largest state. Monolithic Uttar Pradesh (which means 'Northern State') has just under 200 million inhabitants, surpassing the population of Brazil. Indeed, if it were a country, it would be the fifth most populous one in the world. But it would also be the poorest; food scarcity there is more severe than in sub-Saharan Africa. In addition, Bundelkhand is one of the most crime-ridden areas of Uttar Pradesh, as it is (and has been) the home of some of the country's most notorious bandits, who often take the law into their own hands after not receiving justice. Many murder their enemies and then spend a lifetime looting villages to provide for themselves while on the run. It is a common sight to see men casually carrying rifles slung over their shoulders. It is for reasons like these that the Indian government has declared Bundelkhand among the most 'backward' places in the country and, by extension, the world. Vast swathes of Uttar Pradesh are widely considered, even by the government, to be 'lawless'.

Bundelkhand's rocky, uneven landscape, with its bleached-out skies and naked horizon, evokes a place of scant hope. Its muted palette of burnt wheat, ochre, cow-dung brown and ash-grey is relieved only by the greenery from the rice paddies and the abundant tamarind, mahua and sheesham trees. Traversing the land, one encounters apt metaphors for Bundelkhand's harshness: a carcass of a stallion devoured by feral dogs in a roadside ditch, a scarecrow crowned with a horned bull's skull, a farmer relentlessly whipping an emaciated mule.

Babuji and Sampat shared many long rides together on their co-owned, rusty bicycle as they passed through this landscape on their way to nearby villages. It is easy to picture them: Babuji in his cotton tunic and Sampat seated sideways on the back of the bicycle, her sari fluttering in the wind. From a distance, they could look like husband and wife, their conversation like conjugal chatter. It was not so. As they cycled under the searing sun, they spent hours pondering questions like 'How do we get women out of their homes?' or, more fundamentally, 'How do we make a better society?' It was all they ever spoke about.

'Women live in slavery,' Sampat would conclude after their daylong discussions. She hoped that maybe their self-help groups would help women achieve financial independence and, most importantly, freedom.

ONE OF THE HAMLETS in which Sampat and Babuji started their most dedicated self-help group was Uraiya Purva, near where their landlord owned twelve and a half hectares of land. Although Sampat had been setting up self-help groups since 2003, and had groups functioning across the district of Banda, where she lived, it was in Uraiya Purva that Sampat found her most committed members. The proximity of Uraiya Purva to Atarra – it was only a five-minute bike ride away – was one of the reasons for the success of the group she started there. It contained the women who would, eventually, become the first members of the Pink Gang.

There were no toilets in Uraiya Purva, just a hole in the exterior walls of each hovel, out of which effluvia flowed into grey rivulets of sewage that ran along the narrow dirt paths in the village. There was one hand pump, donated by missionaries, from which villagers drew bathing and drinking water. When Sampat and Babuji used to visit the women, there was never anywhere to sit – there was not a single chair in Uraiya Purva – so people simply squatted or dragged their *charpoys* out of the house to sit on and listen to what Sampat had to say.

Sampat is a gifted public speaker who uses effective techniques to seize the attention of even the most sun-lazed farmer for long stretches of time. These techniques involve prodding the people seated next to her, swivelling her head around suddenly and asking listeners rhetorical questions, looking them straight in the eyes when they least expect it, and clapping her hands loudly to bring a point home. If you were to watch Sampat from a distance, out of earshot, you might be able to gauge every flickering emotion within her by watching her exaggerated expressions – the red-hot anger in her scowl, the happiness in her child-like grin and the surprise in her leaping eyebrows. Her expressiveness is what makes Sampat an extraordinary actor and impressionist, a skill that comes in handy during her lively stories about right and wrong.

Sampat's expansive body language is matched by an

equally loud, attention-grabbing voice and *force* of speech –
one almost feels that the power at which her words cata-
pult towards you could, hypothetically, be measured with
the Beaufort wind scale. The sizeable gap between her two
front teeth makes the impression of her speech even more
dramatic. She is for ever speaking in capital letters – bold,
underlined capital letters – followed by numerous exclama-
tion marks. Her voice booms out even when at home, or
when communicating on her brick-sized Nokia, into which
she is for ever shouting orders, advice and admonishments. It
is no wonder that the sustained exertion of her vocal chords,
and the many years of addressing crowds of women sitting
cross-legged under the shade of banyan trees, have permanently roughened her voice, which has a warm, raspy ring to
it and is often hoarse.

In spite of Sampat's public speaking prowess, it took
patience to convince women who had not made independent
financial decisions before to contribute to a collective fund
from which they could borrow money. Some people would
say, 'I don't even trust my own brother! How can we trust
you?' Sampat would respond by explaining that to withdraw
money from the joint savings account would require at least
ten signatories, and that each self-help group would have a
treasurer, secretary and president to oversee the money matters. Babuji's response was more poetic. 'Without faith, the
world cannot continue,' he would implore. 'Thousands have
died before you. Why are you breathing? Every minute you
run the risk of dying, so how can you say you have no faith?'

Babuji would bring a sophisticated flourish to the discussions. The oldest of eight children, he has a bachelor of arts in
English and sociology from the Atarra Degree College and

so is significantly more educated and knowledgeable than Sampat, who, like most people in Bundelkhand, speaks no English and communicates in either Hindi or Bundelkhandi. Babuji's father, though a farmer, was 'the most educated man in the village. He was eighth passed,' Babuji says, referring to the fact that his father left school around age thirteen, after finishing year eight. When Babuji was growing up, his mother, a devout Hindu, encouraged him to memorise passages from religious texts and recite them to her after dinner. As an adult, Babuji has in his memory hundreds of pithy sayings he learned from many places, from the Mahabharata to Dale Carnegie's *How to Win Friends and Influence People*, a translated version of which he had bought in the city of Kanpur. Babuji has a habit of quoting maxims and proverbs out loud several times a day and is known to illustrate his arguments with parables and cautionary tales from folk stories. It is also normal for him to pepper everyday, casual conversation with pronouncements like 'Nostradamus said the twenty-first century will belong to women' and 'Although Gandhi only weighed forty kilograms, he shook the world'.

When Babuji drifted too far into the clouds during the self-help group meetings, Sampat would steer the conversation back down to a practical level so as not to lose the attention of the women. She is always the one with her feet firmly on the ground, anchored, perhaps, by the weight of leadership that rests heavily on her shoulders. It is she who has the courage to stand up to the police, to abusive husbands, even to bandits – Babuji does not. 'He is the first to disappear when there is trouble. He gets very scared!' a friend remarks teasingly.

MOST OF THE WOMEN in Uraiya Purva are aged widows, left behind by younger generations who have migrated to India's bursting cities to seek livelihoods for themselves. Historically, widows are among the most mistreated of Indians; this is the country of *sati*, the now-outlawed custom in which widows were expected to throw themselves onto the blazing funerary pyres of their husbands; untold numbers were pushed into the flames if they did not willingly end their lives. Bundelkhand, a region the size of Belgium, was a stronghold of the *sati* tradition, so much so that in the novel *Around the World in Eighty Days*, Jules Verne's character Jean Passepartout saves a young woman from a *sati* death when he is passing through the region. Now, though immolation is no longer the fate that awaits widows in Bundelkhand, their lives are often extinguished slowly through neglect and abandonment.

'All have left. Only I am here,' said Kodia Dai, a toothless septuagenarian who would go on to become one of the Pink Gang's long-standing members. There was an upside to having been left behind, though – having to fend for themselves, the forgotten women of Uraiya Purva had no meddling in-laws dictating what they should do – they were free, in the winter of their lives, to live as they pleased. The women in Uraiya Purva agreed to take part in the self-help group, and so it was formed, earning Sampat and Babuji an initial government commission fee of two thousand rupees – approximately twenty pounds – which they received every time they successfully set up a self-help group. This fee was divided equally between Sampat and Babuji. As facilitators, the two could earn an additional eight thousand rupees, which was paid out in four instalments, if their group fulfilled all of its obligations and government-set targets along the way. Soon after they started working together, Sampat and Babuji decided, 'Whatever we have, even if it's just one *chapatti*, we'll split it between us.'

In exchange for the government commission, organisers of self-help groups were required to convene the members for monthly meetings, which included lessons on personal finance and entrepreneurship. Sampat and Babuji touched on these matters, but they customised their meetings to suit their own mission: equality and justice for women, the lower castes and the poor. Sampat spoke in her booming voice about various problems she had faced in her life: marrying at age twelve, struggling with a demanding mother-in-law, being uneducated. She talked about the domestic violence she had seen in her life – like her neighbour who used to beat his wife incessantly – and how women should rise up and fight together. 'If we unite, then we will be strong!' she told them, thrusting a clenched fist into the air.

Because of Sampat's strong personality, and her record of helping others, it wasn't long before the women of Uraiya Purva started coming to Sampat with their problems, which were plentiful. Some complained about the lack of a road leading to Uraiya Purva. Others, like Kodia and her friend Lungi Dai, needed help getting pension cards, which the official in charge was refusing to give them until they paid a bribe; without the cards they were going hungry. Sampat started mobilising the women in the self-help group to act collectively in response to these problems. She galvanised the

women, who until then had never taken part in any protests, to march together to confront government officials, to
demand better roads and bribery-free bureaucracy.

In the beginning, officials would deride Sampat and her
cohorts. 'Just *who* are you?' they would ask, with a con-
temptuous sneer whenever the women showed up at police
stations and ration distribution centres. But soon a simple
stroke of genius would turn these women – old widows and
middle-aged gadflies – into the nightmare of corrupt officials
and, very quickly, into the talk of the town.

SAMPAT FIRST CONSIDERED using uniforms to unite the group
in 2005, around the time of Diwali, the Hindu festival of
lights, when Sampat took some of the women from her self-
help group on a small pilgrimage to the town of Chitrakoot.
Though she was not particularly religious, Sampat saw the
trip as a good opportunity to get the women accustomed to
independent travel. Unfortunately, one woman was left on
the train after everyone else had got off. 'I can't remember
her name. We used to call her "Pappu ki didi" – Pappu's sister. She had fallen asleep and went to Jabalpur. We all were
crying when we saw that we left her behind,' Sampat would
recall later. The whole night all of the women worried for
their friend's safety. The most worried of all was Sampat –
she had taken personal responsibility for the women that day
and she feared reprisals from the woman's family. 'In Bundelkhand, people can get you into a lot of trouble. They
could have put a lawsuit on me saying I kidnapped her. It's
very easy to get someone arrested here, so I was very tense.'
Upon their return to Atarra, the women waited together on

Sampat's patio, hoping their friend would show up. As they sat there glumly, Sampat thought to herself that this wouldn't have happened if the women in her group were easily identifiable when they went out in public. 'Maybe they can wear a badge?' she thought, but quickly rejected that idea. Then she came up with the solution of them wearing the same-colour sari, a dress that millions of women in the subcontinent, including Sampat, wear on a daily basis. 'Like that, the women will be easily seen in a big crowd,' she thought. Immediately, the many additional advantages of wearing a uniform became apparent to her. Far from simply helping to make sure people don't get lost, it was a way to build a strong, collective identity – a way to symbolise their unity. Wasn't that what she was always trying to teach the women? 'I thought even the divide between rich and poor will disappear. Often, a well-off member would wear a nice sari while the Dalits wore ugly saris,' she would remember, referring to the low caste formerly known as the 'untouchables'. Drawing inspiration from the sticks the elderly women used while walking, Sampat also considered the benefits of everyone in her 'gang' carrying sticks. She thought they would be useful in case there was any trouble, and also to scare away stray dogs.

Sampat decided she would buy forty saris to start with, enough for the most loyal members of the self-help groups. Each would receive a sari in exchange for a two-hundred-rupee, one-off fee that would also make her a member of Sampat's NGO, the Tribal Women Upliftment and Empowerment of Women Organisation. The Pink Gang would eventually fall under the auspices of this NGO.

Before buying the saris, Sampat shared the novel idea

with her members. 'If we buy them, will you wear them?' she asked. The women promised they would. The cost of buying the initial batch was four thousand rupees – just over forty pounds. This was where Sampat stumbled. 'Where can I get that kind of money from?' she asked her friends. After a few days of thinking it over, Dr Khanna, a good friend who spent a lot of time with Sampat on her patio, came forward to say he would loan the money to her. Being a lower-caste man himself, he supported Sampat's efforts to help the members of society who were mistreated the most. The three of them, Babuji, Sampat and Dr Khanna, set off by train the next day to Kanpur, a nearby city with a large fabric market, to buy the saris.

That day, they walked through the labyrinthine market, which sold cloth of every description. Saris sparkling with sequins hung alongside gold-embroidered and -brocaded wedding saris in rich reds and ochre. Merchants unfurled the intricately woven dresses, nine yards long, as brides-to-be and traders from smaller towns inspected the wares. None of those saris would do, of course. Sampat needed something plain, functional and cheap – artificially dyed polyester would serve their purposes best. When they came across a small stand selling the sort of saris Sampat was looking for, the three friends ran their eyes over the multiple shades. Blues ranged from turquoise to aquamarine, greens from deep forest to the startling traffic-light hue. Which colour should they pick? Sampat initially wanted to buy blue. 'I said no, I didn't like it,' Dr Khanna would remember later. 'Me and Babuji said pink is much better, so she agreed.'

There were some serious considerations to be made in

their choice of a colour. In India, each colour is saddled with political or religious associations. Red is employed by socialists. Green by Muslims. Blue by the Bahujan Samaj Party, the lower-caste party. Orange by Hindus. Yellow by the Gayatri Pariwar, a large religious organisation of which Babuji had been a member. Every colour, even white, seemed 'taken' by some group or another. 'We didn't want people to mistake us for someone else,' Sampat remembers. That is why pink was ultimately chosen – it was the only colour in India that seemed to be free of such associations.

On the train journey back, with the big parcel of saris secured in the luggage rack, the three of them spoke excitedly about the future. 'When we go anywhere, people will be curious!' Sampat said, clapping her hands in delight. 'They'll be even more afraid of us in uniforms!' she exclaimed.

The next morning, Sampat went around to the nearby villages – Uraiya Purva, Gokul Purva, Sudama Purva – where she and Babuji had started self-help groups. 'The saris have come!' she told the women. 'Tell everyone to come and get their saris!' Over the following weeks, one by one, the women came with the money. Those who could not afford to pay for a sari ('Many are very poor,' said Sampat) received one for free.

Why did these women, who had never before rebelled, join Sampat's nascent vigilante gang at this stage of their life? Lungi Dai, one of the elderly women, put it this way: 'Hope is a very big thing. Sampat gave it to us every time she came to the village.' Kodia Dai, Lungi's best friend, said, sucking in her lips over her toothless gums, 'A lot of women were joining, so I decided to go along too!'

ON THAT COLD DECEMBER MORNING in 2010, Sampat, her hair still wet from her bath, walked decisively towards her landlord, Lakhan Upadhyay, who was sitting with Babuji on the concrete patio in front of her office. Lakhan, who owns several *bigas* of fields on the outskirts of town, is a handsome, well-built father of four who is distinctive in his appearance. He dresses in freshly pressed *khadi* suits, which are three times more expensive than the cotton ones sold in the local market, and every morning, during his six o'clock worship, or *puja*, he ceremoniously paints his forehead with two white, horizontal lines made of sandalwood paste and adds a dot of red *kumkum* powder in the centre; these markings, which denote his high rank in the Hindu caste system, remain there for the whole day. At the back of his crown, which is covered in short-cropped, salt-and-pepper hair (though he was greying, his moustache is dyed jet-black), a minute braided tail curves away from his scalp.

Hearing Sampat approach, Lakhan looked up from the newspaper he was reading and a question formed on his lips. The matter that Lakhan wanted to raise had been on his mind since yesterday.

The night before, Lakhan had heard the news of the theft at the legislator's house. News always spread quickly in the town of Atarra. It was exchanged at marketplaces while people thumbed okra and aubergines and lamented the rising food prices. It was discussed excitedly at communal wells, where villagers bathed together under the expansive sky. Or sometimes it arrived on a bicycle pedalled swiftly by a gossiping friend.

Lakhan, who lives upstairs from Sampat's office, had been sitting on Sampat's patio at dusk when a man called Kallu stopped by on his way home to ask if Sampat was around. Kallu, a lower-caste man, was a 'big fan' of the Pink Gang and wanted to inform Sampat of the latest. As she was out, he passed the message on to Lakhan instead, after parking his bicycle on the dusty road.

Both men treated the story with suspicion.

'Who will believe such a thing will happen here?' Kallu asked. 'Put it into Sampat's ears, no? Then we'll get the real story,' Kallu went on to say. '*Hao*' – yes – Lakhan replied in the Bundelkhand dialect. 'I'll tell it to her.'

When Lakhan asked her the next day if she was aware of the news, Sampat waved him off. 'Tsk! Brother, I already know about it!' Sampat replied. She could be brusque at times, but Lakhan took this in stride. Sampat's temper was always a looming presence, bubbling under the surface, and, when it was not employed for the benefit of society (in a shouting match with a corrupt policeman, for example), she tended to scold those around her – often Babuji, with whom she bickered incessantly.

She simmered down.

'Good, now who will read the story out to me?' she asked. Sampat had taught herself to read basic words in a large font, but news articles, printed in a relatively small print, required an enormous effort for her to decipher; the written word was like a foreign language she had never mastered and could understand only in fleeting moments of intense concentration.

When Sampat was a child, many of the boys in her village were enrolled in a small school, in which lessons were conducted under a tree; she and the other girls were never included, however. Sampat often hid behind a bush and watched the lessons enviously, trying to follow through the twigs and leaves what was being written on the blackboard. When the schoolboys in their uniforms sauntered out of class, Sampat stalked them; they were walking repositories of precious gems of knowledge, which she wanted to own too. 'I used to get hold of those small kids and said to them: teach me, otherwise I will beat you! Slowly, slowly we used to learn from them. First we used to see whatever was written on the board and we used to copy it. We used to see that they were studying but that no one was teaching us so we felt like studying too. Like if someone is making a *chapatti*, even we would want to make one. That's how we used to feel,' Sampat remembers.

Sampat had taken her friends Gayatri and Prema along with her every time she forced one of the boys to divulge the secrets behind the symbols and numbers on the blackboard. Together, the three of them would practise their new words. 'We used to write on the mud ground. We used to write and then wipe the words away,' Sampat recalls. Unlike her friends, whose few learned, written words had now sunk into the dark mud of their memory, Sampat etched hers into her mind so that they would never be lost. 'They have forgotten all now, but I remember. They all are in their in-laws' place and have forgotten. They all got mixed up in their family. They are still close to me so when we meet they laugh and say, "You remember everything and we have forgotten!"' One of the boys who helped Sampat and her friends the most, Ramesh Gupta, still recalls those days now whenever he bumps into her at the market. 'He hasn't been able to get a job so now when he sees me, he says, "You took my knowledge from me!"' Sampat recounts with a chuckle.

Back on Sampat's concrete patio, Babuji took it upon himself to read out loud the article explaining the alleged theft at Dwivedi's home – public readings, recitals and pontifications to edify his listeners were some of his preferred activities. In his sleepy voice, using the same cadence with which he recited poetry, this village orator read out the following headline on the front page of *Hindustan*, one of the main Hindi-language newspapers in the country.

HUNDREDS OF THOUSANDS OF RUPEES HAVE BEEN
STOLEN FROM A PEOPLE'S REPRESENTATIVE'S
HOUSE - IT IS SAID THAT A GIRL LIVING IN THE
HOUSE COMMITTED THE THEFT

The author of the article was Amit Tripathi, a local journalist with whom Sampat had recently struck up a friendly rapport. Sampat liked Amit; he was one of few honest journalists she knew.

Babuji read aloud that the unnamed girl, who was allegedly employed as a maid to 'wash cooking utensils', was accused of stealing two hundred thousand rupees (over two thousand pounds), two mobile phones, jewellery and a rifle. According to the article, neither the police nor Dwivedi were confirming the news, though the politician was 'blaming opponents' for what he called a 'conspiracy', said the paper. 'Who was the girl? Where was she from? It was not clear,' wrote Amit, saying only that she had been living and working at the house of the legislator for 'some time'. Babuji read that the news had sparked the curiosity of those living nearby, many of whom crowded around the legislator's house in the hope of seeing something interesting. 'The whole district is in a heated discussion about this,' the newspaper reported.

'A rifle? How is a girl going to walk around with a rifle, tell me?' Sampat asked rhetorically.

By the time Babuji had finished the article, Sampat's mind had already changed gears. She turned to Lakhan and said, 'I'll try to find out about this and, as you are a Brahmin, you should try and collect information from your sources.' Lakhan, like the legislator in the news, is an upper-caste man, and so Sampat believed he would have access to gossip from within the tightly knit community.

After delegating this task, Sampat jumped up and made her way out towards her mission for the day.

CHAPTER TWO

BANDITS ON BALLOTS

NOT EVERYONE HAS THE COURAGE TO BECOME
A SAMPAT PAL AND FIGHT AGAINST A LEGISLATOR.

—Sampat Pal

'JUST WHO DO YOU THINK YOU ARE?' IS A QUESTION THAT Sampat is used to hearing. At times, she acts like she is running a small detective agency; on other occasions, she behaves like a police officer patrolling Bundelkhand. For all of her life, Sampat's endless meddling has nettled many of those around her and left others slightly baffled.

Sampat does not know exactly why she has persistently felt compelled to get involved in other people's business — indeed, it represents one of the greatest mysteries that she has encountered in her life. She once declared that 'not even *I* understand Sampat Pal'. She paused and then, wrinkling her brow as she pondered the enigma that she represented to herself, came up with an idea. 'When I die, the Indian government should look in my brain and find out how I have become like this.' It was an earnest, if somewhat humorous, suggestion. After a moment, she added, 'They should look into my heart too, that could help.'

Sampat is confident that any postmortem examination of her brain would reveal a fascinating, highly developed mind; she is quite possibly one of the most intelligent people she knows. 'That's why people listen to me. They say that if Sampat-ji does something, it's not without any logic. Even good, learned professors fail in front of me, and they agree with what I am saying. They say that although I am not educated, I have gained knowledge from my vast experience. One professor asked me, "Sampat-ji, you don't have any formal education, so how did you get such vast experience? You speak so well nobody has any answer to it. Where did you learn all this?" I said I don't know. Then I asked him, "Where did the person who invented school study? Someone must have come up with it on their own, right?"' she recounts. Few of Sampat's closest friends deny that her raw, intellectual strength was cultivated entirely on her own. 'Sampat is sharper than I am. I am very straightforward. That's why I'm behind. Though, I'm more educated than her, I'm miles behind her,' Babuji willingly admits.

Looking into Sampat's past offers few clues into the origins of her formidable understanding of the machinations of power and society. Her hometown, Kairi, is a small, windswept farming community in the heart of Bundelkhand. When Sampat was growing up in the 1970s, Kairi – like many parts of Bundelkhand – was a place where injustice against women, the lower castes and the poor was an accepted part of life. The cries of a woman being beaten by a drunk husband in the middle of the night; a Dalit denied participation in village celebrations for fear that he and his family, considered 'untouchable', would 'pollute' the communal metal *thaali* plates heaped with biryani; girls married off to widowed, older men who would use them like maids: these occurrences were, for the most part, accepted as being 'how things were'. Parents, grandparents and cousins – everyone – had stoically born life's injustices without so much as a wince. If you could not, there was little hope for survival.

Sampat's parents were farmers. 'They were simple people, they didn't take much interest in things,' she says, but they taught her good values. 'We were all kind-hearted. No one in my family treated women badly.' Sampat had one sister and two brothers. Of the four children in the family, two were precocious and turned into rather remarkable people. 'I was brightest and most dynamic in my family,' Sampat states simply. Sampat's brother, Ram Lal Pal, also differed radically from all the other children in the village – he became a *saddhu*, an ascetic holy man, at the age of ten. 'He used to find small stones and worship them. When we went to the village fair he rang a bell and started praying. He used to collect ants in a box and feed them with sugar and ghee. He burned wood and made a *tilak*' – a Hindu religious marking often made using sandalwood paste or red *kumkum* powder – 'on his forehead,' Sampat remembers. Then one day he ran away to live with a holy man, a *baba*, and became his disciple. 'We all cried. We were very unhappy. He grew his hair and left for Vrindavan' – a holy city. 'I think my mother never recovered from the story with my brother. It was hard for her to have two children who had sacrificed their lives – one to God, another to society,' she adds.

It must have been evident to Sampat's mother early on

that her daughter was not a typical girl; for one, Sampat was the most outgoing of all the children in Kairi, well known among her friends for her bold arboreal explorations, which she started around the age of five. 'There was a mango tree in my village. I saw boys climbing the tree and I thought, Why can't I climb it? One friend, a girl, supported me while I climbed it. That's how I began. Once we were many girls at a jamun tree. I said to them, Come, let's climb. They said, No, we can't do it. They helped me up. The branches of the tree were very fragile, so I fell. When I came back, we hid from the elders as I was hurt.'

Apart from her courage, Sampat also picked up skills very quickly. She was the first person in her town to learn how to sew. 'No one in Kairi could sew. Not my mother, nor my sister. God gave me this wisdom – I don't know why, but he did,' Sampat says. She fell in love with sewing the first time Chunni Lal, her uncle, took her along with him to the tailor. This uncle, who was the only one in her family at the time with a university degree ('He did a BA in Atarra. He was an educated man'), was Sampat's favourite – 'He treated me like a man.' Chunni dispensed life lessons like, 'If someone hits you, hit them back.' Sampat wanted to please Chunni, who treated her better than most people, so it was a lesson she tried to put into practice as often as she could.

Standing with her uncle in front of the tailor's shack, Sampat looked on with fascination at the tailor's sartorial movements, observing the swift up-and-down dance of his feet on the pedal-operated sewing machine and the way he carefully guided the fabric underneath the hopping needle. As Sampat watched him finishing off clothes for another customer, she thought about the doll she owned – her only

one – and its tattered dress. Maybe she could make a dress
for the doll? She thought. When Sampat asked the tailor if
she could take a piece of fabric that had been discarded on
the ground, he encouraged her to, and then pointed to the
rubbish heap around the back that had more scraps she could
help herself to.

After Sampat returned home that day, she stole money
from her parents to buy a needle and thread, and then practised sewing secretly in between her farming work until
it became something of an obsession – she returned every
other day with her friends to rummage through the tailor's
waste pile for scrap fabric. 'I told my mother I was out in the
fields, but I went there instead.' Once, when she couldn't
get her hands on a piece of cloth in the rubbish dump, she
tore off the bottom strip of her mother's sari. 'Back then,
the edges weren't hemmed, so she didn't notice! I had a bad
habit of stealing cloth – I was always scared of getting caught,
so I tucked it into my underwear or armpit when my mum
walked by. Look, even today I have this habit!' Sampat says,
pulling out a rolled-up scrap of fabric from her bra and waving it around, chuckling heartily. This life skill would give
Sampat an advantage in her adulthood – it allowed her to be
financially independent.

More than the sewing, however, it was Sampat's social
consciousness that set her apart from all of the other people
in her village. From her earliest days as a child, Sampat had
always felt keenly the offence of injustice – the sight of it
smarted her. When she was around seven or eight, one of
her friends in the hamlet, a shepherd boy called Chand Pal,
had been slapped by a girl called Gayatri Patel, who was the
daughter of a powerful landlord. The little boy was crying

bitterly and was being consoled by the other children. What had been his crime? He had gone to the toilet, there in the field, in between the raised banks of tilled soil, and was spotted by the watchful eye of the landlord's daughter. Gayatri yelled hysterically that he should conduct his calls of nature off the field next time. The children were expected to defecate on the edges of roads, where the land belonged to no one. Many were killed this way after being hit by passing trucks, especially at dusk or when it was foggy. Yet if they relieved themselves on the property where they were working, they were beaten.

Sampat and her friends hated Gayatri. They thought she was a wicked brat. 'That girl was a bully. The whole family had a fighting nature. She had an abusive tongue too. She quarrelled with everyone. She used a Bundelkhand swearword at me, which meant I was a widow. I said "How can I be a widow? I'm not even married!"' Sampat recounts, chuckling at her ignorance. 'She pulled faces at me. I bit my thumb at her or made big eyes.' Sampat's father had gone to speak to Gayatri's father to complain about what the girl had done. 'My father went to that family and said that they shouldn't beat children,' Sampat remembers. Her father's intervention offended Gayatri's father and resulted in the two men quarrelling. 'After my family had an argument with them, they said we should not walk on their land anymore,' Sampat recalls.

When Sampat heard what had happened, her body filled with rage. She was so cross that the most brazen of plans germinated in her mind. Gathering together a motley group of her friends, Sampat convinced the other children to 'poo' in the fields at the same time the next day, when the young heiress to the farm was sure to be watching. Even at that age, Sampat knew that if her enemies were larger and more powerful than she was, she had to outnumber them. It was easy for Sampat to get the other children to agree: back then, as now, she had a way of melting away their fears with her confidence. Under her direction, the children squatted down and pushed out whatever coils of excrement they could, giggling wildly as they did so.

Gayatri, spotting the defecators, rushed towards them with a menacing look. 'Their house was far but she saw us from a distance. She had a stick with her. When she ran she shouted, "Just you wait, I'm coming!" I said, "*You* wait! I'm going to show *you*,"' Sampat recounts.

'There was a scuffle. She had long hair. I grabbed it and pulled it with all my strength. We all got her and pinned her on the ground and rubbed her in shit. It was like playing with mud. I rubbed it in her mouth. I was so angry. I was a child, so doing these things wasn't disgusting to me then! Some boys who were with me ran away when Gayatri's brothers came. I said, Stay away, this is a girl's fight. Then her father dragged her away and shouted, "Why did you get involved?"'

'My father was away that day but my uncle told him what happened. My uncle said, "You did the right thing. You had a good fight today."'

'People think I am fierce now, but they should have met me when I was a child!' Sampat laughs, when telling the story.

NOW THAT SAMPAT has grown up, the bullies she confronts are bigger and more powerful than those of her childhood. On the morning of 14 December, on her way to investigate the case against Sheelu, the girl accused of stealing from the legislator, she set out to call on the most menacing Goliaths in Bundelkhand: the police. The Uttar Pradesh police force is the largest in the world under a single command, and in the eyes of many, it is one of the largest criminal organisations on the planet. 'There is not a single lawless group in the whole country whose record of crime is anywhere near the record of that organised unit which is known as the Indian Police Force,' a fiery judge and activist called A. N. Mulla once famously said.

'The corruption in the police is high here, and politicians are driving it. Those who win elections and become ministers want to rule the police. They need money, and the police give it to them. These are the issues in Bundelkhand and all over India. Some people say it's only in Bundelkhand, but I see it everywhere. It happens in big cities also, not only in small places,' Sampat says.

Given the meagre pay of policemen – often less than what a sweeper might earn – the police force is particularly vulnerable to corruption. The practice of bribing one's way into the force is common, with aspiring officers sometimes paying anywhere between 100,000 and 500,000 rupees, or approximately £1,100 and £5,500, to be accepted into the force. Such officers expect that their 'investment' will pay off once they have supplemented their incomes with bribes. After an aspiring officer has paid his way into a post, he remains loyal to his political backers, whose favour he has effectively purchased. 'It has become obvious that the police cannot be neutral. Either you comply with every order from the political masters, or you have some strong backing of a leader who protects you. That is how policing is done here,' said one superintendent of the Uttar Pradesh police during an interview for a Human Rights Watch report.

Yet despite their might, the police in Atarra have a fearful respect for Sampat, this woman who barges into their station and demands explanations for their actions like a headmistress descending onto a misbehaving classroom. If all of the police in Bundelkhand know about the Pink Gang, it is because Sampat first made a name for herself and the Pink Gang at this very local police station, causing the very highest members of the country's political elite – the Gandhi dynasty – to sit up and take notice.

ON 2 AUGUST 2006, less than a year after Sampat started the gang, she was sitting on her patio with Babuji and Lakhan when she received a visit from a woman called Sushila, a mother of eight living below the poverty line. Between sobs, Sushila told Sampat that the police had beaten up and taken away her husband, Bare Lal, after a dispute he had had with a neighbour a few days earlier. Sushila's husband was being detained without any charge, and the police hadn't provided his family with any information about the arrest.

Sampat was not surprised by Sushila's story – by then she had handled numerous cases involving illegal detention, which was rampant in many parts of India where domestic law allows the police to arrest individuals on the mere basis of 'reasonable suspicion'. There are virtually no remedies available to wrongfully imprisoned citizens, and offending officers are rarely disciplined. It is a system in which police can wield their power to arrest for a myriad of unlawful purposes, including to extort, to inflate arrest quotas and to silence citizens who dare to make complaints about them. This is why Sushila felt powerless in the face of her husband's sudden arrest.

'I go to the police station to meet him, but they always tell me to go away,' Sushila told Sampat that day, breaking down. 'How will I look after my children on my own? Who will feed them?' she asked tearfully.

After Sushila narrated her story, Sampat promised to accompany her to the Atarra police station. 'I'll beat them with my own hands if they don't listen to us,' Sampat told her confidently as they walked the short distance to the station. Sampat often illustrates how she would make good on such threats by wildly slapping and punching her imaginary opponent, until she snaps out of her violent reveries with a torrent of hoarse, hearty chuckles that make her cheeks rosy.

In India, the majority of complaints are made by travelling to a police station, as emergency helplines are barely functional or existent. Many ordinary Indians, especially women, enter police stations with a sense of dread and anxiety and often refuse to go after dark. Far too often, newspapers carry reports of sexual molestation, rape and even murder carried out by officers in stations. One of the stories that recently hit national headlines told of a woman who alleges she was gang-raped by officers after they forced her to drink alcohol. She had gone to the station because she had been told, erroneously, that she had been offered a job.

When Sampat arrived at the police station with Sushila in tow, Sampat approached the station officer, a man called Zameer Ul Hassan. 'Why are you keeping her husband? You should charge him or let him go!' Sampat snapped.

The officer demanded to know who she was.

'You don't know, what? I'm Sampat Pal, leader of the Pink Gang.' The station officer was not impressed with her credentials. 'He told me many people come here, trying to act like *netas*' – referring to leaders and people with political power – 'don't think I'm going to listen to you,' Sampat recalls.

'If you don't listen now, maybe you will when I come back with a hundred women armed with sticks?' Sampat replied testily. 'Bring, bring,' he said in impatient monosyllables, and sent them away.

As they left the station, Sampat told Sushila to meet her at the office at eleven o'clock the next day. 'Then he'll see who Sampat Pal is,' she said angrily. Leaving Sushila, Sampat marched over to Uraiya Purva, where some of the initial Pink Gang members lived. Uraiya Purva is within walking distance from Sampat's office; if you take a left from her patio and walk half a mile, you get to a canal with dark-green currents where those without running water bathe, wash their clothes and rinse steel cooking pots. If you cross the bridge that goes over the canal and continue a few more miles, you reach the field-rimmed cluster of mud huts.

When Sampat reached Kodia Dai's home, she told her to 'call the others, quick', and Kodia obliged, hobbling across the village and knocking on the doors of all the members with her gnarled, crooked hands. Once they gathered, Sampat narrated Sushila's story. 'This happened to Sushila's husband today, but it could be you next. That's why we have to teach them a lesson,' she said forcefully. The women nodded. Sampat instructed them to report to duty at the office at eleven o'clock the next day.

'Come wearing your pink saris and bring your sticks,' she ordered, and they promised to be there.

'THAT DAY AROUND a hundred people gathered at my terrace,' Lakhan says, remembering the inundation of people choking the entrance of his house and overflowing onto the main road. In addition to the Pink Gang members from Uraiya Purva and Gokul Purva, dozens of passersby had crowded around the house to see what was going on, plus the media had made an appearance. The journalists, whom Sampat had called, were from Sahara Samay TV and the newspapers *Hindustan*, *Dainik Jagran* and *Amar Ujala*.

After everyone had gathered, Sampat addressed the press corps. Behind her, on the wall, was a hand-painted slogan that read, 'For truth and justice our blood will always flow – The Pink Gang'.

'A man has been taken captive by the police with no charge filed against him!' Sampat boomed to the notepad-clutching journalists and then, pointing to an anxious-looking woman, added, 'And this is his wife, Sushila.'

Sampat stood before Sushila, who wore a variegated sari with gold brocaded sleeve hems, and a gold nose stud, and pointed to a darkened bruise under Sushila's left eye. 'How did you get this injury?' Sampat asked in her demonstrative style. The woman explained that she had been hurt in a scuffle with the police. Turning to Sushila and raising her bamboo stick, Sampat said, 'Out here, officials don't listen to us, do they? But they will if we go with a *laathi*.'

Carrying rope ('You never know, you might need it,' she

said), the large stick and a bulky, black leather handbag over her shoulder, Sampat led approximately five-dozen women onto Bisanda Road, which is part of National Highway 71. Behind her was a phalanx of ten pink sari–wearing women, all of whom demurely covered their heads. Trailing the foremost ranks was a long line of around fifty peasant women, without uniforms, who had spontaneously joined in the protest but were not official gang members. 'Down with the police!' Sampat yelled in a scratchy voice, thrusting her fist in the air. The pink-uniformed women raised their hands in response and echoed her chant. 'Let's make more Pink Gangs!' the women shouted.

The television journalists filmed the procession as the women made their way noisily down the street. Men watched from the edge of the road; some laughed, others looked puzzled. All, except those trying to push through the crowd with heavy agricultural loads on their pushcarts or bicycles, stopped and stared.

By the time the group arrived at the entrance to the police compound, a large crowd of male passersby had gathered (the majority of the people out on the streets in Atarra were men, as women tended to stay at home). The women stopped at the threshold of the police station and yelled, 'Down with Hassan Inspector!' – naming and shaming the station officer who had mistreated Sampat and Sushila the day before.

The crowd of women who assembled that day was a motley one. Some, like Kodia Dai, were elderly, with birdlike legs, who leaned shakily on their bamboo stick weapons for support. The Pink Gang members at the front appeared the most focused – their countenances were serious and their chants the loudest. Among the non-uniform-wearing women, at least one protester, dressed in a lime-green sari, carried an infant in her arms; another was heavily pregnant; and one carried her lunch with her in a stainless-steel tiffin box. A number of women looked sheepish and shy, smirking awkwardly under all the attention; others giggled and chatted with one another between the chants.

Babuji and Lakhan had followed Sampat and the women from a distance, but when they arrived at the destination, they hung back – neither daring to get too close to the police compound. 'She told all the male supporters to stay behind the group of women,' Lakhan recalls, referring to Sampat. This order was for their own protection. 'Sampat didn't want people to raise fingers at the men and say, "You've started all this." You see, Sampat thought the police would cook up charges against us.' She deemed women less vulnerable to police attacks. 'There is no women's jail nearby so it is hard to arrest them,' Lakhan explains. The police also 'don't do *laathi* charges on women,' he adds, referring to the police practice of dispersing protesters by charging at them with the large bamboo sticks. A large crowd of people gathered, blocking Bisanda Road. People living opposite the station leaned out of their windows or went up onto their flat roofs to get a better look.

The women entered the compound and then gathered in front of the veranda of the police station, under a red-and-blue plaque that read, 'ATARRA POLICE STATION – 1960'. 'Okay, everyone,' Sampat shouted to her troops, 'Don't be afraid!'

Sampat walked across the veranda and into the narrow, crowded office of one of the policemen. She was followed by at least one cameraman and as many women who could fit into the room – the others hovered outside the door. 'All of you, sit outside,' the policeman commanded, but Sampat overruled him.

'No! We will sit here!' she yelled. Turning back to the women, she instructed them, 'Sit down, sit down,' tugging at Sushila and the other women, who were unsure what to do.

After the women had squatted in the cramped office, taking over all the floor space, Sampat turned to the young officer and, pointing an accusing finger at him, shouted, 'You've kept a poor woman's husband out here all night. I'll take him with me today. What form of justice are the police giving?' The policeman did not answer; he picked up his crackling walkie-talkie and transmitted code messages to his colleagues – 'Delta One, enter mobile from Delta One' – and then sat tight.

Sampat, realising that this junior officer was not the right person to deal with, stomped out of his office and went to speak to the subinspector, a balding, beer-bellied man with a moustache called Sangham Lal Singh. The subinspector was sitting behind a desk overlooking the veranda.

'By shouting in this manner you're not going to achieve anything,' lectured the police officer from his chair, waving his index finger at Sampat.

'No? Then we'll shout more!' Sampat retorted. 'Raise your voices, we're all one! Strength in unity!' she hollered towards the women, her chorus of chanters, who had got up and followed her outside. All of the women raised their fists and joined in Sampat's rallying cries.

With several cameras pointed at him, the officer, looking embarrassed, tried to get Sampat to turn back to him and stop this raucous, impassioned chanting, which was disrupting the calm of his station.

'Come this side, don't cause any drama,' said the exasperated officer, motioning Sampat towards him.

'Without her consent, how did you dare just take her husband? So you've got bullets, have you? I don't care. I don't fear the police. You're a human, just like me,' she shouted, banging her fist on the desk behind which the officer sat.

Just then, Sampat thought she heard the policeman mumble *haram zadi*, which means 'bastard'.

Sampat's eyes grew wild. 'You call me a *haram zadi*? Have you gone mad?' she shouted hoarsely, her voice breaking. Whipping her head around to face the women behind her, she repeated in a hysterical tone, 'He called me a *haram zadi!*' her outrage growing.

That was when all order in the station broke down. 'You've come here to fight . . . ,' the subinspector started saying. But before he could finish, Sampat clasped a large folder she was holding in her hands and brought it crashing down on his head with a smack. She then pushed the folder into Sushila's hands, who was carrying Sampat's bamboo stick and rope, and grabbed the *laathi* from her. Sampat raised the long stick high above her head, bringing her elbows up around her temples; she assumed a position evocative of an axe-bearing wood feller about to reduce a lone tree stump to firewood.

'Hey, hey, hey!' the policeman said with alarm, as he leapt up from his seat and pushed forward the desk that separated him from Sampat.

Seeing this scene unfold, the raucous crowd that had

gathered around the entrance of the police station started cheering and hooting. 'The crowd swelled up. Spectators began entering the station. The road was jammed. People said, What's happened? Something like this never happened before. I stayed outside in a safe place in case of a *laathi* charge. People were watching from terraces and five hundred people on the road were watching,' Lakhan recalls.

In the station, too, everyone was shouting. In the disorderly melee, Sampat, her hair flying wildly around her face, was desperately issuing commands to the women, who were either frozen stiff or sluggish with fear. 'Tie him up,' Sampat shouted to Sushila, who was holding the coil of rope as if it were a slithering python. Jostled by the throng of women who had crowded onto the veranda, Sushila demurred at executing the order; she uncoiled and recoiled the rope nervously and looked around to see if one of the other women might help her tie up the policeman – which was not something she had any experience with. There were no takers. In the meantime, Sampat, agitated and raging against the flustered officer, whacked his forearm, which was stretched out before him to shield himself, with her *laathi*. Some of the women's coloured-glass bangles broke in the commotion.

'Tie him up, tie him up!' Sampat ordered again, her handbag swinging uncontrollably from side to side. Sushila, holding the rope, summoned up her courage and crept around the desk and towards the officer. 'What do you think you're doing? Get away!' he barked at her. Sushila, deflated, slunk back into the crowd. There was growing confusion among both the Pink Gang and the police officers, most of whom by now had stepped out of their offices and were deliberating about how to deal with this unruly group of women.

Outside, the crowd was going wild. 'The Pink Gang has tied up the subinspector with a rope!' people shouted down the street. 'I saw Sampat slap him across the face like this,' another said, grossly exaggerating what had actually happened. 'He was saying, "Please, please! Stop!"' spectators recounted to passersby, in awe of what the women had done. 'They tied him onto a chair with rope! She beat him several times. There was a cop with a rifle but he stood there silently!' Lakhan remembers hearing amid the animated street-talk that day.

It was then that the provincial arms constabulary arrived, along with the subdistrict magistrate, S. C. Sharma, and the circle officer, T. P. Singh – the junior officer had alerted them over the wireless. They decided on the spot that because of the growing mob, it would be unwise to arrest any of the women. 'Even the general public were shouting against the police,' they later wrote in a report on the incident, justifying their decision. The police worried that there would be what they called a 'worsening of the law-and-order situation', so they let all the women go home, to the surprise of people in Atarra.

A case was registered against Sampat, Sushila Lal and another Pink Gang member, also called Sushila, each charged with eleven crimes, including rioting, obstructing a public servant in discharge of public functions and criminal intimidation. Sushila and Sampat spent one night in jail a year later, when the case was finally heard in court, but the other Sushila, Bare Lal's wife, did not have to because the judge accepted her plea that she could not afford to spend a night apart from her eight children.

AT THE POLICE STATION, Sampat had used a well-known technique of protest in India called *gherao*, whereby the public, driven by a sense that they have no traditional recourse to justice, and no power on their side except their sheer numbers and anger, surround an offending government establishment – an electricity department, a police station, a university or, in the case of labour disputes, an office or factory – to demand justice. *Gheraos* sometimes lead to mob violence, a common occurrence in the nation.

In India, mob violence can erupt suddenly and with no prior warning. Often fatal road accidents lead to a spontaneous killing by passersby of drivers presumed to be guilty. Labour disputes are another major cause of violent confrontation. On several occasions, disgruntled, overworked employees burned to death or attacked with iron rods executives and human resources managers.

Men perpetrate most of these attacks, though women too have been involved in sprees of violence. One of the most high-profile women-led attacks took place in August 2004, when a mob of around two hundred women yielding knives, stones and chilli powder brutally and fatally beat the serial rapist and murderer Akku Yadav in a district court. In a mere fifteen minutes, the mob stabbed Yadav seventy times, and an alleged victim cut off his penis with a vegetable knife. The women were from a slum called Kasturba Nagar, where Yadav and his gang had allegedly gang-raped, murdered and tormented residents for over a decade, with full knowledge of the police, who residents claimed were working for the criminals. After the slaughter of Yadav, the women collectively declared their guilt in the murder, frustrating police efforts to charge anyone with the crime.

Despite the frequency of *gheraos* and violent protests in India, Sampat's highly publicised encounter with the police could have spelled the end of the Pink Gang. Apart from the pressure the incident put on the gang members, who were wholly unprepared for what had happened at the station, Sampat could have risked being put under surveillance or faced more serious charges. There were some defections after the protest, most notably Sushila Lal, the beneficiary of the protest. When the police came to arrest her, she denied being present that day, though there was plenty of video footage and witnesses, including the police.

'She was a weak woman,' Sampat recalls with a shrug. 'She came back to me for help again after that. Can you believe it? The other women were saying we shouldn't help her because of what she did. I told them we don't have to let her back in the gang, but we must help her, so we did.'

Instead of the public condemning Sampat, politicians, journalists and large portions of civil society applauded her and the Pink Gang. The *Hindustan Times*, an English-language paper, wrote that her gang played a 'pivotal role in uplifting the status of women'. The most significant encouragement she received came from the powerful Indian National Congress, the political party that has been in government for most of India's post-independence era. The then secretary of the All India Congress Committee, Dr Bhola Pandey, got in touch with Sampat shortly after her confrontation with the Atarra police. 'He wanted to know who that woman was who dared to beat a policeman!' Sampat surmises. 'He told me they liked my work.'

Dr Pandey invited Sampat to local Congress Party events and ensured that Sampat was part of a large delegation of social workers invited to meet Sonia Gandhi, the president of the Indian National Congress, at her house. In 2007, according to Sampat, Dr Pandey said he could secure her a ticket to run as a Congress Party candidate for the Legislative Assembly in Uttar Pradesh that year, but it never materialised. 'Bhola Pandey said that I will get you a ticket, but he wasn't able to,' Sampat recounts.

Sampat does not hold a grudge against Dr Pandey for not fulfilling the alleged offer of a ticket, which was informal and made without assurances. 'I didn't even mention it. They didn't give me the ticket, so I thought I shouldn't insist on it or it will become my weakness. I didn't ask. They didn't give and I didn't take. I didn't even fight with them,' she says.

ON THE MORNING OF 14 December 2010, Sampat walked into the Atarra police station like it was her own house – she was confident and purposeful in her stride, quite distinct from most members of the public who ventured there. When an ordinary, unprivileged Indian comes to meet a police officer, he or she often addresses the inspector in a grovelling, servile way. Many bend to touch the inspector's feet (when coming and then, once again, when going, for good measure) and frequently press their hands together, like one does in prayer, bowing regularly during the hurried conversation with excessive gratitude for being granted an audience.

While being addressed in this manner, the policeman often sits smug and condescendingly on his chair, quite deliberately making signs of boredom and distraction – inspecting his nails, dusting off his shirt or scratching his face. Sampat, however, does not indulge this ritual.

When Sampat made her way into the police station that day, to enquire about the unusual theft charge brought by Dwivedi, she went straight for the office of Rajendra Yadav, the circle officer. Yadav was a middle-aged, clean-shaven man with neat hair that was all but shorn away on the sides, leaving only a stubble of silver and black. His military grooming is offset by his soft, round cheeks and bow-shaped lips, which always appear to be on the verge of a smile. That day, he wore a khaki-coloured shirt with three silver stars on his epaulettes, denoting his rank. In his past dealings with Sampat, he had proved to be friendly, honest and helpful. 'He's a good man. We're not friends – I don't make friends with police – but he is good,' Sampat concedes.

One of the first cases for which Sampat had approached him was a spurious rape claim made by a woman. It was evident that the man she was accusing of rape was innocent – he was nowhere near the scene of the crime when it was said to have happened – and Sampat felt that he was being framed. She presented the evidence to the circle officer, who concurred that the man was indeed innocent. When the officer tried to have him released, however, the superintendent at the time told him to back off from the case. 'He was probably paid off,' snorts Sampat. The circle officer did not give in to the pressure of his boss, however, and released the innocent man anyway, winning great respect from Sampat in the process.

That December morning, Yadav ordered a low-ranking constable to bring two fresh cups of tea, one for Sampat and the other for Yadav. Unlike so many other citizens, Sampat is relaxed in the presence of police officers. Whenever she visits the station, she installs herself in a chair with a confident air (often bringing up her feet, so that she is sitting cross-legged and comfortable) and starts out by making small talk in her chatty, lively way about current affairs, drawing out lessons from misbehaving politicians and scandals and dominating the direction of the discussion. That morning, however, Sampat got straight to the point. 'What's this story about the legislator?' she asked soon after sitting down. 'Have you found the stolen objects? The rifle? The mobile phone?'

Sampat found Yadav uncharacteristically rigid when he learned why she had come. Yadav sat behind his desk, which was bare. Indian police suffer from such a colossal amount of underfunding that many stations have no stationery at all. The public is often expected to bring its own paper if a report is to be filed.

Yadav hesitated before answering her questions. He finally said that he was not the one handling the case, that it was Radhe Shyam Shukla, the subinspector, whom she needed to speak to. He raised his eyebrows when he spoke the name 'Shukla'. Sampat did not need to be prompted, however – she knew from experience that Shukla spelled trouble.

IT WOULD BE AN UNDERSTATEMENT to say that Sampat and Shukla were not on good terms. The subinspector had arrested Sampat's landlord in 2006 under a fabricated murder charge. The reason for the false accusation was clear in Lakhan's mind: he had helped Sampat uncover a scam involving the ration distribution shops, called *kothedars*, which were illegally selling government grain, intended for people living below the poverty line, on the black market.

According to data compiled by Bloomberg News, which ran a long, investigative piece in 2012 on the scam, corrupt politicians in Uttar Pradesh had looted $14.5 billion in rationed food over the previous decade. India runs the largest rationed food distribution system in the world, yet most of the food never reaches the plates of the hungry. Sampat's operation against the corrupt rations distributors in Atarra went on for several weeks. Along with other Pink Gang members, she not only collected information on the secret redirection of rationed grain from government warehouses to private ones, but also on two occasions halted trucks suspected of carrying stolen food and raided the home of a ration shop owner who was hiding grain in his house. A large chain of corruption spanned the police force, ration and welfare officers and politicians, and tons of grain was being siphoned off this way each year. The Pink Gang's meddling in this lucrative business ruffled many feathers, and so Shukla was sent to convince Lakhan to 'rein' Sampat in.

Just who sent Shukla is not clear, but it is safe to assume that politicians or business owners paid off the subinspector, like many other officers in the force. Shukla put pressure on Lakhan to kick Sampat out of his house and make her stop her investigations into the large-scale food robbery. When Lakhan refused, Shukla warned him that he would pay for his mistake. A few months later, the police arrested Lakhan for murdering a businessman at the Atarra train station.

Lakhan was ultimately released owing to a lack of evidence, but the shadow of the allegation still hangs over him.

THAT DECEMBER MORNING, Radhe Shyam Shukla wore a light-green felt beret with the red and blue insignia of the Uttar Pradesh police. The greying officer, with a moustache and pouches under his eyes, told Sampat he had no time for her. 'I am busy – come another time,' he said, before showing Sampat to the door.

'You can send me away once but, you listen to me, I'll come back,' she warned, slamming the door behind her.

Rebuffed by Shukla, Sampat marched back to Yadav's office demanding answers.

'He told me, Sampat-ji . . . this case is very difficult, I don't want to be involved,' Sampat remembers.

'I said, You don't want to be involved? You think I want to be involved? You think the girl wants to be involved? *You're* police. You locked her up. How can this case be difficult for you?' Sampat recalls.

Yadav insisted that it was and that there was 'a lot of pressure coming from the top.'

Sampat pressed for more details.

'He told me quietly-quietly that the theft charge is false. . . . Shukla is doing everything they are telling him, he registered the case and is following their orders. . . . He said there are much bigger forces at play. . . . Yadav said I cannot do anything, or I too will be in trouble.'

Yadav was not exaggerating. Given the systemic ways in which political representatives have historically exercised influence and pressure over the Indian police force, the police could not be trusted to fairly handle the case. Officers who stand up to orders coming from politicians often find themselves transferred. Indeed, so common are transfers that Union Home Secretary G. K. Pillai told *Tehelka*, an Indian investigative journalism magazine, that the 'average tenure of an SP' – a superintendent – 'in UP is almost two months.'

Knowing this did not make Sampat any softer on Yadav. 'Maybe you've been paid off not to interfere,' she retorted.

'He told me, Sampat-ji, it's not like that. I have to think of my job – they will fire me if I go against them,' Sampat recalls.

'If that's true, then losing your job is more honourable than being corrupt!' Sampat quipped.

Yadav was silent, and then he said, 'I won't be able to do anything to help Sheelu. Neither will any other police officer. If anyone can do anything, it's you.'

Sampat shook her head in disappointment at the cowed man.

'There is no courage in you,' she snapped, and then marched out.

THE VISIT TO THE POLICE STATION confirmed that Sampat was right to assume Dwivedi's theft claim could not be trusted, but that was no surprise to her. 'I'm always right,' she says nonchalantly, as if her instincts are a compass that never fails.

Unlike the police, Sampat would not let herself be intimidated by any politician. Politicians from Uttar Pradesh have a deeply entrenched reputation for being gangsters; in Hindi films they are often represented as villainous, pot-bellied men with oil-slicked hair, wearing dark sunglasses and gem-studded gold rings on their fingers. In real life, as in films, they are often surrounded by a coterie of gun-toting musclemen, also wearing shades, who drive through their constituencies with rifles sticking out of car windows and fire shots into the air after election victories (leading to casualties and deaths of passersby). Some politicians ride bareback on horses into train stations, where on crowded platforms they exhort people to vote for them, effectively bringing everything around them to a standstill until they have got across their ominous election slogans.

'Who can be a bigger bandit than he who wields all laws? Have you ever seen a CBI' – Criminal Bureau of Investigation – 'investigation give justice to a poor man? Every day so many incidents happen. Many people die. Many die in big pain. People walk free from the biggest scandals. A legislator is the biggest person. No one is bigger than him. A legislator is the biggest thug with the most money. He has five thrasher machines and six land mafias. He is a big man. He can buy two or three villages. No one is more powerful than him. Second is Sonia Gandhi or UP' – Uttar Pradesh – 'government or the central government,' Sampat once said. Many would agree with her.

Things came to a head between 2002 and 2007, the period in which Sampat formed the Pink Gang. During this time, the Samajwadi Party ruled Uttar Pradesh, and nearly half of its electoral candidates either had criminal charges pending against them or had been convicted. The culture of criminality within the Samajwadi Party, whose chairperson is a former wrestler, spread across the state and led to a dark era referred to as the Goonda Raj, or the Rule of the Gangsters. 'You punch me four times and snatch my money, that is Goonda Raj. You kick me out of my house, that is Goonda Raj. Raping my daughter is Goonda Raj. Work which is done by muscle power or power of position – all that is Goonda Raj,' explains Babuji. Ministers in the party did little to rein in the free-for-all that governance had become; one even went on record saying, 'As long as you work hard and get things done, you can steal a little.'

During the Goonda Raj, some so-called gangster politicians campaigned from behind bars and, when they won, proceeded to represent their constituency from jail. Like powerful mafia bosses, being in jail did not stop the *goonda* politicians from conducting business as usual. One legislator, jailed for murdering his lover, reportedly shuttled between his cell and a private hospital room, where he allegedly held court, spent time with his wife, and ate home-cooked meals. 'Prison is where UP politicians go for a holiday,' remarked one newspaper. Politicians locked up while awaiting rulings on their cases were still allowed to run for office given that criminal cases in India's backlogged courts can last up to fifteen years.

Ironically, protection was the one of the main reasons why many voters in the world's largest democracy allowed hoodlums into power – they thought that they would be more secure if a don were ruling over them. Another was corruption. 'A good person never wins here. People are fools; they just want money and alcohol. Politicians give them these things in exchange for votes. This is the kind of public we have,' Sampat laments, adding, 'Neither the government wants to change anything, nor the people. We can't blame it all on the government. In a democracy people form the government they want. But what happens here is that people cast their votes for someone if he offers them alcohol. Those who give away alcohol win and go to Delhi while the rest continue to live like dogs in the village. Corruption is increasing.'

Sampat had, in the past, taken on *goonda* politicians more powerful than Dwivedi. In fact, she had run against one in local elections. In 2007, after Dr Bhola Pandey, the then secretary of the All Indian Congress Committee, had backtracked on his offer to give Sampat a ticket, and after she had buried any hopes to run for office, word spread that Piyaria Patel, the mother of Ambika Patel, a feared bandit, would be running for a seat in the state legislature. It was evident to all that she was just a dummy candidate and that if she won, it would be Ambika – whose alias was Thokia, derived from the Hindi verb *thokna* (to hit) – who would actually be in power. In India, it is common for powerful villagers to put puppet candidates on the ballot in their place, especially since affirmative action policies meant that some *pradhan*, or village head, seats were reserved for lower-caste or female candidates only. The political class often abused this system; there were countless cases of wives or even servants standing in as proxies for the real candidates.

'In the villages, there was Thokia's terror,' Sampat remembers. 'He threatened that if his mother did not win the election, he would kill people with his gun and burn their houses. People were scared of him.' Thokia was an elusive, Robin Hood figure. Legend has it that he turned to banditry when he couldn't get justice for his sister, who was brutally raped. Thokia, who had been on the run since 2001, was known for his extortion of wealthy landowners and so was feared among the upper classes. Though he reportedly had 147 criminal charges against him, including looting, kidnapping, extortion and murder, many of the poor loved him, and it is believed they helped him hide from the police in remote ravines and dense jungle areas. Among his good deeds, he would often settle village disputes and donate money to finance wedding celebrations for humble families.

Thokia's mother was running with the Rashtriya Lok Dal, or the National People's Party, a left-leaning party that was previously aligned with the Socialists and brands itself as the defender of poor farmers and the landless underclasses. Her election slogan, which appeared below an illustration of a hand-operated water pump, the party's symbol, on her campaign posters, was an unveiled threat: 'If you want to live in peace, vote National People's Party.' The entry of the bandit's mother into the political class spelled the very opposite of peace, of course. 'It is unfortunate that in our country people threaten others for votes. There is no joy in being an independent country so far,' Sampat says.

Sampat was concerned about what would happen to law and order – already tenuous – if the proxy of a bandit came into power. The state had already endured five years of the Goonda Raj during the reign of the Samajwadi Party, and if prominent criminals were to come to power again, it would mean that thugs would lay down the law of the land once more; no one would be safe under their reign. 'If bandits are ruling, imagine how much worse it would get? People would think that it is normal to have these people in power, and maybe even more of them will get votes next time,' she says.

The canvassing techniques of Thokia's gang offered a taste of what would come under their rule. Sampat's own gang members had alerted her to the unchecked abuse of villagers by the bandits. One Pink Gang member, Munni, who lives in Panchampur, a small hamlet in the Naraini constituency, came to Sampat in tears. Thokia's men were abducting her son every morning and forcing him to canvas for the bandit's mother. They told him that if he did not co-operate, he would never see his family again.

Sampat, along with local Pink Gang members, Lakhan, and Babuji, went to Panchampur to investigate and found out that the abuses were widespread: 'It wasn't just Munni's family. The entire village was being threatened. I went to that village, called the people together, and asked them why they were so scared of Thokia. They said, "*Didi*"' – a respectful way of addressing an elder sister – '"we live in the jungle and he can do anything during the night. Neither the police comes here nor does anyone take care of us, that is why we are scared," adding "This is a forest area, there is no education, we are cut off by a river . . . there are too many difficulties. One cannot find a police station nearby and people are not ready to help each other."'

'Many people were forced to work under him but not all complained to me, only Munni did. However, when I used to go to the village, people used to tell me, "*Didi, what can we do? If we don't vote for him, Thokia will kill us."*' Perpetuating their fear was the rumour that Thokia was able to obtain records of people's votes. 'I also used to explain that when your vote is cast, no one goes there, only the voter goes there to cast their votes, so who will see who you have voted for? He used to scare them like hell. He also used to go to the extent of saying that CCTV cameras are there, so if you vote for someone else, police will arrest you, so they used to get scared. But I used to tell them, just like this, that there are no CCTV cameras and that people could come out and vote against him. He is a bully and will kill people.'

It was after visiting Panchampur, and seeing the fear of the villagers there, that Sampat decided to run as an independent candidate – her sole mission would be to defeat Thokia Patel's mother. 'I did not have it in my mind to contest the election. I did not even have money to do so, but I was very worried that if people continued to be scared of these bandits, then they will become slaves of these thugs. I called all women of the village, held a meeting and told them that people will become slaves and they will continue to be killed. Bigwigs will continue to run for office and poor people will be killed everyday. That is why we cannot let them win,' she says.

'The women said, Let's all go together. I said, Let's go. We did publicity, talked to people, and asked them for votes. Mainly we told them not to cast votes out of fear.'

Sampat chose a defiant election symbol – a stick. Political symbols were plastered along the walls in Naraini during the campaigns, and each of them appealed in coded terms to the voter's dreams, aspirations or identity. The symbols of other parties included a kite, scissors, a glass tumbler, an airplane, a sewing machine, a banana, an elephant, a cabinet, an axe, a ring and a lotus.

In case people did not understand what the stick represented, Sampat spelled it out for them in one of her gutsy slogans, which caused much talk across the villages.

Mera chunao chinh chhadi
aur Sampat Pal maidan mein khadi
agar Thokia karega gadbadi
toh marni paredi chhadi

My election symbol is a stick
and Sampat Pal is standing on the election field.
If Thokia causes any trouble
then he'll get the stick from me

Sampat's canvassing efforts were helped by the fact that she was already renowned for her work with the Pink Gang. 'When I reached there, women came out and said, "*Didi* has come, *didi* has come." They all know me by name. I am known there thanks to the newspapers.'

Of course, Sampat did not expect to win. How could she compete with the cash handouts, fanfare and elaborate promises that the other parties were offering? It is well known that apart from threatening voters, candidates also bribe them to ensure their support. Many voters consider election time to be the only period in which they ever get anything from the politicians, so people were hardly going to forfeit the freebies flooding the villages by supporting Sampat, who had nothing to offer.

Sampat hoped that as both she and Thokia's mother appealed to a similar demographic, she would be able to split the votes enough to prevent her from winning. She also was banking on the fact that her outspoken campaign would embolden villagers not to vote for Thokia's mother out of fear.

Sometimes, the *pradhans* she encountered during her canvassing would try to persuade Sampat not to run against

Thokia (few referred to Piyaria as being the contender, despite her name being on the ballot), or even encouraged her to join 'his' campaign. One *pradhan* from Naugawan invited her to tea at his place one day and told her, ' "*Didi*, do one thing, either give support to Thokia or accept support from him." I said I don't want to do either,' she remembers. The *pradhan* then told her that Thokia wanted to meet her 'face to face'. 'I said I don't want to meet him. I am not here to win or lose. I am entering the elections to give confidence to people and create awareness that they should not vote for people who scare them. That's why I am standing for election. I won't support him, he is a bad man, later police will torture me, I don't want to support him or have his support, he is not a nice man,' she recalls.

Apart from campaigning, Sampat was also actively trying to limit Thokia Patel's reign of terror on the villagers in the district of Naraini. She complained to the police, citing the threats that people in Panchampur were facing, and asked that they intervene. 'I complained to the police that he is threatening people, beating them, burning their houses. I gave a written complaint to the police to stop his vehicles. I made the application on my behalf,' she says, explaining that no one else dared to make a complaint under his or her own name. Sampat's pleas were successful. 'With the help of the police I stopped all his propagandists; the police stopped their vehicles and asked why they were threatening and blackmailing people to vote for them,' Sampat recalls. When Thokia's campaign machine ground to a halt for two days, it put a serious dent in his campaign efforts; for the first time, Sampat was hopeful that his puppet candidate, his mother, could be defeated on Election Day.

There were sixteen candidates to choose from on that searingly hot day at the end of April, when elections in Naraini took place. The whole country watched the Uttar Pradesh Legislative Assembly elections closely; all wanted to know whether the Goonda Raj would continue to reign over this large, populous state.

When the ballots were counted two weeks later, Sampat and Piyaria, Thokia's mother, were the only women in the gathering of candidates awaiting the results in the counting station. 'Both of us were looking at each other. I recognised that she is Piyaria, but she did not recognise me because she never came out in public nor did she go campaigning. She asked me where I came from. I told her I am Sampat Pal. Then she asked me, "Are you also running for election?" I said yes. She asked, "What was your election symbol?" I said my election symbol was a "stick". Then she knew that I was the one who was opposing her,' Sampat remembers. The women treated each other with mutual suspicion. 'She asked whether I got my lunch or not. I said I'll not eat. She gave me a few cashew nuts, but I did not eat them. I kept them in my hands. She kept on eating and asked me why I am not eating, so I said I'll eat later, but I threw them away.' Why did Sampat refuse the snack? 'Because I was hating her from inside. I thought this food was bought with some corrupt money. My inner voice says that I should not accept food from such people. It does not matter how much they butter me up,' she explains.

The women eyed each other closely while the ballots were being counted. 'She was proud that she was leading against me, as when she had one thousand votes, I had only one hundred,' Sampat says. When the results were announced, it was revealed that 27,251 people voted for the mother of Thokia. She did not win, however; she came in second behind Puru-shottam Naresh Dwivedi – the same man who would later accuse Sheelu of theft – who had won by 4,443 votes. By comparison, just under three thousand people voted for Sampat, but she is convinced that those votes would have otherwise gone to Piyaria, and so was pleased with the result. She also believed that many more would have voted for Piyaria out of fear had Sampat not repeatedly visited villagers and urged them not to give in to the bandits. 'Had I not contested, he would have won, but I defeated him,' Sampat said referring to Thokia, adding, 'I considered his loss my victory.'

'I was clapping when Purushottam Naresh Dwivedi won. Everyone was happy – not that he had won, but that Thokia lost.' Now, Sampat looks back on the celebrations with regret. 'There is no difference between Dwivedi and Thokia. If anything, Dwivedi is worse.'

CHAPTER THREE

THE RED ROOM

I AM SUFFERING WHATEVER HAS BEEN
WRITTEN IN MY DESTINY.

—Sheelu

THE STORY OF HOW SHEELU ENDED UP AT THE LEGISLATOR'S HOUSE begins in Shahbajpur, a remote, impoverished village dotted with mud and thatch houses and surrounded by lentil fields, where she grew up. To reach Sheelu's hometown, one has to drive down winding, narrow roads, beyond which deep, red-earth ravines are carved into the barren, bush-and-shrub landscape. An anaemic river called the Ranj, a tributary to the sacred Yamuna River, runs through the gorge. Approaching Shahbajpur, before you cross the Ranj, someone has carved the word 'WELCOME' vertically into the bark of a birch tree standing on the right side of the road.

The majority of people in Shahbajpur are Kewats, members of the lowly boatman caste who traditionally spend their days on the steep embankment of the river, where they earn a living making ropes out of stringy river reeds that they left to dry in the beating sun. These days, with water levels in the Ranj being so low, many try their hand at farming. 'We are farming people. We husk grain, we grind, we chop,' said one villager. Shahbajpur has a tumbleweed tranquility to it, where the silence is more likely to be punctured by animals baying than human activity. It is a place where a seventeen-year-old girl like Sheelu might have felt she was wilting away.

Sheelu was known in her hometown as a bold, spunky young girl, not as demure as many of the other village girls her age. She had carefully plucked eyebrows that arched slightly, and smooth, flawless skin, except for a handful of small pockmarks on her cheek, upper lip and at the inner part of her left eyebrow. She owned a small mirror with a plastic frame and spent hours looking at herself, from this angle and that, trying out various affected expressions of coyness, similar to those seen in Hindi soap operas.

When Sheelu laughed, she did so with a cackling abandon, throwing her head back and clapping her hands with mischievous delight. More often than not, she found comedic value in something said that was slightly naive or half-baked. When her mouth was not flung open with laughter, it was more often than not twisted into a wry smirk. Sheelu had a caustic sense of humour – the fact that her intelligence had been stifled when she was pulled out of school early caused her to grow bitter and resentful. She had a habit of rolling her eyes when figures of authority, like her father, lectured her, and talked back when she disagreed with them.

Sheelu's impertinence started soon after her mother died, which she believes happened when she was around nine or ten years old. Her father, Achchhe, pulled her out of school so she could look after her three brothers, who continued going to school. She also helped to run the household while her father, a subsistence farmer who earned twenty-five rupees a day (less than thirty pence), ran a small shop out of the house. There, he sold one-rupee worth of consumer goods packaged in colourful sachets the size of a condom packet – 'Good Time Tea', 'Lux Shampoo' and several brands of chewing tobacco.

As Sheelu grew older, she became bored with her domestic chores – drawing well water, cleaning and cooking. When her father was out in the fields and her brothers were in school, she would take the family bicycle and ride it along the narrow dirt lanes that snaked along the river – 'I went out quietly, without telling anyone. It didn't matter where I went, I would just drive around on my own.' When her mother was alive, Sheelu was forbidden to ride the bike. 'You'll get hurt,' her mother said one day. 'I need to be hurt to learn,' Sheelu replied. When she refused to listen, the family sold the bike, only replacing it much later. By then, she had already had a taste of freedom and wanted more.

After Sheelu's mother died, there was little left to keep Sheelu firmly rooted in the house. She frequently argued with her father, and after their rows, she often went to live with a maternal aunt in a village called Lacchapurva, across the state border in Madhya Pradesh. Other times she would leave home for weeks on end with the excuse of wanting to attend religious festivals or village fairs near Harnampur, where her grandparents lived. The sojourns away from home grew longer and more frequent until, by the age of seventeen, Sheelu had been absent for almost one and a half years.

THE RED ROOM 67

Achchhe, who was known to have an alcohol problem, did not do much to bring Sheelu back into the fold. He assumed she had been living with her aunt.

When Achchhe finally decided to send his son Santoo to pick Sheelu up, Santoo returned later that day empty-handed. Sheelu, the boy told his father, was no longer living with her aunt, but was now living in Pathara.

THERE ARE CONTRADICTORY VERSIONS of how Sheelu ended up in Pathara. Achchhe claimed that the aunt Sheelu was staying with in Lacchapurva (who was feuding with Achchhe over land left by his deceased wife) sold his daughter to a young man called Rajju Patel – thought to have links to bandits – for fifty thousand rupees, approximately five hundred pounds. At other times, he said a *pradhan* sold her. Sheelu claimed that Rajju kidnapped her, holding her in Pathara for one and a half months. Others, like the villagers in Pathara, would tell a very different story. They asserted that Sheelu had fallen in love with Rajju and eloped with him – it was widely acknowledged in India that a large proportion of kidnapping complaints are in fact from parents trying to cover up the elopement of a daughter. Indeed, the state government of Uttar Pradesh reportedly pressured the police into registering all cases of runaway marriages as kidnapping.

People in Harnampur had informed Achchhe where Rajju Patel lived, but Achchhe did not want to retrieve Sheelu on his own – what if Rajju threatened him? Achchhe considered going to the police, but he feared he would need to pay a bribe to guarantee their help. With his negligible earnings, he was in no position to grease the palms of the

local police, nor did he have the stature to demand that the
police help him without payment. He did know one person
who could accompany him to the police station, however.
Someone who was so powerful that he could even order the
police around. This man was Purushottam Naresh Dwivedi,
the legislator.

Both Achchhe and Dwivedi are members of the Bahujan
Samaj Party (BSP) – Uttar Pradesh's ruling party, which represents lower-caste voters like Achchhe. Full of hope, Achchhe joined the party after it was formed in 1984, when he
was sixteen – 'I've been a member since the days of Kanshi
Ram,' he says nostalgically, referring to the founder of the
party.

Many in Shahbajpur are part of the BSP. Indeed, the
bridge that crosses the river Ranj, just outside of the village,
is dedicated to Kanshi Ram. Achchhe joined for many of
the same reasons that others in his village did. 'You see, no
one listened to the poor. There was no work for poor people
either. I heard that if one joins BSP, they will get some help,'
he remembers. 'I gave regular donations, been working for
the party since my youth. . . . Do you want to see my card?
I have it here,' he says, reaching into his wallet and carefully
taking out a folded piece of grey paper.

In 2007, the BSP gave Achchhe a small-time role as a
'sector warden' – which meant that he acted as the party's
voluntary organiser and representative on the ground in ten
small villages, one of which was Shahbajpur. Achchhe's job
was to help local residents in whatever way he could. 'I meet
the public, I listen to them. Like if someone has beaten a
poor person or if a poor person has beaten someone, I listen
to both of them. I ask for justice from the government. . . .

This is the kind of work I do.' When he needed help, however, he would turn to Dwivedi.

Achchhe first met Dwivedi in 2007, in the run-up to the state Legislative Assembly election. As a party loyalist, Achchhe campaigned tirelessly for Dwivedi and earned his favour when he won. Both men have described Achchhe's relationship with Dwivedi as that of 'guru and disciple' – 'I obeyed him and called him "guru-ji, guru-ji",' Achchhe says. As a lower-caste man addressing a Brahmin, Achchhe used the religious term guru as a sign of respect. But Achchhe's use of this appellation was somewhat ironic. Despite the party giving nearly a quarter of the election tickets to Brahmins in 2007, the BSP claimed to represent the Dalit (formerly known as the untouchable) caste and was, in theory, vehemently opposed to caste discrimination.

Not knowing who else to turn to for help with his daughter, Achchhe called Dwivedi – whose number was saved on his phone under the entry for vidhayak, or 'legislator' – on 8 December 2010. After Achchhe told Dwivedi his predicament with Sheelu, the worried father asked whether Dwivedi would accompany him to the police station. The legislator snorted at the idea that Uttar Pradesh's law enforcers could be of any help to Achchhe. 'Don't go to the police. They can be bribed and come back with empty hands,' he reportedly told him. There was another reason why Dwivedi thought Achchhe should not report the incident with Rajju. 'If you make a report, you will have a bad name,' he allegedly said, referring to the shameful nature of the incident.

'I will send my men to Rajju's village, we will get her – no need to involve the police,' Achchhe remembers Dwivedi saying. The men, accompanied by Santoo, headed out to Pathara that day. Achchhe had a feeling in the pit of his stomach that this would not end well, but he couldn't have predicted just how disastrous this course of action would prove to be.

SAMPAT'S FIRST MATTER of business was to find out what Sheelu's connection to the legislator was. After leaving the police station, Sampat decided to make her way to Pathara, the town where the newspapers said Sheelu had lived, to investigate. Sampat had a good source there: the father-in-law to her second daughter, Ambrawatti, was the village chief. Because Pathara was at least two hours away, Sampat decided to get an auto-rickshaw to drop her off at her family home, in Badausa. From there she could get a youth called Nati, a friend of her son's, to drive her the rest of the way.

Badausa, with a population of about five hundred, is arranged in an undeveloped strip, often just a few houses deep, around National Highway 76. Badausa, like Atarra, has little signs of urban planning – raw sewage flows into open canals, and almost no households have running water. Electricity is only available for a few hours each day.

Sampat travelled down the congested main road, past carts displaying pyramids of pomegranate and sweet lime. As noon approached, people milled about the *chai* stalls and the vendors pushing oil-stained glass vitrines on wheels full of savoury snacks like *samosas*, with flies whizzing around them. Underfoot, on pavements made of stamped-down dirt, roosters pecked on small mounds of waste speckled with colourful plastic wrappers; old men on rope-beds sat smoking and watched their bare-bottomed grandchildren play near the edge of the road.

As Sampat neared her family house in Badausa, she crossed a bridge that cuts across a low river, called the Baghein; it runs through a wide gorge, on the sloping, silt-laden banks of which people cultivate land for farming. When the hot season starts after April, young men swim in the river to cool off. In the winter, those without water at home can be seen bathing and washing clothes and cooking utensils there.

Shortly after crossing the bridge, Sampat stopped in front of her family house, which is perched atop a bank of soil a few yards back from the motorway. All the houses on this road are joined together in a row and look identical – they each have a metal shutter running down the front of them, a plain, windowless facade, a sheet-metal front door and a flat roof, good for flying kites and sleeping when the nights are hot. Sampat's house differs only in its colour – it is painted pastel pink.

The front door opens into a narrow entranceway, which leads to a spartan room with a concrete floor. One of the candyfloss–coloured walls is crisscrossed by clotheslines from which hang dozens of school uniforms – red trousers, white shirts, red-and-white-striped ties and red belts with aluminium buckles – all belonging to Sampat's many grandchildren.

At the back of the room, two metal doors lead out to a bare concrete terrace overlooking fields, smokestacks of brick kilns and, half a mile in the distance, a train line. Inside the house, at the bottom of concrete steps is a lower level, where cooking and washing are done, and a small bedroom, in which Sampat's family takes turns to sleep.

Sampat's house teems with people at all hours of the day, which partly explains why she rarely spends time here

– 'This is not a place to do work! That's why I go to my office.' Sampat's husband, Munni Lal Pal, her eleven grandchildren, nieces and nephews live in the house, along with four of her five children. The eldest, Prabha, is followed by Champa, Munna (Sampat's only son) and Nisha, the youngest. Ambrawatti, the second eldest, is the only one who lives with her in-laws. 'I have the whole world's kids growing up in my house,' Sampat once said with a tired laugh.

Now that she is older, Sampat is free to drift in and out of domestic life; she is no longer entangled in maternal duties. 'There is no pressure on me from my family. I focus on that which needs more attention. If there are problems in the house, I solve them and move on. My family's pain and someone else's pain are the same,' she says practically. When they were young, her children did not understand why Sampat's attention was divided between so many strangers, who used to unload their problems on her. 'Before, there were problems with the family. They said, Are you more concerned about them or us?' Sampat recalls. Her answer to that question was a difficult one for a child to hear. 'I am everyone's mother. I do not put my family first.'

Today Sampat's daughters – along with her granddaughters, daughter-in-law and two nieces – run the household. Sampat has not cooked a meal, or made herself a cup of tea, in many years. She is the proverbial man of the house. Whenever she sleeps at home (generally about half of the time), she expects the food to be ready when she arrives after a long day of work. Perhaps she feels that she deserves it, given that she works almost every day, Monday through Sunday, sunrise to nightfall. Her only holidays are weddings and religious feasts.

When Sampat all but moved out of her family house and into the office she shares with Babuji, in 2005, leaving her husband to look after Nisha, her actions did not provoke the kinds of threats that other women in her place would have received. Not even when Sampat informed her husband that she would be living with Babuji, himself a married man, did she experience the kinds of problems one would typically expect.

'I explained to my husband that a man should lend a hand in a woman's growth. If I get out of the house, of course I will have to make friends, but there is no wrong relationship that I share with Babuji. If we are living in one room, it is because there is no other room available or because it is too costly. If we stay in one room, what's wrong with that? Babuji has a very good character. I have never seen him have bad intentions towards a woman; his character is like a diamond. Who would work so honestly with a woman? That's how I explained it to my husband,' Sampat says.

Place Sampat next to her husband, and the inexplicable – how a married woman in Bundelkhand could live with another man without social sanction – becomes easier to grasp. Munni Lal, with his sunken cheeks and several missing teeth, spends most of his waking life sitting sullenly inside the house, shrouded in an enduring, diffident silence. He resembles a shrivelled husk of a man, resigned to his insignificance. Munni Lal, who was often high on marijuana during the early years of his marriage, can usually be found in a quiet corner of the house, lying on a rope-bed from where he issues forth alternating coughs and groans, usually owing to his bad back. Whenever Sampat returns home, he offers a faint grunt acknowledging her presence. It is rare to ever catch Sampat and Munni Lal talking, or even exchanging glances, but then again Munni Lal is not much of a conversationalist.

One might say that Munni Lal tolerates the current state of affairs thanks to a feat of self-delusion. 'One thing is sure, God has made pairs,' he once said about marriage. When talking about married life with Sampat, he gets nostalgic. 'When we are together, there is a feeling of togetherness. It is a great feeling, we can eat and drink comfortably, sweep the house, go for a shit in the morning, have a bath, light two incense sticks in the morning and evening, life goes on nicely . . . ,' he trails off as he remembers the good moments. Then, inevitably, he remembers that they hardly live together anymore. 'It's okay. I work and eat two *rotis*' – flat, unleavened bread – 'What more do I need? I have worked hard since the beginning. I have many qualities; it is not that I am sitting here without any qualities,' he adds, defensively.

By the time Sampat moved in with Babuji, she was already her own woman – a far cry from the scrawny child who had been married off to a widower a decade her senior. Back then, Munni Lal's age gave him an advantage over Sampat, but that has long since evaporated. Just as he began wilting away after a lifetime of working the fields, Sampat found herself blossoming. Her booming voice, firm footfalls and growing involvement in public life had pushed Munni Lal into the shadows. Their children rarely sought his permission or advice in important matters. Behind his back they call Munni the 'Buddha', because all he does is sit in a meditative silence. Since no one listens to him anymore, he has taken to muttering to himself and occasionally shouting at his grandchildren. 'Today no one obeys me. My son is out of school. My daughter says, "Do you have money or not?" Is money everything? That behaviour I am getting. I didn't behave bad any time in my life, I never wished bad for anyone.'

When Sampat spends the night in Badausa, she and Munni Lal never sleep beside each other. Instead, she nestles in with her grandchildren on cold nights or sleeps alone on the roof, where faint breezes offer respite during stifling summer nights.

Munni Lal was 'around eighteen or twenty' when he married the first time, but before his wife could move in with him, she died. 'I never saw my first wife. I saw her once during marriage but she never came. She died there, in her parents' home. I don't know how, she must have been diseased.' After the death, his first father-in-law offered Munni Lal another daughter to marry, but he turned him down. Soon afterwards, his marriage with Sampat, who was from the same community – they are both in the Gadaria, or shepherd, caste – was arranged.

Sampat was only twelve on the day of her wedding. 'I didn't know what marriage meant, no one explained it to me. Me, I was enjoying myself that day! Playing around, eating many, many sweets that people brought. Mother told me, "Sit down! Don't play like this!" but I did anyway. I thought it was fun. I didn't know anything about what came after,' Sampat shrugs.

Up until then, 'marriage' was a game she played with her friends. 'We used to go to the farms when it was the season for growing trees; there was so much grass. There was a wide strip so we used to pluck it and make grass jewellery, weaving belts, anklets and toe rings. It came out looking very beautiful and we too looked very nice. The whole day long we played like this in the fields. We made one girl the boy, one girl the bride. Then we watched them pretend to get married. They would say, "Okay, bye! We are going to our in-laws' place now," and then wave to us,' Sampat chuckles. 'What did we know back then? Nothing!'

Sampat was renowned in Kairi for inventing games and for her incurable tomboy spirit. She once collected dozens of grasshoppers for a unique radio made out of a carton, with a stick for an antenna. The 'music' came from the chirruping insects Sampat had caught; she tied together their legs with fine thread, which was fed through a hole in the box. 'When I pulled the string, they started singing – *tee, tee, tee, tee*. It was like Chattarpur Radio!' she says, laughing at her ingenuity.

The games ended when, after the wedding, she arrived in Gadarian Purva (Shepherd's Village) to live with her in-laws and husband. Gadarian Purva is a hamlet composed of an austere collection of mud huts near Badausa. It is surrounded by stony hills, atop of which are perched countless boulders. On the outskirts of the village, hardened men and women, enveloped in clouds of grey dust, arduously broke rocks with sledgehammers to sell to local construction businesses. The deserted, narrow mud-brick lanes of Gadarian Purva made a negative impression on the young Sampat. It was much smaller than her parents' village of Kairi, people were stern and, to her disappointment, 'no one was excited that I had arrived!'

In the centre of the hamlet was a well where people bathed, drew their cooking water and washed their clothes. Tethered to the doorposts of houses were mottled goats and cows. Naked children, their eyes lined with *kajal*, a type of eyeliner believed to offer sun protection, often ran around in the dirt lanes, chasing each other with sticks and other implements. Behind the wooden doors of the huts were the women, who remained out of sight except when, with veils drawn over their faces, they made their daily trip to the well. This was where, and how, Sampat was expected to live. Hunched over a fire, stirring *dal* and curry in a large pot, feeding a brood of preferably male children.

Everyone who lived in the settlement was a member of the Pal community and were traditionally shepherds. Nearby were other hamlets: Charmaran Purva, where the low-caste leather-tanning Charmars lived, and Yadavan Purva, where the land-owning Yadav caste lived. Sampat's village Kairi was multicultural – there were Charmar, Kori, Nai, Lohar, Ahir and Darzi castemen, and 'even some Muslims!' In Sampat's view, the small-mindedness of the people in Gadarian Purva was heightened by the fact that members of only one community inhabited the village.

Sampat may not have received the reception she had hoped for in her new home, but her husband was genuinely happy to have her. After the disappointment of his first marriage, Munni Lal was pleased with the new mate that had been found for him. 'Our second marriage was very good. The new girl was good looking, and that other girl was dark-skinned,' he says.

For three years, however, Sampat was not fully his, for she travelled back to her parents' village every two weeks until she started menstruating, following a custom called *gaona*. 'These days the girl follows the groom immediately after marriage, but in those days she used to go to the husband only after a few years, when she was grown-up. See, *gaona* happens when the girl's body is not completely matured. When the girl is fresh and plump, that's when she joins her husband,' Munni explains. The final trip of Sampat's *gaona*, when the young bride was finally meant to belong wholly to Munni, never culminated in the marital bliss he had hoped for. Just like in the early days when Sampat would shuttle back and forth between Kairi and Gadarian Purva, she was perpetually slipping through Munni's fingers. Sampat was an elusive woman, with itchy feet and grand dreams in which he played no role. 'When a husband does not get to see the wife, he keeps thinking about her. Where is she? How is she? The wife also thinks the same about her husband. When they become one, their thinking changes. Two attachments become one. There is no one except the husband and wife,' says Munni idealistically.

With each year of their marriage, Sampat, famished for freedom and with an insatiable desire for independence, ventured further and further out into the world until, inevitably, the moment came when she maintained but the faintest whiff of a presence in Munni's life.

SAMPAT TOOK HER FIRST STEP towards independence before the age of fifteen, soon after the *gaona* period ended. In those days, when she was still young and skinny, Sampat was 'put to work' in her in-laws' kitchen, making *chapattis* and preparing meals for the family. Sampat was often tasked with grinding the grain, an arduous, thankless job that she hated – 'I was still small and couldn't do it well.' Towards the end of the *gaona* period, it dawned on Sampat that she would be trapped in Gadarian Purva for the rest of her life, that very soon she would not undertake those frequent trips back to Kairi, during which she threw off her constricting wifely skin and jumped once more into the familiar body of the carefree child. 'I won't stay here as a slave,' she decided resolutely. 'I wanted to keep my same nature and spirit that I had as a child – I didn't care about what people thought about me,' she later said.

The next time her mother-in-law ordered her to grind the grain, she flat-out refused. 'This shameless girl won't listen!' bellowed her mother-in-law, for all to hear. Munni Lal's brother was particularly offended by Sampat's stubbornness. 'This one needs a slap to listen,' he concluded, and swiftly smacked her in the face. Sampat refused to eat for two days until, seeing that her spirit could not be broken, her mother-in-law convinced her to eat something.

Munni's stance in the standoff between mother and wife was neutral – he was neither friend nor foe. The shy, mildly ineffectual man never deliberately harmed her – 'He has never hit me,' Sampat will concede – though he lacked the conviction to stand up for her in the face of tradition. He blames this on his lack of education. 'I am an illiterate village person. The educated people have four eyes, two are these,' he says pointing to his eyes, 'and another two is their knowl-edge. What do we have? Only two eyes. It's like that, isn't it?' he says. Sampat, however, was one of those people with four eyes. 'She was very clever since the beginning, your Sampat. She used to teach me about behaviour and good conduct. "One should not scold the other," she used to tell me. Also said not to doubt each other. She used to scold me though . . . now also it is the same.'

Munni Lal wasn't the only one Sampat 'scolded'; her mother-in-law was a frequent victim of her untamed tongue. In Gadarian Purva, it was customary for newly wed women to observe *purdah*, a practice by which women pull their sari fabric over their faces so that they are fully hidden from view. Sampat, not accustomed to being curtained off from society, would sometimes forget to cover herself. 'But how can you forget?' shrieked her mother-in-law when she first caught her uncovered. 'You are acting shamelessly!' Her admonishments left Sampat fuming. A few months into her marriage, Sampat was speaking to a distant male relative who had stopped by to pay a visit. In a conciliatory mood she had covered her face, but the cloth reached only to the tip of her nose, leaving her mouth exposed. When her mother-in-law saw her, she barked, 'What! Just half *purdah* you're doing?' to which Sampat responded by throwing back the veil completely. Glaring at her with her uncovered face, Sampat shouted, 'Forget it – I'm not doing *purdah* anymore! What is so wrong with showing my face, tell me?' and stormed away.

The disputes grew louder and more frequent until the relationship with her in-laws crumbled after she gave birth, 'around fifteen', to her first daughter, Prabha. 'This daughter-in-law is useless. See, she has given us a *girl*,' complained Munni's mother to all who would listen.

'In our Bundelkhand, we sing songs when boys are born, but for girls no one sings. My in-laws were the same. They taunted me and made comments about why I didn't give birth to a son.' Sampat's mother-in-law expected her to bear these scornful remarks, as other women of her generation had, and was livid when Sampat would pounce on those who slighted her daughter. 'What's wrong with a woman? You're one, aren't you?' Sampat would say.

Once Sampat had regained her strength after the birth, she informed Munni that she was moving out. 'If you want to live with me, then it won't be in your parents' house.' In a country where living with the extended family was the norm, for a wife to demand that her husband leave his family house was unusual; in a place as bound to tradition as Bundelkhand, it was unheard of. Torn between his family and his headstrong wife, Munni Lal felt it would go against the laws of nature to live apart from his wife. 'Where my wife lies down, there I also lie down. No one can say, Why have you gone there? If something happens to the husband, the wife looks after him, and if something happens to the wife, then the husband will look after her. The husband will think about the sorrows or sicknesses of his wife, the husband will wash her clothes, will give her a bath, food . . . no one else will do that. Husband only will do. Come whatever may, husband will bring food. And when he brings food he won't eat alone; they will eat together.' Such were Munni's feelings. His agreeing to move out would mark the beginning of a lifetime of concessions and defeats that he would experience in his marriage.

THE FIRST TIME SAMPAT created a group of women in Gadarian Purva that resembled a gang was when she fought against a man called Ram Milan, a distant relative of Munni's who used to beat his child-wife, Dookli, viciously. Sampat, who lived next to them, would hear the lashings and Dookli's cries of anguish. For a long time, Sampat did nothing to intervene – 'I didn't get involved immediately back then, it wasn't easy.'

One day, however, she stood outside their front door and shouted, 'What can she have done that you're beating this girl up day and night?'

Ram Milan emerged from his hut, shouting, 'What do you know? This girl never does any work!'

'Maybe that's because she is still young!' Sampat snapped – Dookli was, by her estimation, no older than fifteen. 'She also secretly eats our food!' the man added.

'Secretly eating your food? You must not be feeding her enough then!' Sampat shouted back.

This back and forth continued until, according to Sampat, Ram Milan shouted, 'Don't start acting like you're the president of the village council here, you whore. This is none of your business,' and slammed the door.

The next day, Sampat called together her friends, Bijma, Kesariya and Kusuma. 'I took them to the fields with the excuse of cutting grass,' she remembers. Sampat told them about Ram Milan's violent ways, but did not mention her plan. When they spotted him in the field, carrying a heavy load of wheat on his head, they crept up behind him. Sampat, who is remarkably strong, shoved Ram Milan forcefully so that he staggered forward and, losing his balance, dropped the bushels of wheat he was carrying. Before he could turn around, Sampat elbowed him powerfully in the ribs. 'I didn't slap him though – that would have been a bit much,' she later said.

'He fell and started shouting, "These women are beating me, come!" That was great work!' Sampat chortles. 'After

beating him we said, "From now on, don't beat your wife."
The women who were with me told everyone that Sampat Pal had given him a beating for what he was doing to
Dookli. It was known by all in the village, and Ram Milan
didn't beat his wife ever again.'

Shortly after the incident with Ram Milan, Sampat heard
that there had been a murder in the village of Rauli, which
was nearby, on the other side of the neglected state motorway, a badly paved two-lane road traversed by screeching
trucks, oxen and carts, and shepherds. Rumour had it that
an upper-caste landlord had sexually abused a lower-caste
tenant, a woman named Dulariya, and that he had murdered her son for getting involved. Sampat went out with
her friends Bijma, Kesariya and Kusuma to meet the woman,
without telling her husband. 'I felt like we had to do something, but we didn't have any power in our hands back then.
There were not many women with us at that time, and we
did not know about courts and legal procedures,' Sampat says.

As much as she wanted to, Sampat could not do much
for Dulariya, but she did try to encourage her and the other
women in Rauli to stand up to oppression together. The
murder of Dulariya's son had caused them all to realise
that their rights and life would continue to be trampled
on unless they learned to protect themselves. So it was that
Sampat gradually reached out to women across the hamlets surrounding Gadarian Purva and tried to help them
in their struggles. It was a slow process, not least because
Sampat was not allowed to wander around freely without
her husband's permission. She was still, as she describes it,
'in chains'.

———————

AFTER GIVING BIRTH to five children, Sampat, only in her early twenties, was starting to feel suffocated by the restrictions placed on her. 'I was cooped up in the house like a rat,' she says. Over the years, she thought with ever-growing urgency about how to become independent, until the question consumed her. One day, as her children played in the courtyard of her mud hut, Sampat withdrew inside to be alone. Lying there, looking up at the thatched ceiling, she searched the shadowy gaps between the spindly twigs, across which were stretched thick cobwebs that had trapped feathers and small insects. She and Munni had built this house from scratch with their own hands in three months. It had felt like freedom at the time – 'I had my own kitchen, my own field. My in-laws didn't tell me what to do,' Sampat recalls – but that feeling soon evaporated and she started to grow restless. 'This is not freedom,' she thought. 'Freedom is when I have my own money, but how do I do that?' she wondered.

Sampat had one skill that no one else in Gadarian Purva had, 'not even the men': she could sew. That childhood obsession, which her mother had considered a nuisance, turned out to be a valuable skill from which she could earn her own money.

Happenstance had revealed Sampat's sewing skills. One day she had taken fabric to the tailor in Rauli so he could make clothes for her children to wear at a relative's wedding. Sampat also provided the designs. 'It was a very different style I had instructed him to make. One of the designs had many buttons and another had frills,' she remembers, explaining that she had been inspired by clothes she had seen someone in town wearing. Weeks went by, and every time Sampat went to the tailor, he gave one excuse after another for why he still was not done. With the wedding day fast approaching and her patience all but gone, Sampat grabbed the fabric back from him. 'Enough. I'll sew this myself. You're useless,' she shouted at him in front of the other villagers.

'Think you're better than me, do you?' the insulted tailor shouted back.

'Of course! At least I'll do the work, instead of just talk about it,' she said and marched off. She managed to lay her hands on a needle and thread and then took the measurements of her children when she got home. Improvising as she went along, she marked the fabric with a piece of chalk and then, for want of scissors, cut it with a sickle, which she pressed between her knees with the blade curving towards her. It took her two days to finish the outfits by hand. When she was done, her husband brought the crudely constructed garments to another tailor in Rauli, a Muslim man, for finishing touches. 'Who did this?' the tailor asked, inspecting the seams of the garments. When Munni told him it was Sampat, he replied, 'Your woman is very clever, you should buy her a sewing machine!' It was a casual, off-hand comment, but when Munni repeated it to his wife later that day, a storm of possibility swirled in Sampat's mind. Now, all she could think about, day and night, was how she was going to purchase a sewing machine and become a self-employed seamstress.

The sewing machine that Sampat wanted was produced by an Indian company called Kapoor, and it cost 660 rupees – 'That was a lot of money back then.' Where could she get the money from? Munni would never agree to give it to her. Not that he was spiteful or mean, but he was overly cautious with money, especially since, unlike everyone else in the village, he and Sampat ran their own household, independently from their extended families, and so had higher costs.

That day Sampat resolved to acquire the money secretly, the way she had done as a child, by selling some of the family grain without telling Munni. In the small attic where they stored their produce, she pilfered 110 rupees' worth each of wheat, split red gram, mustard, rice, chickpeas and barley.

She went to see the grocer, a man called Mahesh, who sometimes bought produce from women without telling their husbands – but at a substantially lower rate in return for the favour. 'I am selling you these sacks. They are worth 110 rupees each,' Sampat told him. Mahesh eyed her suspiciously and then gave her the money. Once he paid her, Sampat said sternly, 'And don't tell my husband about this.'

'He will come and shout at me if he finds out!' the grocer protested.

'Don't worry – I am not a thief, am I? I have the courage to face him if need be,' Sampat assured him.

WHEN MUNNI ASKED Sampat how she'd been able to afford the sewing machine, Sampat lied to him, saying that she had found the money lying on the road. After Sampat finally taught herself how to operate the machine, it opened the door to financial independence; soon, Sampat was earning as much money as her husband. However, this did not make Munni more amenable to her demands for even more freedom, such as when she wanted to join a local, cash-strapped

NGO based in Badausa called Prabhat Samit. Raja Ram, the head of Prabhat Samit, which ran small schools and raised awareness about women's rights, had courted Sampat when she became renowned for her sewing skills, and had told her that he could use women like her in his organisation. Sampat went to the organisation's meetings without Munni's approval, finding excuses that would keep him unaware of her comings and goings. 'My husband didn't know about it. Nothing he knew! He wasn't letting me go freely at that time, so why tell him? Just for him to break my head?' One day, however, she was caught.

'I'm going to take the rubbish to the fields,' Sampat told Munni, picking up a heap of litter and walking outside, as if nothing were amiss. After walking towards the spot where they normally dumped their waste, Sampat pulled her sari fabric over her face so that she was well hidden, and turning around, she headed towards Rauli. 'This was my way of going quietly-quietly to places; no one knew who I was when I walked around like this – that was the good thing about the *purdah*,' Sampat chuckles as she pulls her sari over her face to demonstrate her disguise.

Hidden behind her veil, Sampat walked down the main brick lane that ran between the cluster of austere white-washed adobe huts that made up Gadarian Purva. When the village fell away, she continued along a raised dirt track (high enough to still be navigable when the rice paddies were flooded with water) and past the stone crushers, who were surrounded at all times of the day by a faint cloud of pulverised granite.

Sampat crossed the state motorway and walked the short distance towards the one-storey, white-washed brick school set in the centre of a large, dusty yard. The NGO had set up hand-painted posters exclaiming slogans about equality and justice. Some of the members from Badausa were already inside, sitting on mats on the floor. Many of the women there already knew Sampat, like Dulariya, whose son the Brahmin landlord had murdered. That day, Sampat had been asked to address the crowd.

'We are strong when we are together. Do you see this hand?' Sampat asked when she stood up before her audience, with her palm open and fingers splayed, as if about to deliver a slap. 'What will hurt more? If you hit someone like this? Or . . . ,' – bringing her fingers together in a fist – 'if you hit them like this?' she asked, punching the air. 'This is why we must form groups. Only then will we get our freedom.' Her words were directed at the women who had come to hear her speak, though many of the men listened attentively too.

Sampat sang several songs that day, mostly Hindi sing-alongs she had composed herself. 'Women learn a lot through songs. That's why I sing them,' she says. Some, like the one about the inability to understand English, were humorous. Others, which were delivered in the undulating, mournful style of Bundelkhand's folk songs, were more serious, such as the one about affirmative action and the rise of women.

> *Wake up, wake up you Indian women*
> *This is era to become awake*
> *We should do our job, where sisters can work we*
>   *won't call men there*
> *We will solve our problems on our own, We will*
>   *make our lives better*

The time has come to wake up, we will educate both
girls and boys together
We will allow no difference between them, we will
improve their lives
The time has come to wake up.

Listening to Sampat with great attention that day was a man called Gulab, a politically aware member of the Charmar community, who are Dalits. Charmars had been mistreated in Bundelkhand and, indeed, across the country for generations; calling someone a Charmar was an insult in many circles of Indian society. Sampat's lament about injustice filled his heart with sorrow as he remembered all of the social problems plaguing the lower castes and women alike, and he saw in her a kindred spirit.

Gulab had never before seen an uneducated woman speak with such confidence, especially in an area like Bundelkhand. 'This woman was spreading good awareness. I was agreeing with what she was saying. Later I heard that she was a courageous one also, and doing good work, so I wanted to meet her husband and congratulate him,' Gulab recalls. He asked the people in Rauli if they knew where Sampat lived, and when he found out her house was nearby, he set off to meet Munni, who was unaware of his wife's double-life.

'Gulab didn't know about my secrecy and told my husband everything! He put my husband into doubt. My secrets were out. Now that one started asking me about what I was doing, and I became worried. How did you go to Rauli when Rauli is two kilometres away? I first made excuses that I didn't go. He was saying, If you didn't go, then why did Gulab say so? I was worried. Gulab had gone, but my husband troubled me at night. I controlled him slowly. I said, "Don't you doubt me,"' Sampat recalls.

After being exposed, Sampat stopped trying to hide her comings and goings, which led to a string of loud, public arguments between the deceived husband and the stubborn, strong-willed wife. Sometimes, she says, Munni would follow her to meetings with a stick and shout at her in front of the other women. 'My husband would curse at me a lot. I decided either I will become weaker than him or stronger than him. What do you think I chose?'

'Find another husband. I will not keep you,' Munni shouted at her one day in front of a group of women.

Sampat shouted back at him. 'I have no other husband. You think I am so stupid to do this at the cost of my home? I am doing this to save women and the poor.'

'Who are you? The saviour?' Munni snapped, before spinning around to go back home.

When Sampat came back that night, Munni hadn't eaten dinner, out of protest. To irritate him, Sampat helped herself to a large meal, ignoring his sulking fast. 'I ate nicely. He looked at me with a long face. I said, "Okay, don't eat! It won't change anything. I will go to meetings every day."'

During the long silence that existed between them, it briefly crossed Sampat's mind to beat Munni into submission with the help of other women. She rejected the idea because, she thought, 'If I do this, I will become weaker.' Physically assaulting her husband would not bring lasting peace to her household, nor would it eliminate the domestic distractions that were keeping her from engaging with the world as she wanted to.

That evening, as Munni was lying on his *charpoy* with an empty stomach, Sampat instead besieged her husband's parochial mindset with her words, employing reason, her art of persuasion and a plainly spoken threat.

'Let me explain some knowledge to you,' she said, drawing close to him. 'Men and women are like tyres of a car. We cannot go separate-separate. Are you understanding? If we work together, our kids will get a better life. They will study and will go to good schools. If you quarrel and fight with me, I will go back to my parents and the kids will become orphans. Even if you want to get married again, I won't let that happen. I will be finished and you will be finished.'

Munni rarely found the strength to confront the tempestuous storms of Sampat's temper; he did not have her cunning or her command over language. When he did summon the courage to shout at her and hail her with abuses, his anger was mere drizzle compared to the hailstorm of Sampat's response. Munni lacked the resolve to stand his ground, and so, after a token amount of resistance, he would inevitably withdraw into himself, leaving his wife to go forth unhindered in whichever direction she liked.

WHEN SAMPAT WENT OUT to investigate Sheelu's case on 14 December 2010, she did not have to sneak out or get permission from her husband. If Munni wants to know where his wife is these days, he rarely dares to ask Sampat directly; he prefers to learn of her whereabouts from their children. Had he asked, he would have learned that she had gone to Pathara.

As soon as she arrived in the village, she went to meet Nattu Lal Pal, Ambrawatti's father-in-law, to ask him about

Sheelu. Nattu was the *pradhan*, and Nattu's older brother ran a small street stall, where he and his wife sold packaged snacks and chewing tobacco. Sitting behind the stall from sunrise to sunset, Nattu's brother was nothing less than the eyes and ears of the quiet settlement, watching the comings and goings of the villagers and trading small-time gossip with the customers who stopped to chat.

The day she questioned him, Nattu told Sampat, 'When Sheelu came here, no one knew her. The neighbours used to think she might be some relative of the family. She used to go to farm the land, cut grass and bring back the processed paddy.' Apart from her sudden arrival in Pathara, there was nothing about the girl that attracted any suspicion among the closely knit villagers.

One morning, about a month and a half after Sheelu had moved to Pathara, the calm of the village vanished when a large jeep arrived carrying Dwivedi's men and Achchhe. 'Sheelu's father said Sheelu was being kept forcefully,' Nattu would later recall, adding, 'The legislator had sent his brothers to see who the goon was who was keeping her captive.' Nattu categorically denied that claim. 'Everyone used to see her out of the house, working and going here and there. She would go to the well to get water. She was living openly; she never lived as a captive. Why else did she not look for an opportunity to run away? The truth is she that had a relationship with Rajju; there was a love relation,' he said.

The legislator's men searched the village for Rajju and when they found his father, Gaya Prasad, the men demanded to know where Sheelu was being kept. When the old man refused to give them any information, they allegedly picked him up by his hands and feet and dangled him over the well in front of his house. 'They gave him several blows, kicks and slaps,' said Nattu. Rajju's mother, who Sampat later met, told her that the men 'kicked him, punched him and tied him up'. After being assaulted by the legislator's associates, Gaya Prasad confessed that Sheelu was hiding nearby, in a small outhouse belonging to Rajju's uncle. Nattu maintains that she had run there herself when she heard the men were looking for her, while Sheelu and her family insist that she was taken there against her will.

After Rajju's father gave them the information they were after, the musclemen threw him on the ground and then made their way to the outhouse. When they stood outside the door, 'they called for Sheelu but she did not respond. The men were convinced that she was inside, so they broke the lock. She started crying in fear. If she were taken captive, she should have responded from inside when she was called, no? She should have said, I am here! Free me!' offered Nattu.

Apart from that, Nattu could tell Sampat no more about the matter. He informed Sampat that once the men had dragged Sheelu out of the house, they shoved her into the jeep and sped off.

'That was the last that time we saw Sheelu,' he told Sampat.

AFTER HEARING NATTU'S ACCOUNT of Sheelu's stay in Pathara, Sampat made her way back to Atarra, taking the very same road that Sheelu had taken the day the legislator's men took her away. When Sampat passed Dwivedi's house, she pressed her face to the window to search inside it, as she imagined all that might have transpired behind those walls.

Dwivedi lived in a three-storey house on Atarra's main street, not far from where Sampat and her Pink Gang head-quarters resided. His house was an eggshell colour with black stripes resembling prison bars painted down the entire front of the building. Despite the drab architecture the house offered subtle clues about the profession of its owner. A hor-izontal stripe of blood red and royal blue, the livery colours for many governmental bodies in Uttar Pradesh, ran along the facade immediately below the terrace on the second floor, while on the roof a bare flag pole stood in wait of an official hoisting. Apart from those political trappings, the exterior was bare save for a satellite dish and a swirling stucco om sign that was flanked on either side by a swastika, a Hindu symbol ubiquitous in India that is considered auspicious.

From Pathara, the legislator's men took Sheelu to this house, one she had never seen before, belonging to a man she didn't know. When her father told her that she would be living there, Sheelu started to cry. 'I want to go home,' she said, but her father broke it to her that she would be staying at the house 'for some time'.

'Don't cry, Sheelu. This is a legislator's house. It will turn out good for you here. If anything happens, you tell me,' Achchhe remembers telling his daughter.

Dwivedi was allegedly irritated by the suggestion that something inappropriate might happen.

'"What are you saying, Achchhe Lal?"' Sheelu later remembers him asking. 'You're my man, my disciple. What bad could happen to your daughter in my house, you tell me?' Turning to Sheelu, Dwivedi said with some finality, 'Daughter, you are staying here.'

Sheelu's memories of that conversation are blurred from

tears and from waves of nausea ('I think they gave me some
sleeping-type medicine, you know the one?'). She does
remember pleading with her father to take her home. When
Achchhe suggested to Dwivedi that perhaps it would be best
if he took his daughter back with him, Dwivedi allegedly
dismissed his idea.

'What place could you take her to that is better, and safer,
than here?' he demanded. Dwivedi then promised that apart
from housing Sheelu, he would also arrange for her marriage
– an offer that entailed not only finding a suitor but also
helping to finance the dowry. 'He told me, Achchhe Lal, you
are my disciple. You are a good helper; you made me win.
Leave your daughter here. I will arrange for her marriage. I
will find a boy for her; I will look after it,' Achchhe says the
legislator promised. 'I am giving you a helping hand. I will
spend one lakh' – which is one hundred thousand rupees –
'for your daughter to study.'

This was the offer that disarmed Achchhe. Sheelu was
one year away from turning eighteen, and Achchhe still
had not found a husband for her. After the incident with
Rajju, Achchhe probably feared that he might never be able
to marry off his daughter, or that he would have to pay an
exorbitant dowry for Sheelu now that she was considered
'spoiled goods'.

Once the matter was decided between the men, Achchhe
left. A man called Cheddhi, one of the servants who lived
in the house, then took Sheelu upstairs to her room. The
room was windowless, and from the ceiling hung a solitary
red bulb, which gave the room its blood-hued colour. The
cold room was soulless and bare, save for a bed, television and
bedside table.

Before leaving, her father had told her that he would check up on her in a few days, but that was hardly a consolation. Sheelu was unwell – 'I was feeling strange. I had aches all over my body and head. I felt quite weak, also' – and decided to go to sleep. Cheddhi gave her a bed sheet but no blanket, so she took the shawl that she was wearing and wrapped herself in it tightly.

WHEN SHEELU OPENED her eyes, she was disoriented – it took her a moment to realise where she was. She had slept late; it was already early afternoon. She looked around, and her vision forced a reality onto her that she, fleetingly, hoped was just a bad dream: that she was left on her own in a foreign house inhabited by complete strangers. Her first thought was, 'When will my dad take me away from here?'

A young woman came into her room shortly after she awoke and suggested that she wash up. She later learned that this was Rani, the politician's daughter-in-law. 'I'm not feeling well. I'll take a bath later,' Sheelu told her despondently. After some time she finally got out of bed to wash.

Cheddhi gave her a bar of soap, toothbrush, toothpaste and a towel. The bathroom was next to her room. When she emerged after bathing, the afternoon sun was strong enough that she could dry her hair on the terrace, where she sat alone.

Once her hair was dry, she ventured downstairs to have lunch. It was the first time she had gone down since she arrived. Cheddhi gave her some *dal*, which she ate slowly and on her own. Rani, who was in the house, did not join Sheelu.

After lunch, Sheelu dragged herself back up to the sun-lit terrace, which overlooked Banda Road, named after the nearby town. The street was busy with people. Bicycle rick-shaws, pedestrians and cows made their way up and down the littered road lined with stalls selling freshly squeezed fruit juice, tobacco and tea. Amid the crowds, Sheelu spotted a group of girls in pale blue and white uniforms making their way back from school. Sheelu felt a yearning as she looked at the girls with pigtails and satchels. 'If only my mother were alive, I would be studying too,' she thought with sorrow.

Sheelu had attended the village school – a white concrete building with murals depicting the lower-caste political hero Bhimrao Ramji Ambedkar – for only a few years. The school was not a rigorous institution of learning; Sheelu had on many occasions convinced the teacher to let the students skip studying to play sports and games, from which she often emerged as the winner. Standing on the terrace that day, watching the schoolgirls walk past, with their minds soaked with new facts and thoughts, she felt a wave of regret wash over her for having wasted a single hour of class time. 'Now it's too late. My father keeps saying he'll send me to school again, but he doesn't do anything,' she would later say.

When they vanished out of view, Sheelu's gaze wandered towards two unusual architectural features on the street. The house to the left of Dwivedi's had a large concrete model of a helicopter, which was about her size, perched on the top of the roof. Opposite that house, on the other side of the road, another building had a large decorative sculpture of an aero-plane, slightly larger than the helicopter, on its roof. 'When I saw them, I thought, if only they were real, then I could escape,' she remembers.

After some time, Rani came up, and Sheelu asked her who she was. Rani said she was the politician's daughter-in-

law. The women did not speak much – 'I was not very talk-
ative,' Sheelu would later say – but she did have one question.
'Does the legislator have any daughters?' Sheelu asked. Rani
remained silent and then walked away without answering
the question.

When dusk fell, Sheelu wandered back downstairs, where
she met the legislator's wife, a middle-aged woman called
Asha Dwivedi. The women exchanged a few pleasantries –
neither was in the mood for conversation – and then Sheelu
asked the woman the question that Rani had so mysteriously
avoided answering. 'How many daughters do you have?'
Sheelu asked. No sooner had the words crossed her lips did
the woman burst into tears. Between sobs she told her that
her daughter had 'burned herself and died', and then she
rushed into her room.

Asha Dwivedi's wording had not been clear. Had the
daughter set herself on fire on purpose or was it an accident?
Either way, Sheelu became very worried after that conversation. She went up to her room feeling a deep unease, a
dread sinking into her. When young women across India
die in flames, the assumption is always that there is some foul
play at hand. That is why if a woman dies in a fire within
the first seven years of marriage, the police are required to
rule out the possibility that it was a 'dowry death', which
is the killing of a daughter-in-law who did not bring a
high-enough dowry with her after marriage. These dowry
deaths, which are often disguised as 'kitchen fires', are so
common that they received their own section in the Indian
penal code in 1986. 'I thought something bad must have
happened to that girl, and tears came to my eyes. I wanted
to escape that house.'

ON SHEELU'S SECOND NIGHT at Dwivedi's house, she alleges
that the politician came up to her room after she had gone
to bed. Sheelu says Dwivedi asked her how she was settling
in and whether she was fine in the house. Sheelu believed
this question was insincere. She thought that he must have
remembered the tears she shed when her father left her there,
and heard her say, repeatedly, that she did not want to stay.
Dwivedi, Sheelu claims, had plans for her to stay in the house
for the rest of her life.

According to Sheelu, when she said she wanted to go back
to her father's house, Dwivedi responded by telling her that
this was her new home. Then he informed her of the marriage he was arranging for her to Cheddhi, the servant who
had shown Sheelu to her room and had brought her toiletries
on the day she arrived. Cheddi lived a serflike existence in
the house, and the idea that Sheelu would be wedded to him
revolted her.

'I told him I didn't want to marry Cheddhi. I said that
my father would find someone from our own caste for me,'
Sheelu would later say.

Sheelu's flat-out rejection angered the legislator. He
barged out of the room, and Sheelu was worried that that
wouldn't be the last she heard about the matter.

THE NEXT DAY, while Dwivedi was out, Sheelu slipped out
of her room and went downstairs. There, she met Dwivedi's
wife for the second time, and that time, Sheelu remembers,
'she treated me quite nicely'. She prepared the girl a *thaali* of

basmati rice, lentils, pickled mango, green chilli and *chapatti*. Asha waited on Sheelu, who was famished, and refilled her dish generously each time she finished the previous serving. Asha's motherly doting put Sheelu at ease for the first time since she had arrived, and the young girl opened up to her. Sheelu told Asha about Dwivedi's marriage plans for her and Cheddhi. Asha's face, which was gentle and warm until then, grew stern. 'Don't you agree to it, you understand me? Say no,' the woman instructed her. When Sheelu asked if Asha could dissuade her husband herself, she allegedly refused to.

Sheelu could not eat more – 'How was I supposed to eat with all these problems on my mind? I wasn't even thinking about food. Just how do I get out of here? How?' – and Asha, seeing Sheelu looking weak and sickly, suggested that she go have a nap, which she did. Rani followed her up the stairs, and before going into her room, Sheelu lingered at the terrace, looking down at Banda Road, with its bustling activity. 'Which way is Naraini?' she asked Rani, who stood beside her – Naraini being the biggest town near her home. 'That way,' Rani responded, pointing left.

That evening, Sheelu joined the women of the house – Asha and her daughter-in-law Rani – for dinner. To Sheelu's relief, Dwivedi was out again, so she hoped that another uncomfortable conversation about marrying Chiddhi could be delayed until at least the next day, by which time she hoped to be out of the house.

After dinner Sheelu retired to her room to plan how she might escape. As she lay in bed thinking about what to do, her door, which had no lock, opened suddenly. It was Dwivedi.

The legislator allegedly told Sheelu again that he was arranging for her to marry Cheddhi, and that she should accept. When she refused, the politician allegedly started beating her. Trying to escape his blows, Sheelu says she leapt up and ran to the bathroom next door. She managed to get into the bathroom, but before she could close the door, he thrust his arm through the crack and grabbed her towards him. The next minute, she says, she was against the wall with his thick-fingered hands clamping her mouth closed. Dwivedi told her she was going to marry Cheddhi. 'And when you do, we both will be screwing you,' he allegedly told her with a snarl.

With one strong arm clasping her body and keeping her mouth covered, Sheelu says Dwivedi led her to the bed. Sheelu's throat felt as tightly knotted as the drawstring of her *salwar*, loose-fitting cotton trousers, and her stomach clenched. Dwivedi reached for the remote control on Sheelu's bedside table with his free hand and turned on the television, pushing up the volume until the room was bathed in a flickering blue light and reverberating with shrill voices advertising the latest consumer products in Hindi.

CHAPTER FOUR

LOVE IN BUNDELKHAND

WHAT IS LOVE? LET ME TELL YOU.

L IS FOR LAKE OF SORROWS.

O IS FOR OCEAN OF TEARS.

V IS FOR VALLEY OF DEATH.

E IS FOR END OF LIFE.

—Babuji

IT WAS DARK WHEN SHEELU WAS BROUGHT TO THE BANDA DISTRICT Jail on 14 December at 8:16 p.m. A decrepit colonial-era lockup initially constructed by the British in 1860 to house 'dacoits murderers and cattle-thiefs', the jail was a reminder of Bundelkhand's history of unruliness. It was a terrifying place for a young woman to find herself in, though the past few days had hardened Sheelu and had prepared her for the worst.

Sheelu alleges that after the first night she was raped, the legislator violated her another time the next day. It was around three in the morning on 13 December, when Sheelu claims he tried to rape her a third time, that she had seized the opportunity to escape. 'He wanted to rape me again. He was in the bathroom . . . I heard the bathroom door and I thought, This is my chance,' says Sheelu.

Before Sheelu fled the house, she took a mobile phone that was charging in the house, which she claims she thought was her own. Sheelu then made her way southeastward by foot down the unlit roads. It is not clear where Sheelu was headed, but she was caught in the village of Turra, a few miles from Atarra, after Dwivedi discovered her location through tracking his mobile phone.

While Dwivedi's men were looking for her, Achchhe was called to Atarra, and it was then that he was allegedly threatened and dangled over the fire. According to Achchhe, after Dwivedi received word that Sheelu had been found, he sent Achchhe back home, refusing his request to see his daughter. Sheelu was brought to Dwivedi's house, where she says Dwivedi's men sexually harassed and threatened her before she was taken to the police station. It was only twenty-four hours later that the legislator's son, Mayank, registered a theft complaint against her, on 14 December at 9:30 a.m. By then, news of Sheelu's arrest had already spread across town.

'Those people were drunk. They beat me. They took me to the police station and accused me of being a thief. Even the inspector beat me, despite me telling him the truth. He created a false report and sent me to jail.'

At the time, the *Hindustan* had noted the veil of secrecy drawn tightly around Sheelu's arrest. 'What is the reason why Sheelu has been kept away from the media glare? What is the reason why her family has not been traced? When the police arrest smaller thieves, they proudly parade their catch, but why not with Sheelu?' It would be some time before those questions were answered.

ON 19 DECEMBER, Sampat made her way to the Banda District Jail in an attempt to meet Sheelu there. 'She was stuffed in jail . . . I wanted to meet her myself to see what it was all about. Until you speak to the oppressed, you will never hear them,' she says.

Sampat knew the jail very well, though she wishes it were for a different reason. Her son-in-law, Tirath Pal, had been incarcerated there for nine years for a murder she claims he never committed. Tirath's family had been involved in a feud with their Brahmin neighbour after the upper-caste man's goatherd wandered onto their land. Sampat alleges that when Tirath's family chased the goats away, a quarrel erupted between Tirath's uncle and the Brahmin, after which Tirath's uncle was shot dead. The family 'filed a complaint and there was a case, but the neighbour was so moneyed that he bought the police. He got bail immediately,' Sampat recounts. After the neighbour was released, the antagonism between him and Tirath's family raged on until, according to Sampat, they falsely implicated Tirath in a murder that occurred in the town of Fatehpur. 'Poor thing has been in jail for so long for a crime he didn't do,' Sampat says. Sampat regrets that Tirath never asked for her help, and believes the worst could have been averted had she intervened in time. 'He never asked for any help from me. He didn't think I could help him; he didn't see me as anyone special. He used to think I was an ordinary woman,' Sampat says with a shrug. Tirath was arrested in 2004, two years before Sampat started the Pink Gang.

Tirath's imprisonment had devastated Prabha, Sampat's eldest daughter, who now looked after their four children on her own. 'After what happened, life was very difficult for her. She has spent her life in tears.' Prabha is a beautiful woman in her early thirties, with sorrowful almond-shaped eyes, soft lips and long, tousled black hair. She is slow to warm to people and carries a melancholy air that flees when you make her laugh, but only momentarily. Prabha moved back home to her parents' house after Tirath's arrest so that she would have help with her children; few wives want to continue living at their in-laws' house when their husband is absent, though most do, as it is socially unacceptable for women to move back in with their parents after marriage. To while away the time, and contribute to the household kitty, Prabha stitched *cholis*, fitted camisoles for saris, on a pedal-operated Singer sewing machine. After sewing had bought her a measure of her own freedom, Sampat had always insisted a woman should know how to sew in order to earn her own money, and the same applied for her daughters. Now, in hard times, Prabha turned to the sewing machine to make ends meet.

Unfortunately, Prabha was not the only one of Sampat's daughters to have been struck by a tragedy. Prabha's small, wiry younger sister, Champa, also was a single mother who spent her days at the sewing machine. 'I sleep and I stitch, that's all,' Champa says. Champa has sharp cheekbones and a strong jaw line, marked by a prominent crescent-shaped scar, which she acquired in her childhood. She had been running to get an axe for her uncle when she fell and landed on a shard of glass she had been holding in her hand. Sampat left her newborn son, Munna, alone when she rushed to her daughter's side, causing one woman in the village to censure her. 'They told me, Today a son has been born! Why are you leaving him for your daughter?' Sampat remembers. She replied that her daughter was just as important as her son.

Champa was once married to a man called Rakesh Pal, whom everyone called 'Doctor Saheb' because of his rudimentary training in Ayurvedic medicine. After their wedding, Champa moved into Rakesh's house, which was haunted by the memories of the violent death of his first wife. When still a child, Champa had actually witnessed what had happened. One day when Champa was on her way to the well, she saw smoke rising from Rakhesh's house. 'I ran and I told mum, "Look, Ram Vilas's house is on fire!"' she recalls, referring to him by his nickname. 'When the fire was doused, I saw her. People said, "This is Rakesh's wife, she has burned herself." Many people were gathered in front of the house.'

Rakesh's first wife was one of countless Indian women to have died engulfed in flames. Even if Rakesh's wife's death was a suicide, everyone wondered whether the young bride had been driven to kill herself. As Champa would find out when she married Rakesh, his mother seemed to view any woman married into their house as little more than a servant.

'When I married, I stayed for a year, then I came back. I didn't want to do much grinding of grains or housework. If I didn't want to work, my *saas*' – mother-in-law – 'beat me,' Champa recalls. 'Once, I was sick, and she knocked over the bed and said, "She's always sick!"' Her younger sister Nisha arrived at that moment and saw what happened. 'Nisha ran with tears to our mum. My mum came and carried me away in her arms like a child. She said to my *saas*, If anything would have happened to my daughter, I would have showed you,' Champa remembers. 'My *saas* said, One daughter-in-law has already died. *Nothing will happen to me if another dies.*'

For the next four years, Champa lived with her children at Sampat's house in Badausa. Her husband, who was away earning money at a carpet factory in Varanasi, returned to live with her at Sampat's and then, after becoming accredited, opened an Ayurvedic doctor's clinic next to Sampat's office in Atarra. Once they had saved enough money, Champa and her husband built themselves a house that was within walking distance of Champa's family home. It looked as though they had finally overcome all of the difficulties of their early married life.

Then one morning Champa awoke to find that Rakesh had not returned the night before from visiting friends in a nearby town. Champa's youngest child, a delicate, doll-like girl called Himanshi, told her over breakfast that her father was never coming back. How did she know? Himanshi replied that her papa had come to her in her dreams and told her. A few hours later the police informed Champa that her husband had been found hacked to death by an axe. The case remains unsolved.

Though these tragedies were out of Sampat's control, others weren't. Three of Sampat's daughters claim they were married off when they were still teenagers. Champa says she was married at the age of thirteen. 'I was in class eight,' she says. 'I went from my in-laws to give exams. One or two exams I couldn't take, but I got a pass because the teacher suggested I give a doctor's note,' Champa says, remembering her last days in the school system. 'Our position was very bad back then. The elders started saying, Your daughters are getting old, they should get married,' she recalls. 'My mum feels bad that we got married so young. Sometimes I quarrel with her about it. I say, My body is damaged from having children so early. My health is bad. She says, "What has happened has happened. I am your support for you and your children."'

Sampat has sometimes denied that her children married below the legal age. Other times, she acknowledges that it happened but says that she could do nothing to stop it. 'I always knew it was wrong, but it was my in-laws who forced my children to get married so young. I couldn't do anything then,' she says.

That might be why the only one of Sampat's daughters who escaped child marriage is Nisha, Sampat's youngest child, who was raised in Badausa, not Gadarian Purva. Unlike her sisters, Nisha succeeded in enrolling in university and obtained her parents' guarantee that they would not marry her off before she graduated.

It is ironic that the woman who has helped empower so many women across Bundelkhand was not able to protect her own daughters from the hell of child marriage.

'I never enjoyed my youth because I got married at the age of twelve. What does one know at that age? Then I had children at a young age also. My entire youth was lost in that. My childhood was spent in hate because when it should have been time to play and study, I was tied to someone. Then, I became a mother at the age of fifteen. So, I was bound even more,' Sampat remembers.

When she gave birth to her first child, Sampat had many hopes for her. Like all parents, she wanted Prabha to have a better life than she did. 'People felt sad when a daughter was born, but I was happy. I used to dream during my pregnancy that God should give me a daughter first. I thought, I will teach her things. Above all, I wanted to give her a proper education. My parents didn't allow me to study. I said I will educate my daughter.' It took giving birth to four more children before she could realise that dream for any of her daughters.

THE DECEMBER MORNING Sampat arrived at the Banda District Jail to visit Sheelu, Tirath was at his desk. 'Your mother-in-law is here. She wants to meet you,' his colleague told him.

Tirath, a tall man with coppery-brown hair, broad shoulders and a lean physique, spent most of his days hunched over the desk in his jail office, where he was paid to do clerical work. His duties included entering into the register detailed information on new convicts; noting the time inmates were given dinner and what time the jail gates opened and closed for the day; recording the time that inmates left jail for court appearances; and completing paperwork for inmates who had been freed – 'They call me the *writer*, because it is my duty to write.'

Seeing him at his desk, surrounded by stamps, pens and a large ledger, you wouldn't think he was an inmate, except for his yellow uniform. The humdrum office job, which kept him busy every day from six in the morning to six at night, helped him to forget the true reason he was there.

Tirath was glad Sampat had come, for he had some confidential and valuable information to share with her. He guessed that the purpose of his mother-in-law's visit had to do with Sheelu, the young woman who was now the jail's most famous inmate. Like everyone else in the jail, he had been closely following Sheelu's story since it had first come out in the newspaper. 'Which kind of girl could do something like that?' he asked himself, referring to the theft.

'She'll come soon, then we can all see her,' one of his colleagues had said, looking forward to a diversion from their monotonous workday.

The day Sheelu arrived, Tirath gleaned more information about her case than he had expected. He saw the new girl in the office adjacent to his, talking to the jail's medical doctor, a man called R. C. Sahu, accompanied by Tirath's friend Shahjehan Begum, a female constable. The girl had swollen eyes and held her head in her hands, crying, as she spoke to the doctor. Tirath guessed that the girl was Sheelu and that she was undergoing a routine medical interview for new inmates. After the interview with the doctor was over, Tirath caught a moment with Shahjehan in the corridor to ask her about the new inmate. 'She said a very wrong thing had happened to the girl. . . . A *rape* had happened to her. She was bleeding also,' he later recalls. Worse still, Shahjehan told Tirath that the doctor refused to report the matter to the police. Everything pointed towards Sheelu's incarceration being part of a cover-up.

THAT MORNING, when Sampat greeted her son-in-law, she confessed, 'I'm only meeting you as an excuse. I've come to see Sheelu.' Sampat was sure that Sheelu would be in the visitor area of the jail that day because she had it from Amit, the journalist from the *Hindustan*, that Rajju's mother, Sunaria, was planning to visit Sheelu in jail. This would give Sampat the opportunity to speak to Sheelu in the common visiting area. Amit also told her that he would run a story on Sampat's jail visit, in order to bring more attention to the case.

On her way in, she met journalists from local dailies who were trying to gain admission to the jail to meet Sheelu, but they were unsuccessful. Sampat, however, had a way of steamrolling obstacles with her will and resourcefulness. On a recent journey to a small village near Atarra, where she had gone to visit a Pink Gang member, the car Sampat was travelling in had encountered a tractor on a narrow, raised mud bank, which served as a road. There was not enough space for both vehicles to pass, and Sampat made sure she was not in the one that would have to reverse. 'Get out of the way! Get back!' Sampat hollered out the window, gesticulating to the farmer to back up, which he did. Turning to her fellow passengers at the moment of victory, she chuckled, 'I'm used to getting my way.'

That day at the Banda jail, however, her mission required discretion. She was purposefully alone; she did not want to attract unnecessary attention by arriving with other gang members – the time had not yet come to get them involved. She hoped to sneak into the jail and speak to Sheelu undisturbed. She was not wearing her pink sari, partly so as not to be recognised by any of Dwivedi's men, who she thought might be lurking around the jail entrance, and also because she wanted to give the impression that she was there for personal reasons and not for 'business'.

Sampat and Tirath walked together to the visiting area, a long outdoor shed with a corrugated tin roof where prisoners and their families sat on floor mats. The inmates sat in two long rows, with the women sitting near the entrance of the shed and men sitting at the back. Guards stood by the entrance, gathered around a small fire for warmth.

As they lowered themselves down onto the mat, Sampat asked whether Tirath could see Sheelu. Tirath replied that he could and pointed her out.

Sheelu was sitting cross-legged with Sunaria, who was caressing her on the crown of her head and murmuring in her ear. In front of her were clothes and *lai*, a sweet snack, which Rajju's mother had brought for Sheelu. Inmates were allowed cigarettes, *gutka* (a mild stimulant consumed like chewing tobacco), biscuits and *laddu* (a sweet ball of flour, milk and sugar often sold at Hindu temples), but edible gifts had to be tasted by the visitor in front of the jailer to prove they contained no poison. 'That's Rajju's mother,' Sampat said under her breath. 'Yes. How do you know?' Tirath asked, surprised. 'Because Amit told me she was coming,' she replied. 'This is proof that Sheelu ran away with Rajju,' Sampat thought to herself. 'Why else would his mother be here?'

Sampat got up from the mat and walked over to Sheelu. The two had never met before, and Sheelu would later say that she had no idea what Sampat wanted from her. 'Sheelu, I am Sampat Pal,' she said, bending over the girl. When introducing herself to people, Sampat enunciates her name with such confidence that, even to those who have never heard it before, it gives the impression of a sturdy, reliable rope, capable of hauling weak souls out of the deepest quagmires. When she promises help, her gestures echo the valiance in her voice: she places her hand on her heart, or raises a strength-imparting clenched fist as she focuses her forest-green, amber-speckled eyes on her listener's. Sampat told Sheelu, 'I am with the Pink Gang; we will get you justice. Don't speak here; tell everything in court. Don't change your statement and don't be scared if they put pressure – '

Before she could finish what she had to say, word had spread to one of the guards that Sampat was talking with Sheelu.

'Sit down!' he ordered Sampat. 'Stay on your side!' he commanded, pointing over to where Tirath was sitting. Before the guard reached Sampat, she turned to Sheelu one last time. 'Do not fear. I am here and I will fight for you,' she remembers saying.

When the guard, who recognised Sampat as the Pink Gang leader, arrived to lead her away, he gave her some advice. 'Sampat-ji, if you want to meet Sheelu, go to court on the twenty-fourth of December,' he said, adding, 'She will be there then.'

When Sampat sat back down, Tirath whispered to her the news that Sampat had suspected since the beginning, that Dwivedi had raped Sheelu. 'This case is very sensitive,' he told her. Sampat was not surprised. 'We're going to get her out of here, you'll see,' she said confidently. 'Keep your ears open and tell me if you hear anything else,' she instructed, before getting up to leave.

ONE OF THE FIRST PEOPLE Sampat updated on her investigations into Sheelu's case after her jail visit was Geeta Singh, the twenty-six-year-old Pink Gang district commander who had alerted Sampat to Sheelu's suspicious arrest before anyone else, and who was especially interested in the case. Geeta is a tall, apple-cheeked woman who lives in a ground-floor, one-room apartment in the pilgrimage town of Chitrakoot, twenty miles southeast of Atarra. Chitrakoot is a town of incense clouds and tinkling prayer bells where, according to Hindu mythology, the deities Sita and Ram lived together in exile. Geeta's front door opens straight onto a narrow side street, at the end of which is a Hindu temple flying triangular orange flags. She lives here with her two-year-old daughter and Deepak, her husband. At least once a day, a zebu cow with crescent-shaped horns and blinking, black-rimmed eyes lazily sticks its head into the living room and stares for a few moments before ambling away. Geeta's days are composed of a series of similarly unannounced house calls. Apart from the vagrant cows, visitors include women in need – some who have run away from violent husbands, others who want to run away with lovers – and customers of her husband, a small-time moneylender. On the road running perpendicular to the lane, saffron-robed pilgrims often pass by, in or sometimes atop crowded buses, as they make their way to the Hanuman Dhara – a holy site on a hill outside the city dedicated to the Hindu monkey god Hanuman.

Geeta and Sampat speak at least once a day. If Sampat needs to get word out to gang members that there is a protest they need to attend, she calls Geeta and the thirteen other district commanders. They, in turn, call Sampat for advice on local cases they are handling. 'Sister is our leader, isn't she?' Geeta says. The local Pink Gang leaders meet only if there is a large protest that requires collaboration between the various branches; otherwise they stay in touch over the phone and operate as separate units. Travel, even over short distances, is too cumbersome and expensive to do regularly. Geeta and the other women heading up district-level Pink Gang groups handle small cases, such as 'ones where we can come to an understanding, like a family dispute', says Sampat. For the bigger cases where the gang might, for instance, confront senior members of the district-level administration, the local Pink Gang commanders call Sampat. 'If they go on their own, the government people often say, "Bring your leader," so then I've got to come,' Sampat explains matter-of-factly.

Geeta juggles motherhood and her vigilante commit-ments with seeming ease. When she is busy, her daughter is often kept entertained by the television, which is propped up on a stool opposite what is the seating area by day and family bed by night – it takes up half of the floor space in this cramped flat. Behind the television are a plastic tricycle, a bouquet of limp peacock feathers, steel cooking pots and large plastic vats of cheap cooking oil; the rest of the family's possessions are in a large metal chest at the foot of the bed. Geeta's daughter splits her time between here and Deepak's parents' house in Atarra to ease the financial burden on the young parents. 'She likes eating very expensive sweets – every day we spend fifty rupees on her and we don't always have the money,' Geeta complains in her languid voice. Geeta has taught the little girl to chant Pink Gang battle cries. 'Long live Sampat Pal! Long live the Pink Gang!' she shouts in a squeaky, giggly voice when prompted by her mother, who sometimes entertains visiting gang members with the antics of her aspiring vigilante daughter.

Geeta's work is facilitated by Deepak, a moustached young man in his early thirties with fine black hair, which he combs upwards with gel. Deepak dresses 'modern' – in jeans and button-down, pastel-coloured shirts of polyester-cotton mixed weave. He is also a gifted cook who expertly spices his dishes and carefully scouts the market for the freshest produce, chicken and fish. A true gourmand, one of his favourite ingredients is peach-coloured bird fat, which he keeps in a jar on the shelf above the stove. 'This is the best fat, just smell it,' he entreats visitors. Among the many dishes he knows how to cook is turtle meat curry, a rare dish unheard of in most of the country. Deepak often promises his friends that if they catch a turtle for him at the nearby wildlife reserve, where he has been told giant turtles roam near the river, he would cook the dish for them as a reward. The offer, which entails the risk of a poaching fine, remains untaken.

For Deepak, cooking is not just a leisure pursuit or 'time-pass', as he calls it. It is a labour of love that forms part of the unspoken division of work that exists between this enlightened househusband and the local Pink Gang leader. Deepak, whose work allows him to be home most of the day, also looks after their daughter when she lives with them. 'The first word for most children is "*ma*"; for our daughter it was "*pa*",' he chuckles, amused at this incongruity. Geeta is often away, and her hours can be unpredictable, though sometimes she takes her daughter to protests if no one is available to look after her.

Deepak is as unconventional at work as he is in his private life. He has two hundred thousand rupees – over two thousand pounds – of loans circulating among fourteen people, and sees himself as a moneylender with a social purpose. Not only does he fund Geeta's Pink Gang activities (he covers the cost of transportation to and from protests; medical treatment for battered wives; and meals for women who stop by the house), but says he refuses to pressure poor people to pay back money if they can't afford to. This charitable approach, however, has failed to take away the uneasiness he feels towards his job. 'It makes me sick, living off the interest I earn,' Deepak says sadly. 'I don't want to have bad blessings, so I spend the money quickly.'

WHEN SAMPAT TOLD GEETA that Sheelu was accusing the legislator of rape, the local Pink Gang leader was not surprised. She had heard from Deepak that the legislator was a man without scruples. Deepak knew what he was talking about – he used to work for Purushottam Naresh Dwivedi when he was widely known to have been a liquor don. In fact, that was how Deepak started his moneylending business – by allowing hard-up alcoholics to pay him for their booze at a later date, with considerable interest. When Geeta met him, Deepak was also a heavy drinker on the verge of alcoholism, but she helped him overcome his addiction.

Deepak started working in the sleaze-laden liquor business when he was around eighteen. Back then, he reported to his distant relative Lala Ghanshyam Singh, a notorious Atarra underworld figure who styled himself as a Wild West villain – he was known to wear large cowboy hats and ride through Atarra on a stallion. Lala Ghanshyam was close to the Dwivedi family and allegedly hired the future politician and his brothers to work with him.

Deepak was the manager of three liquor stores – one in Atarra and two others in Badausa and Khorand – owned by the politician's brother, Ram Naresh Dwivedi, whose street name is 'Little Ali the Prince'. 'He has a bad reputation,' says Deepak of his former boss, but that is an understatement.

Deepak alleges that Little Ali the Prince, who suffered from a heavy stammer, often visited prostitutes in a small hotel owned by Deepak's relative. Deepak remembered an incident when the police raided the hotel and found Little Ali the Prince with a prostitute. A mob got hold of him and forced him to march down the street wearing a 'garland of shame' called *chappal ka haar*, which was a wreath of shoes tied by their laces. 'He also likes boys!' claims Deepak tittering. He was once accused of molesting a boy – 'He was put on a donkey and his face was blackened by soot by people that time,' a common form of mob justice. 'The whole family are dirty people – all of the brothers – dirty, dirty, dirty!' he said.

According to Deepak, Dwivedi was no better. 'He has a mistress he keeps in Chitrakoot – I saw her whenever I dropped off the cash earnings at the office, which is where she lives,' Deepak said, raising his eyebrows as he narrated the family's titillatingly scandalous behaviour.

Among those who know Dwivedi, it is sometimes rumoured that he entered politics through outbidding a candidate named Ram Sewak Shukla, for a BSP election ticket. Many in India believe that their candidates pay their way onto the ballot.

'I know them well enough to know this story of Sheelu is not true! You tell me, wouldn't all eyes be on a girl running away with a rifle? This can't be!'

Geeta, who has an earnest, unshakeable faith in Sampat, assured him, 'Sister will get to the bottom of this. Definitely.'

Geeta knew that it was only a matter of time before Sampat would uncover the truth. Conducting proper investigations had been one of the first rules that Sampat had laid down when she took on Geeta as a district commander. 'The gang is strong, but we must use our strength wisely,' she had said. Sampat did not want her Pink Gang members to fight against people without having acquired adequate information: 'Speak to everyone – neighbours, family, village heads, even the police, to find out the truth about a story. Don't just believe what you hear.' She taught her gang members to be good investigators and to avoid ending up on the wrong side of an argument. 'I've never misjudged a case in my life,' Sampat has boasted. 'I always get to the bottom of a story.'

AS SAMPAT UPDATED GEETA on her investigations into the case, Geeta's ears perked when Sampat told her that Sheelu had eloped with Rajju. Tangled love stories were Geeta's 'speciality' – perhaps because her own marriage was born out of one.

Geeta met Deepak for the first time seven years ago, during *holi*, the popular Hindu spring festival. Hindus celebrate it by throwing colour powder and water at friends and family, as if participating in an enormous Technicolor snowball fight. Celebrants chase each other, trying to rub fistfuls of bright pigment into the faces and hair of their squealing targets. During *holi*, the streets are splattered with all the shades of the rainbow, and revellers are covered from head to toe in vivid hues. In all its chaos, *holi* is the festival that allows the most opportunities for playful flirtation and is undoubtedly the most romantic holiday.

During *holi* it is also a widespread practice for people, including children, to consume *bhang*, an intoxicating beverage made of cannabis, sweetened yogurt and milk that is often sold at Hindu temples. Deepak's body was buzzing with *bhang* and butterflies when he first walked up to Geeta and smeared a small mound of coloured powder on her cheek. He had often seen Geeta visiting her aunt in the neighbourhood, but he had barely exchanged a word with her, and yet there he was, running his fingers along the smooth curve of her cheek in a dreamy, soft-focus high. To his horror, Geeta shouted at him and batted Deepak away angrily with her hands. 'I am a fighter, I don't take nonsense from anyone,' she would later say about the incident. Deepak slunk away with shame and spent the rest of the day trying to avoid Geeta.

When he awoke the next day, head pounding with a hangover, Deepak received a call from an unknown number. The voice he heard on the other end made him sit up with a start. It was Geeta. The two youths spoke for approximately half an hour, and by the end of the conversation, Geeta had all but asked Deepak to marry her.

Pouring her heart out to this perfect stranger without so much as a preamble, Geeta confided to Deepak about the hopeless situation she was trapped in. A few years back, her father, a labourer, had been electrocuted and suffered permanent brain damage. Geeta, her mother and her three sisters, no longer provided for by their father, went to live with Geeta's paternal uncle, who thought it a curse to be a guardian to so many girls and did not disguise his desire to get rid of them as soon as he could.

Those were dark times for Geeta's family, and her mother could barely cope with the strain. One day she beckoned her daughters to her and, sitting them down, gave them all a plate of food to eat. 'Let us die,' she said, with a reckless, vacant expression. 'Let us have poison and die,' she repeated wildly. Geeta, the eldest of the four daughters, looked to her plate and understood what her mother had done. 'We were small and innocent and scared of death,' Geeta remembers. Geeta threw the metal *thaali* plate to the ground and ran away. Her mother ran after her and slapped her, and 'then she cried and cried, saying, "I will look after you even sacrificing my life."'

Then, just as Geeta's mother had feared, her uncle told Geeta that she was going to be married. She was still a young teenager – only fourteen years old. The worst part was that her groom-to-be was an older widower who already had two children, one of whom was her age. 'I don't know his name . . . no one told me,' Geeta says. At the time, Geeta did not know what child marriage was, or that it was illegal. 'I was so ignorant back then. I didn't even know what marriage was. People in my village were even more ignorant than me – they did not even know what trains were!' she says wide-eyed.

On the day of the wedding a conscientious villager alerted the police, and in a rare incident of responsiveness, they intervened by fining the uncle and the middle-aged groom and prevented the marriage from taking place.

When Geeta met Deepak at *holi* a few years later, she knew it was only a matter of time before her uncle would try to marry her off once again. 'I've opened my heart to you on these matters,' Geeta told Deepak on the phone that day. 'You decide what you want to do now,' she told him, and hung up. Weeks of secret conversations at village pay phones followed, in which the two bared their souls to each other. Geeta learned that Deepak's life was in disarray too; his mother had died that year, he was drinking heavily because of his grief, and his father was pressuring him to get married so they could use the dowry to pay off some of his mother's medical bills. Realising they both needed each other equally to escape from their families' plans for them, Deepak accepted Geeta's marriage proposal and the two ran away together.

WHEN GEETA AND DEEPAK ELOPED, they spent their first night as fugitive lovers huddled at an all-night snack stand on the main road in Chitrakoot. The hostels they had approached made a scene about letting out a room to an unmarried couple, and as Deepak reminded Geeta, 'We wouldn't be able to afford a room anyway.'

Neither of them thought running away would be easy, but they had it better than other fleeing lovers. Newspapers across the country reported daily on honour killings by families who felt disgraced by their children's romances. The problem was so pronounced that the courts in some states had responded by ordering the government to set up safe houses in which eloped couples could live – they were not exactly honeymoon suites, but better than death. Geeta's uncle was unconcerned about her whereabouts, and though Deepak's parents were furious that he was marrying a girl with no dowry, they did not go as far as to threaten them with murder.

At daybreak, the bleary-eyed couple made their way to one of the temples in Chitrakoot where Deepak's uncle worked as an acolyte. The temple was an imperious but aged building with grand steps leading up from the street to a scalloped, arched entrance. Inside the temple a myriad of marble courtyards led to side rooms and halls filled with idols and bare-chested priests in loincloths poring over ancient holy books. It was not a place where a couple living in sin would ordinarily seek refuge, but Deepak hoped his uncle might take enough pity on them to let them sleep in the small lodgings kept for travelling pilgrims.

The young couple ended up living in the temple for several months, paying only a nominal amount for what used to be the shed where the holy cow was kept. Despite the humble living conditions, they led an undisturbed, peaceful existence until someone informed the police that they were living together unmarried. From then on, police came by on a weekly basis demanding bribes to keep them out of trouble.

In a bid to protect themselves from predatory police, Geeta and Deepak got married at the temple. Deepak's uncle officiated the ceremony. Although Deepak and Geeta invited their parents, none of them came. Unlike the grand weddings that are common in India, theirs was a simple ceremony, attended only by the temple staff they had become friends with during the months they lived in the shed.

The years following the marriage were as hard as the ones preceding it. Without any family support, the couple faced homelessness several times, first when they had to vacate their room at the temple for arriving pilgrims and later when they could not make enough money to pay for a tenement. It was a tumultuous time, but they eventually found their footing and were able to move into a small room in a shared house as lodgers. In their new home, neighbours often harassed the young couple after they learned the two had eloped. People called Geeta a prostitute, and other times referred to her simply as Deepak's 'mistress'.

'This suffering has made me strong and this is why I can help people today,' Geeta later realised.

THREE MONTHS AFTER GIVING BIRTH, Geeta was watching television in a rare moment of downtime in the brick lodging she was renting with Deepak for five hundred rupees a month, the equivalent of about five pounds. When the news bulletin appeared, Geeta beheld something that could have flown straight from her idealistic imagination and onto the television screen. The news item featured a group of women dressed in pink officiating a 'love marriage' – a union between two people not orchestrated by parents or community elders but arising from the free will of the couple.

In India, love and marriage don't always go hand in hand. Most marriages in the country are 'arranged', taking place after the parents initiate a formal introduction of each spouse. Love can develop after marriage, but it is not a necessary prerequisite. Very rarely do men and women actually fall in love and choose their partner independently of their parents and extended family. When they do, such passionate unions bring with them a whole host of thorny problems.

Love marriages – the bread and butter of Bollywood films – can attract extreme reactions from traditional members of society. In 2012, a village council in Asara, in Uttar Pradesh, even went so far as to ban love marriages for residents. Sattar Ahmed, a member of the village council, was quoted as saying that love marriages were a 'shame on society'. To prevent romance, the village council also banned women under forty years old from leaving home unaccompanied.

Love marriages have become a highly contentious battleground on which some of the country's most pernicious practices play out: caste discrimination and the dowry system. Though caste discrimination is outlawed in the Indian constitution, caste divisions in society are maintained through the institution of arranged marriage. Hindus are born into one of four hierarchical castes, which are believed by some Hindus to have originated from various parts of the body of Brahma, the creator-god. According to this account, Brahmins, the priestly caste, originate from his head; the Kshatriyas, the warrior caste, emerged from his hands; the Vaishyas, or trader caste, from the thighs; and the Sudras, who perform menial labour, from his feet. Hindus born outside of the system are Dalits, formerly known as 'untouchables', and are traditionally considered the lowest of the low. Within the four castes there are thousands of subcastes – fishermen, laundrymen, leather-tanners – which are traditional hereditary professions that are often revealed by one's last name. For many who live outside urban centres, where social mobility has somewhat diminished its importance, caste determines one's profession, social standing, who one can marry and even who one can dine with (those with 'dirty' jobs are considered 'unclean'); it is therefore evident that people falling in love and marrying outside of their caste threaten the entire system.

Love marriages also undermine the dowry culture, which the bride's family does not pay in the case of love marriage. It is no surprise either that in Hinduism, love marriage or

Gandharva, is described as 'the voluntary union of a maiden and her lover' and deemed the lowest of all eight forms of marriage because it arises 'from desire and has sexual intercourse for its purpose'. Another, the Rakshasa, is described as 'the forcible abduction of a maiden from her home, while she cries out and weeps'. The ideal marriage is the Brahma marriage, which is 'the gift of a daughter, after decking her (with costly garments) and honouring her (by presents of jewels), to a man learned in the Veda', referring to the body of ancient Hindu scriptures.

Couples whose love marriage is officiated by the Pink Gang stand better chances of having their union accepted in society than those who do it alone. In India, it is communal acceptance that truly validates a marriage, and this is what the Pink Gang is able to offer couples whose parents and relatives have denied their right to marry: the Pink Gang publically stands by them during their nuptials, thereby backing their choice and dissuading people from harassing the newlyweds, as is often the case. The impact of Pink Gang weddings goes beyond just the couples who benefit from them and their families, however. The fact that the couple does not receive a marriage certificate from the Pink Gang at the end of the ceremony is not a deterrent: only a minority of people register their marriages in India, a country where it is common not to have a birth certificate. As Babuji put it, 'We have social power, not legal power.'

When the Pink Gang hosts a ceremony for a love marriage, the women sometimes erect a wedding tent on an empty strip of land on the outskirts of town. On other occasions they simply organise the festivities at an accommodating temple. Sampat calls the local district commander of the area and gathers a hundred of her Pink Gang members for the occasion, which invariably attracts the local media. She uses these weddings to deliver speeches on the ills of the caste and dowry systems and to demand why, in this day and age, young people do not have the right to choose their spouse. She often rails against Bundelkhand's older generations, who blame the television for giving the young people 'all these ideas about love'. 'Everyone knows TV isn't real. If it were, why isn't everyone running away then, hm?' Sampat demands. 'I don't think the TV is bad – at least it says that if you fall in love, you should stay together. You shouldn't leave each other, right? Here, men aren't loyal. They keep you for a while, then they leave you. If it weren't for TV, Bundelkhand would be *more* ignorant – we'd be *more* deaf and dumb,' she proclaims, thrusting out her index finger to bring her final point home.

In these happy-go-lucky weddings, Babuji has the duty of chanting the wedding *shlokas*, verses from the Bhagavad Gita, one of the Hindu holy texts, and Sampat presents the bride and the groom with large garlands strung with marigold, jasmine and gerbera daisies to place around each other's neck as a sign of respect. Once the rituals are completed, the Pink Gang hands the couple whatever money the women have been able to pool together to help the newlyweds, who are often only eighteen or nineteen years old, pay their first few months of rent.

To Geeta, the unusual television news bulletin about 'love marriages' was a revelation – she was amazed by what the Pink Gang was doing, but what made an even deeper impression on her was that these women looked just like her. 'If they can do this, why can't I?' Geeta asked herself.

When Deepak, who was still drinking considerably, arrived home that day, the first thing she told him was that she was going to become a Pink Gang member, which provoked a flurry of drunken giggles from him. When he was inebriated, he was particularly prone to silliness. Once, when Deepak contracted malaria, he had crept out of bed to drink with his friends, ignoring the two-dozen calls he received from Geeta. When she asked him the next day where he'd been, he replied, 'Getting bottles', which was how he usually referred to receiving malaria medication via an intravenous drip. His friends rip-roared and high-fived Deepak for his wittiness when they heard the story. 'You told the truth, *bhai!*' they told him, slapping him on the back.

The same day that Geeta told him about her intentions to join the Pink Gang, and when he was finally able to straighten up, he informed her that he knew Sampat – Deepak used to manage a liquor store in Badausa, where Sampat's family lived, and Sampat had run a small tea stall back then that Deepak frequented. 'Yes, yes, she's a good woman,' Deepak said happily to his wife, by way of blessing the idea, and then, after telling her where to find Sampat, he stumbled to bed.

WHEN GEETA WENT to Atarra to meet Sampat for the first time, a few days after seeing the Pink Gang on TV, she wore a pink sari, the only one she owned, to please the Pink Gang commander in chief and to signal her seriousness about joining the gang.

Those who knew Geeta appreciated how rare it was to see her in a sari, for she had refused to wear one for most of her life, which was unusual for a married woman in Bundelkhand. What had caused her to avoid wearing the carefully draped dress was an embarrassing moment that occurred at a wedding in the nearby city of Aligarh a few years earlier. The wedding guests had piled into tractors to ride to the wedding venue, but as Geeta stood up, her sari got caught in a crack, causing the dress to come partially undone. Saris, she felt, were not favourable to women. 'With saris, the belly is seen, the body can be seen, from here, from there,' she complains prudishly. 'This is not good.' Later, Sampat would try to convince Geeta to wear her uniform. 'She always scolds me saying, "Wear a sari, wear a sari," but I don't!' Geeta laughs.

When Geeta told Sampat why she had come to see her, Sampat showered Geeta with questions. The first was whether she had any problem she needed help with. When Geeta said no, Sampat did not believe her. 'No, you must have some problem. Without that, no woman comes here. There must be something. Is your husband bothering you? Do your neighbours bother you?' Sampat pressed.

When Geeta insisted there was nothing troubling her, Sampat changed track. 'So, have you come to me for commercial purposes? I will get you employment? Do you think that?' Sampat continued. 'You say there is nothing but, in my Bundelkhand, there is no such woman who comes on her own without any selfish motives. You won't tell now, you will tell tomorrow!' she chuckled.

Sampat continued grilling Geeta. 'If somebody says something wrong about you, how will you answer him? Will you come to me later and say Sampat-ji, that person said this to me, and that to me? Now if a girl comes to you, will you be able to listen to her problems? If she doesn't have the money, will you be able to go with her to the police station? Where will you get your money from? I will not be able to give you anything. I hope that's clear?' she asked.

The new recruit tried to answer all of her questions as best she could, starting with why she wanted to join the gang. Geeta, whose voice is languid when casually conversing at home, switches into a fast-talking, decisive mode of conversation when discussing important matters.

'It feels good to fight other's fights and to stand up against injustice. To fight with the police is a good thing because the police do all the wrong things. These days they take money and release a guilty person and do not fight for justice. Nowadays whoever has money wins the fight, the person who doesn't have money will lose – his case will be closed by police. Even if he has not done anything wrong, he will be behind bars!' she remembers telling Sampat. Sampat had nodded, pleased with her passionate answer.

'So, do you know about unity?' Sampat asked, as if it were a new product that had just appeared on the market. 'That is how a strong organisation is made. When we fight, we fight together,' Sampat continued. These were not complicated matters, and most women understood quickly, but Sampat always made sure to go over the basics with new recruits.

Geeta was eager to show that she did know about unity and the power behind organisations, or *sangatans*. When she was younger, bandits raided many homes in her village of Param Purva. The people in Param Purva were unusually close. 'It wasn't that this caste had a group, and another caste had a group – we were all one,' Geeta remembers. When the bandit menace started, the villagers came together. The well-off villagers bought revolvers for everyone, and before going to sleep, all the villagers would shoot in the air, the sound of the bullets tearing through the sky. 'They used to fire in the wind, not to kill anyone,' she says reassuringly.

It was natural to Geeta that the villagers confronted the bandit menace themselves, rather than going to the police for help. She had always felt there was no law in her village, and on the rare occasions when a law was implemented, the results were violent and dangerous. As a child, near the field where Geeta's mother, a daily-wage labourer, used to crush stones, she once saw a man beaten as he was hung upside down from a tree in front of the police station. 'They are the keepers of the law; they beat thieves,' Geeta's mother told her, when she asked what had happened. For a long time after that, whenever Geeta saw policemen walking around in groups, she hastened her step and looked down. 'I feared their uniform,' she remembers. Deepak was the one who finally taught her not to fear the police. 'They won't eat us; they are not animals,' he reasoned.

Sampat was impressed by Geeta's story and her zeal. Most women became members of the Pink Gang when they were in trouble and every one else – the police, their community and their family – had let them down. Women whose 'cases' the Pink Gang had solved don't always join, however, as membership is not a prerequisite for support. 'When we solve their cases, they forget about us,' Sampat sighs. To have a woman eagerly offer herself to the service of the Pink Gang without any strings attached – to give and not to take – was rare, and especially valuable to Sampat. Before accepting her into the gang, however, Sampat gave her a task to complete.

'If you can make four women join, then we will think that you can strengthen the organisation. If you cannot, then it will be very difficult for you to join,' Sampat told her, emphasising the importance of members to be fully committed and able to recruit other women into the gang.

THAT DAY, WHEN GEETA returned from Atarra, she recruited twenty-five women – all friends of hers – to join the Pink Gang. Many of these first recruits were from Aarogya Dhaam, a small, undeveloped settlement on the outskirts of Chitrakoot. Aarogya Dhaam consisted of mud huts sitting on an uneven patch of land just off the motorway. Geeta had lived there in the past. Just before she joined the gang, she had helped a woman named Shanti in a dramatic incident that won Geeta the admiration and praise of many women.

Shanti was raising her daughter on her own after her husband abandoned them. She managed to make ends meet by renting out a spare room to lodgers, which worked well until one of her guests started spreading rumours that the single mother was a prostitute, pointing to the fact that she rented her room mostly to men. One day the verbal bullying escalated into the lodger physically assaulting her. Geeta was on her way to buy medicine for her daughter that day, and as she passed Shanti's house, she happened to witness the fight.

'It happened like this. He threw the woman on the ground and lifted a big stone to hit her. I left my daughter and hit the man from behind. After that, three more women came and beat the man together. Only then he left her,' she recalls. Geeta took Shanti to file a police report and promised to protect her in case there were further problems. It was shortly after that incident that Geeta met Sampat for the first time, and so when Geeta started looking for women to join the Pink Gang, they willingly signed up. 'Shanti and ten more women became members immediately. They were thinking that today Shanti is affected, but tomorrow we might become victims and need someone for support. Now I have made at least five hundred members,' Geeta says, referring to her district-wide recruitment.

Geeta brought the new members to Sampat that same week, and each of them received a pink sari in exchange for two hundred rupees – about two pounds – the one-off membership fee. When some of the women asked Sampat what to do about husbands who did not want them to join, she gave them the following advice: 'Talk to your husband. Don't fight with him. If you fight with your husband, then it will be very difficult. He will gradually understand. If he doesn't understand, then call me. I will come to you. I will talk to your husband. He will understand gradually and will definitely send you out.'

Sampat also recommended that Geeta and the women go to the forest and chop bamboo to make themselves *laathis*, explaining that 'they can be useful'. The women did, braving the snakes and wild beasts.

All the women were then invited to attend the next Pink Gang meeting in Atarra. 'A meeting is when we call everybody, and the first thing we do there is sing,' she explained. In a region that still had a very strong oral culture, and where many couldn't read, songs were a good way to educate people. 'Women learn a lot through singing. The songs are about education, like why does a mother treat her daughter differently to her son? Why do women feel sad when a girl is born?

The first person responsible for a daughter is the mother. We all ask each other to sing in the meeting,' Sampat said.

One of Sampat's songs at the meeting was about how the suffering of women continues in homes, from her parents' to her in-laws', and is perpetuated through the generations.

'*The world is bad for girls, why isn't it bad for boys?*' the song starts, before narrating the story of a child whose mother mistreats her because she was born a girl. Then, when she is married off, her mother-in-law harasses her for years. When this woman finally bears a son and he marries, this very same woman goes on to torture her own daughter-in-law, just as she had been tortured. '*That poor girl was a slave from her childhood and remained a slave till old age*' went the final lines of the song. 'There are some women who start crying in this song. They realise that truly we are the ones who are weak, and if we continue to be weak like this, then we will never be able to overcome this in life. So, this song is very good for women,' Sampat says. She instructed them to memorise this song for their own meetings, which she said should be held every month, and to teach the moral of the story.

'Explain that this song tells us that we should educate the girl in her childhood and that if she gets married, her husband should be educated too. The girl should also be independent so that even if her husband leaves her, she won't have to beg him to stay. If we keep begging them, then we will keep being exploited for our whole life.'

In addition, Geeta and her recruits were instructed on how to defend themselves with the *laathis*. There were even lessons on how to ride a bicycle, as being self-reliant was an important part of being a gang member. Throughout the meeting, Sampat drilled home the idea that even though the problems facing women are far too large for them to tackle alone, in a united group they can be victorious. Geeta and her friends felt excited about the idea that they could change their communities; that they too had power and a voice that could be heard.

SOME TIME LATER, Geeta attended a Pink Gang protest rally that the press was covering. Seeing the photographers, Geeta took her *dupatta*, a long scarf, and wrapped it around her face so that she wouldn't be recognised. 'What will my in-laws say if they see me?' she thought, worried that her relationship with them would deteriorate further. Babuji approached her after the rally to say, 'Don't hide! Show your face. You're doing nothing wrong.'

For the next protest she attended, she left her face uncovered, and her photograph ran in the newspaper along with her name.

'You're in the newspaper!' Deepak told her excitedly the next day. 'You're becoming famous now,' he added proudly.

'Won't it be a problem?' she asked nervously.

'It's better than you staying home all day, don't you think? You'll see the world this way. I think it's good. Have courage. . . . I am here. You go.'

WHILE SAMPAT WAS OCCUPIED with investigating what had happened with Sheelu, Geeta had many cases she was attending to herself, one of which concerned a love marriage. The case was brought to her by a woman in her twenties called

Sudha, whose brother Mahesh was in a bind. 'She said my brother has done a mistake,' Geeta recalls about the first time Sudha arrived at her door. Mahesh had eloped with a higher-caste girl, and now the two teenagers – who were living with Sudha – needed help to get married. Sudha's house was in Aarogya Dhaam, and because of the popularity of the Pink Gang there, many neighbouring women told Sudha that Geeta would be the right person to assist the couple.

Mahesh was a strong-jawed, taciturn youth with chestnut-coloured skin who, at eighteen, had a steady job as a brick-layer. He had known Kamini, a girl with soft features, all his life, for they grew up in the same neighbourhood. They started developing feelings for each other once they hit puberty, and for five years before eloping, they had been meeting secretly at the temple. 'We would go there because our parents would not stop us from going there to pray,' Kamini says.

A lodger who stayed at Kamini's house informed her mother, a widow, that her daughter was seeing a boy. When she confronted Kamini about it, the young woman declared that she was in love with Mahesh, which angered her mother. 'Mummy didn't like him because they are poor. I said they are not poor. Money cannot buy everything. She thinks money is a big thing,' Kamini says. After Kamini confessed that she was having a relationship with Mahesh, problems with her mother escalated rapidly. 'She threatened me, scared me, and scolded me. She used to say, I will send you outside. I will kill you. I will throw you out of house.'

The threats from her mother were not uncommon. 'If some girl has a love marriage, she is threatened with murder.

Yes, murders do happen. Here it is like this: if someone likes someone, and their brothers or parents don't agree to the match, then they murder them very fast. Here love marriage is a taboo. But when marriages are arranged, everything is accepted, even if the boy is blind or a drunkard. . . . The truth is that parents don't have to spend their life with the chosen one. The boy and the girl have to,' Kamini says.

Kamini, however, was undeterred. 'When you want each other, then there is no need to get scared. If my mother doesn't approve, what could be done? How could we forget each other? Why should we be scared? We didn't commit any crime. We didn't steal. There was no point to be scared. We kept our courage and relied on each other. If we were scared, then it would not have been possible.'

Kamini quarrelled with her mother for weeks, and during that period her mother often kept her locked up in the house. One night, Mahesh snuck in to see her while everyone was sleeping, to make sure she was all right. The sound of him entering awoke Kamini's mother, and when she discovered Mahesh in the house, she kicked Kamini out. Since then, the two had been hiding at Sudha's so that Kamini's family could not find them.

Continuing to live at Sudha's house in their unmarried state entailed many risks, however. If the couple were found, Mahesh would be taken for questioning, during which time Kamini's mother could force Kamini to falsely accuse her lover of kidnapping. Given that Mahesh was a lower-caste boy who had eloped with a girl above his station, he would almost certainly be up against a legal and police system that was biased against him. Even if after a long trial he managed to prove his innocence, by then Kamini's mother would very likely have already married her off, thus preventing the couple from reuniting.

Marrying would have given them some, but not much, protection from prosecution, given that the police often reject marriage claims by eloped couples, especially when there is no certificate. Even if they did want to marry, however, it would not have been a straightforward affair. In India, the state gives Hindus two options if they want to marry. The majority have a religious wedding, which explicitly requires 'the consent of the guardians of the wife' in order to register a marriage under the Hindu Marriage Act of 1955. Given that runaway couples lack their parents' consent, their only other choice is to have a 'court marriage', which is officiated by the state. Unlike religious weddings, where the ages of the bride and groom are rarely checked, the state would demand proof that Kamini and Mahesh are above eighteen and twenty-one, respectively.

Although Kamini alleges that she was eighteen at the time of her elopement, the date of birth on her school report – the only document she had certifying her age – incorrectly had her down as sixteen. Such errors are very common, as India does not have strict practices on recording births, and parents often deliberately underreport the age of their daughters, since it is helpful when it is time to find a suitor. Even if Kamini's school report had confirmed that she was older than eighteen, there were other strong disincentives for the couple to marry in court: the law required a notice period of one month, allowing time for any objections to the marriage to be made and increasing the risk that the couple would be found by their parents before they had the chance to marry.

'To do a court marriage, it is a long route and one has to take it alone. You have to get help from many people. So my sister said it is better to take the help from the Pink Gang. If we are helped by the Pink Gang, then the law can say nothing to us,' Mahesh said.

Geeta told Mahesh and Kamini that she would speak to Sampat about their case. She also warned that the Pink Gang would not be responsible for anything that happened after the wedding. 'If you abandon each other, then that is not our fault,' she told the couple.

After consulting with Sampat, Geeta offered to marry Mahesh and Kamini on the most important day of the Pink Gang's calendar: Pink Gang Day, held on 14 February. Despite being chosen without any reference to St Valentine's Day in the West, it had nonetheless become synonymous with love, as young couples flocked to the Pink Gang to get married on that day.

CHAPTER FIVE

EVERYTHING WRONG HAS HAPPENED

WILL SHEELU BE ABLE TO RISE
ABOVE THIS OR WILL SHE BREAK?

—HINDUSTAN

THE DAY AFTER SAMPAT'S VISIT TO THE BANDA DISTRICT JAIL, Amit, the *Hindustan* reporter and Banda bureau chief, wrote an article about Sampat's attempt to meet Sheelu. 'The commander of the Pink Gang, Sampat Pal, has declared that she will start a movement for Sheelu's release,' he wrote. 'The lady who fights for women's causes has asked "Where is the rifle which she has stolen?" If the rifle has been stolen it should be produced in the court. Where has the police kept these things? If they have been returned to the legislator, under which law has that happened? Sampat will also go and meet Sheelu's father. Sampat said that the police should seriously look into the matter, otherwise the Pink Gang will start a movement,' he went on to write.

It was thanks in part to Amit's relentless reporting of the story, and to Sampat's public declaration of support for Sheelu, that dozens of journalists and hundreds of curious members of the public gathered outside the Atarra District Court on the mist-shrouded morning of 24 December to catch a glimpse of the young woman against whom outlandish accusations – including stealing a rifle from a politician! – were being levied. Sheelu was due in court because the judge was to decide whether to grant the police department's request for her to be remanded for an additional fifteen days, to enable them to gather more evidence for the trial. Many of those outside stood shivering in the damp chill that hung in the air as they waited.

The district court is a plain concrete bungalow with a corrugated iron roof. The structure stands at the end of a long, dusty road lined with wooden lawyers' shacks and stalls offering photocopying services, official stamps and the transcription of letters for those who have not mastered the written word.

Sampat arrived on the periphery of the crowd with her landlord, Lakhan, who had given her a ride on his motorbike. Like everyone else there, Lakhan was curious to see Sheelu. Although he was not very close to Dwivedi, the families of the two men were on amicable terms, primarily because they were both Brahmins and had friends in common. 'My father is friends with the Dwivedi family. We go to each other's weddings,' he explains.

Journalists from all the major local newspapers were there to cover what was revealing itself to be murky political intrigue. As Sampat elbowed her way to the court entrance, some people recognised her and helped her get through; some even wished her luck. '*Hum tumhare saath hai*' – We are with you – several people shouted towards Sampat.

Sheelu arrived in a police convoy, which included two vans and several patrol jeeps. As they drove down the shack-lined dirt road, they turned on their sirens to get the large crowd out of the way. In the commotion, Sampat and the journalists did not get to see or speak to Sheelu, who was escorted from the jeep into the courthouse by a male officer and a serious-looking policewoman in a khaki *salwar kameez* uniform.

Sheelu emerged from the court around twenty minutes later, still escorted by the officers. The court had granted the police request and declared that Sheelu was to be detained a further fifteen days. Sheelu's presence that day was a for-mality, and she was not required to make any statements to the court. When she exited the building, the crowd saw her properly for the first time. The ashen, weary-looking seventeen-year-old wore a turquoise *pajama kurta*, a tunic top with loose-fitting trousers, a black embroidered cardi-gan, gold hoop earrings and a shawl; she looked petrified. The female guard led her towards the jail-bound, navy-blue police van, but before she could get into it, a television journalist from Sahara Samay TV asked her what her name was. Sheelu turned around and, with a tense, determined look, said, 'I'm Sheelu Devi.' Before the journalist could ask another question, the policewoman hastened her into the van. As she sat down, Sheelu extracted something from her pocket, and after pausing for a moment to build up courage for her next move, she thrust her hand out of the window and attempted to hand the journalists a carefully folded note.

A policeman seized it before she could do so, and according to one *Hindustan* journalist, 'He ripped it up and threw it into a nearby fire.' Journalists scrambled to save the scrap of paper but managed to retrieve only a few charred, illegible shreds.

In the resulting confusion Sampat managed to push her way to the front of the crowd and say to the guards, 'One minute. Let us talk. Let us talk!' Standing outside the opened passenger door of the van, she beckoned Sheelu towards her. Sheelu bit her lips in a moment of indecision, and then scrambled over the guard seated on her left and stepped out of the van and into Sampat's arms, which were stretched wide open to receive her.

A semicircle of television cameras and outstretched voice recorders tightened in around the women, catching every word of their exchange. '*Namaste*, daughter,' Sampat started. 'Sheelu, you will get justice, don't you worry. I will bring thousands of women . . . ,' she said, wiping Sheelu's tears and stroking her hair. One journalist called out, 'Sheelu, what would you like to say about all the accusations on you?' 'Everything is wrong,' Sheelu responded. 'There are many accusations . . . ,' the journalist continued. 'They're *all* wrong,' she insisted.

'What has happened with you?' the journalist asked.

'Everything wrong has happened with me,' she replied.

'Who has done wrong with you?' he asked.

'The legislator and his men – they beat me a lot.'

'Who beat you?'

'The legislator's men.'

'The legislator beat you?'

'Yes.'

'What did he say?'

'He said that he will kill me once I am out of jail,' Sheelu said. 'I am suffering whatever has been written in my destiny,' she added tragically before she climbed back into the van and was driven away.

The journalists then turned to Sampat.

'Sampat, what do you think about this?' a journalist asked her.

'It is all wrong. They are just accusations. The girl is saying that she has been wronged. I am also a woman and I will help her. Sheelu has been badly abused,' Sampat said.

'What about the allegations that she stole a gun from the legislator's house?' one TV journalist asked.

'If she stole a gun, then why was it not submitted in the police station? I have investigated in the police station also. They don't have the gun,' Sampat replied.

Sampat then told the media that she demanded to know why the legislator had taken Sheelu from Pathara himself instead of getting the police involved.

'When I went to Pathara, people told me that they' – the legislator's men – 'broke the door and took her. But it wasn't necessary to break the door. They should have told the police. The police should have received it in writing if the girl was captured by goons or some other people,' she said.

'The legislator is not above the law,' Sampat boomed. 'No matter how powerful you are, punishment should be given.'

AFTER THE CROWDS DISPERSED, Lakhan's phone rang. It was Dwivedi's brother, Ram Naresh Dwivedi – this was the same man that Deepak, Geeta's husband, had worked for at the liquor store in Atarra.

Ram's tone was cordial yet serious when he asked Lakhan if he could come over to his house. 'The legislator wants to talk to you,' he said. Lakhan was uneasy about the meeting. 'I was afraid. I thought, This matter is getting very complicated now.'

After he hung up, Lakhan took Sampat to the side and told her about the telephone conversation. 'What should I do, Sampat-ji. Should I go?' he asked. Sampat was unequivocal in her response. 'Go! Find out what he wants from you and then let me know,' she instructed.

It was afternoon by the time Lakhan reached Dwivedi's home, where he was told to wait in the yard, or *maidan*, behind the house – the same place where Achchhe Lal claims to have been assaulted and threatened. 'There were twenty people sitting there. Security people were there. His brother was sitting next to me. With a lot of respect they made me sit and told me, "*Vidhayak* wants an audience with you." There was a lot of rubbish. Buffaloes and cows were tied back there. Everyone was very serious.'

Dwivedi was not ready to meet Lakhan immediately, as he was giving a press conference inside the house. After the court appearance, journalists had flocked to Dwivedi's home to get his statement on the alleged robbery.

'What do you have to say on all this?' asked one journalist.

Dwivedi paused and then delivered his response in a slow, dreary tone. 'There's been a robbery. . . . This is all a political setup. The things have been recovered . . . ,' he started before he was interrupted by the loud ringing of someone's mobile phone. Dwivedi glanced over towards the noise and then, after the call was cut, continued speaking. 'Since elections are near, this is all a political conspiracy. The opposition is raking up this issue. I don't want to say much more about this now. . . .'

'Sheelu has come out with a lot of allegations. . . . What is all this about?' another journalist asked.

Dwivedi's eyes darted upwards, as if he were trying to recall who this person Sheelu was and what allegations people were talking about. 'What allegations she has made I do not know,' he finally replied, cutting short the press conference.

When Lakhan saw all the journalists exiting the house, it put him even more on edge. It crossed his mind that perhaps the press was colluding with the politician. When he was finally shown into Dwivedi's house, Lakhan found the politician standing in the courtyard wearing a beleaguered expression.

Lakhan recalls the following exchange taking place: 'He told me, "I've called you to ask why Sampat is doing this? Why is she standing up against me? What wrong have I done to her? I haven't ignited anything out here. I've tried to calm things down. Although I'm doing good, my hands are getting burned. I want an audience with Sampat Pal. Can you tell her to meet me?"' Lakhan says.

Lakhan, sidestepping the role of intermediary, offered Dwivedi Sampat's number and said he could get in touch with her directly. The legislator allegedly did not want to call Sampat from his own phone, however, and made his personal assistant ring her.

After the connection was established, Lakhan listened in on the conversation. '*Bhen-ji*' – sister – 'what wrong have I done? I've done no *galat kam*. If you want, I can resign from my legislator position. Why? Because it looks like you don't like my work! Let's meet. I don't want to discuss on phone. I can send a car to fetch you,' Lakhan heard him say.

'If you are innocent, why are you acting like someone who has blood on their hands?' Sampat demanded.

The politician persisted. 'I am coming to you like a brother, with my head bowed and asking for forgiveness,' he said. This angered Sampat even more. 'You should be asking Sheelu for forgiveness, not me!' she shouted. Dwivedi grew frustrated with how the conversation was progressing.

'It is not good to talk about this on the phone. Where are you now?' he demanded. 'I'll send a car to pick you up. Hello? Hello?'

Sampat had already hung up. 'Go find her and bring her here,' Dwivedi barked at his driver, who was standing mutely by the door.

'Lakhan-*bhai*, I've done no wrong. You can speak to your father. Ask him about my reputation. We are a respectable family. I would never do such a *ganda* thing,' Dwivedi said. 'Tell Sampat that I can offer five *lakhs* of rupees' – five hundred thousand rupees – 'from my discretionary fund for her not to speak about me. I can give that money to her son, to help develop his village. Just tell Sampat I'll come to meet her wherever she wants,' Dwivedi allegedly told Lakhan.

Lakhan promised to pass on the message.

WHEN BABUJI HEARD about Dwivedi's offer, he was uneasy. He didn't like that the legislator had offered money to Sampat's son, Kamta, known as Munna – it was only a few months ago that Munna had entered politics and already people were trying to corrupt him. More fundamentally, however, it bothered Babuji that Munna was in politics in the first place.

In October of 2010 Munna was elected *pradhan* of Rauli, the same village near Gadarian Purva where Sampat had first begun work with the Prabhat Samit NGO, which had scouted her after she became well known through her sewing skills. Munna was one of twenty-one Pink Gang–supported candidates who had recently been voted in as *pradhan*. Often these candidates were not members of the Pink Gang, but, like Munna, they were related to members. The duties of a *pradhan* included overseeing the construction of village roads, installing water hand-pumps, building medical centres, and helping villages gain access to money from the government for rural development. At twenty-two years old, Munna was unusually young to be a village chief, a job typically given to experienced, senior men in their forties or fifties. 'People saw hope in him,' explained his wife, Beenu. 'See how many people believe in mummy?' she said, referring to Sampat. 'It is for that same reason that they voted for him.'

A year before, however, Munna was preparing Beenu to run for the local elections. In case Rauli was declared a woman's seat, Munna wanted to make sure Beenu would win it. 'I'm interested in fighting elections,' Munna had told her when they were engaged. 'If it's a woman's seat, would you like to run?' he asked. Beenu had said yes. Munna had married Beenu in January 2010 while he was still a year away from graduating from his course work in agriculture at Bundelkhand University in Jhansi. The hasty marriage was unusual, and Beenu attributed it to the elections – she had to be Sampat's daughter-in-law if she wanted to stand a chance at winning. That year both Beenu and Munna had put forward their names to be candidates, but once the Rauli seat was declared to be 'general' – meaning that there was no reservation that year for women or lower castes – Beenu withdrew her name and Munna won, thanks to Sampat's support.

Munna's political ambitions have put a strain on Babuji's relationship with Sampat's family, which used to be amicable. Babuji had been growing increasingly concerned about Sampat's children, in particular Munna, seeking to profit from the Pink Gang.

Munna, the second-youngest child, can come across as the baby of the family. The playful young politician seems most in his element when lounging at home, teasing his doe-eyed new wife or listening to Bollywood music off his mobile phone speakers. He does not, at first sight, strike one as a person passionate about education.

Yet, in 2008, during his first year of university, Munna started a local school in the nearby town of Rauli and called it the 'Pink Gang Children's School'. 'It was my idea. My mum didn't know about it at first, not even Babuji,' he says. Munna had opened the school to cover part of the costs of his tuition, which came to two hundred thousand rupees (approximately two thousand pounds) for the four-year course.

'I thought, How can I earn money for fees? Then I thought of a school,' he says. 'I first thought of charging fifty rupees a month [approximately fifty pence], but people are too poor, so I just charged twenty-five rupees.'

Sampat, despite being unschooled, used to run a very basic school that Prabhat Samit administered in the nearby town of Gora. It was not a lucrative job – Sampat made five hundred rupees per month – but it may have inspired Munna to consider education a stable source of income. For Munna to open a school, he had to register it under the name of an NGO; affiliating himself with the Pink Gang's NGO – a legacy of the gang's origins in a self-help group – spared him from having to set up his own charity. Contrary to what the name suggested, Pink Gang members did not run Munna's school, nor was Sampat involved in its administration.

He hired eight teachers and enrolled local children from Rauli. In India, even the poor try to give their children a private education because government-run schools are notoriously bad. Often, teachers in the government schools do not appear for class – there are countless cases of teachers receiving monthly pay cheques for teaching at schools they have never set foot in.

The Pink Gang Children's School enrolled 250 children. The students learn from a national curriculum while sitting cross-legged under banyan trees in the yard, where the classes are held – a common setup in many Indian schools. The students, who are divided into eight classes, all wear school uniforms composed of light-pink shirts and black pants, or a dark-grey skirt for girls. Children are admitted regardless of background and of whether or not their mothers are Pink Gang members, and they do not receive any ideological training. The school, in other words, is not a recruiting ground for future gang members.

When he found out about the school, Babuji was deeply upset with Sampat and criticised Munna for exploiting the Pink Gang's name for his own commercial venture. In Munna's eyes Babuji was just jealous that he had opened a Pink Gang school first. 'He wanted to open a school too,' he says.

Now with Munna in politics, however, the school was the least of Babuji's problems. He remembered the days when, before Munna's election, Sampat was a scourge to *pradhans*, who often run villages like their own fiefdoms, siphoning off money from the budgets they manage for their own benefit. Recently a *pradhan* in a village near Mahoba had moved into the local school and declared it to be his house; he continued living there until the Pink Gang kicked him out. Since Munna's victory, however, Babuji felt that Sampat's attitude towards *pradhans* had softened. He did not think that Sampat and Munna were corrupt, but rather that she risked being compromised by him.

Indeed, following the 2010 elections, Babuji felt that Munna's position was already affecting Sampat's ability to check up on the other recently elected Pink Gang members, who in his eyes were not living up to their election promises. Babuji had hoped that with the victory of Pink Gang members in the local elections, they would be able to fight corruption together by alerting the rest of the organisation to any bribery they witnessed. 'If we lead by example, we'll grow and there'll be a social change. But this has not happened because Sampat's own son is a *pradhan*. Now it's hard to tackle these things,' Babuji says glumly.

To his disappointment, several months had gone by without a word from the Pink Gang *pradhans* elected in October. Not only had they not reported any bribery attempts, but they had also failed to inform the rest of the Pink Gang on improvements they were making in their own villages. 'If I speak up against a *pradhan* now, Sampat doesn't like it. Bharat's wife Chandrakali' – a member of the Pink Gang in Duwaria – 'is a *pradhan* and isn't doing much work. Sampat just tolerates this. She doesn't talk back. We hoped that when people try to corrupt *pradhans*, our Pink Gang members would inform us. We haven't heard anything though, so they must be taking cuts too.'

'I love the Pink Gang. I don't want to open this can of worms. It should be Sampat who takes this on. I tell her it's not about winning. It's about how good you do your work. This job is like walking on a razor's edge. The slightest veering off path is dangerous.'

IF POLITICS WAS DANGEROUS, then there was reason to believe that the Pink Gang would be treading on even more delicate ground in the future. In August 2010, Sampat received a momentous piece of news. She had been invited to a private meeting with Sonia Gandhi, the head of the Gandhi-Nehru political dynasty, in her New Delhi home. There are few people in the world who wield more political clout than she does. The elegant, Italian-born Sonia Gandhi, who was named the twelfth most powerful person in the world in 2012 by *Forbes* magazine, became the head of the Gandhi family after her husband, former prime minister Rajiv Gandhi, was assassinated in 1991. Seven years later, she became president of the Indian National Congress, the independence-era party of Mohandas Karamchand Gandhi and Jawaharlal Nehru. Nehru, the first prime minister of India, was the grandfather of Rajiv Gandhi; his mother, Indira Gandhi, also a prime minister, dropped the name Nehru when she married. After the 2004 general elections, Sonia Gandhi was chosen to lead a fifteen-party coalition government called the United Progressive Alliance. She was widely expected to become prime minister, but she turned down the post and appointed Manmohan Singh instead.

Sampat had remained in touch with the Congress Party ever since 2006, when the secretary of the All India Congress Committee, Dr Bhola Pandey, first contacted her following her assault of the Atarra police officer. Sampat was also part of a delegation of social workers who attended a minor event Sonia Gandhi hosted in 2007, but until a few months back, she had never been invited to a one-on-one meeting with the head of the Congress Party.

'Madam Sonia-ji is a very good woman. She has made a name for herself in the entire country,' Sampat says respectfully. Sampat was deeply honoured that Mrs Gandhi had called her to her home. 'She invited me because she felt that I am a strong woman, and if all the strong women are united, then women exploitation will be reduced,' she says, adding, 'She is a very brainy woman and a lady who doesn't have a pride or ego. That's why she embraced and accepted me.'

To get to New Delhi, Sampat and Babuji travelled by overnight train in the 'general class', which is the least expensive and is typically crowded with the same number of people you would find in a suburban train during rush hour. Neither of them had ever gone to New Delhi. Sampat had packed a tiffin full of *puris* and potato curry, and *samosas* wrapped in newspaper. In her overnight bag she had packed a pink sari, to present to Sonia Gandhi as a gift. She also had some newspaper clippings profiling her work to show the Congress Party leader.

The dishevelled couple got off at Paharganj station, the busy terminal that is the confluence point for all of the train lines carrying mostly migrant workers from the impoverished

northern states of Uttar Pradesh and Bihar to the capital. In
the mornings the station is a cacophonous hub of activity.
Hawkers sell everything from combs to colanders; rows of
shoe-shiners bang their buffing brushes on their footstools to
attract the attention of passersby; and women carrying emaciated babies, their heads lolling back on feeble necks, stick
out their grime-covered palms at travellers.

Sampat was unfazed by the madness. She and Babuji wove
through the crowds and made their way to the auto-rickshaws.
The Congress Party had booked a room for them near the
central train station. From there a car came to fetch Sampat
after she had freshened up.

Sampat arrived at 10 Janpath, the official residence of
Sonia Gandhi, after a pleasant drive through the immacu-
late, tree-lined avenues of the exclusive South Delhi neigh-
bourhoods. There, some of the most powerful people in the
country live in imposing modernist villas built in the 1950s,
hidden behind high walls, but not high enough to conceal
the satellite dishes perched on the rooftops.

Sampat went through a security check at the entrance of
Sonia Gandhi's property and then walked down a driveway
that overlooked a vast, rolling lawn of manicured grass. She
was whisked through multiple doors and then, after a short
wait, into the personal study of Sonia Gandhi. The meeting
could not have lasted more than half an hour, but it had
the most profound impact on Sampat. She sat in an elegant
upholstered chair – a far cry from the uncomfortable seating
on the train – and Mrs Gandhi offered her some *chai* in 'a
very nice cup'. The sun-lit room they sat in was decorated
with framed photographs of the Gandhi family, and it had a
large bookshelf off to one side, near the polished wood desk.

EVERYTHING WRONG HAS HAPPENED   155

Sonia Gandhi radiated warmth and had many questions for Sampat. How did the Pink Gang come into existence? Why did she start a gang? Why did she choose a pink sari uniform? 'Then she asked, "Why do you use the word *gang*?" I said, We beat up a policeman and the media called us a gang. Since then the name has stuck and it cannot be changed. She started laughing and said, "Very well." She listened to me. It's not like she didn't discuss with me. She didn't just encourage me and say, "You have done a good job." She slowly understood our strength and then understood that through this women's group, women can take their rights themselves. Otherwise, men will never give it,' Sampat remembers. The head of the Congress Party also had some advice for the vigilante leader. 'It is not good to beat police,' Mrs Gandhi chastised, but Sampat defended her actions. 'If that person does wrong deeds and is taking the law in his hands, what is the problem if we beat him?'

The women spoke about social issues in Bundelkhand. Before she left, Sampat gave Mrs Gandhi the pink sari, which she graciously accepted.

In their last hours in the city, Sampat and Babuji visited India Gate together, an Arc de Triomphe that served as a war memorial. 'At India Gate I saw so many boys and girls sitting together. I was just sitting a few feet away from them, and when they kept hugging, I found it uncomfortable because this was the first time that I had seen something like this. I was feeling shy inside,' Sampat recalls.

Back then, Sampat and Babuji were still not fully comfortable around each other. That particular day, surrounded by flirting youths, they kept a cautious distance between themselves. Things have changed since then. Now, Sampat will often fall asleep in Babuji's lap if they are journeying somewhere by bus or train. If Sampat is exhausted after a day of travelling from one village to the next, Babuji will frequently knead the muscles on her calves and shoulders with care. When she applies mustard oil to her hair, he is often the one to rub it in for her, massaging her head vigorously in the process. Trips, like the one to visit Sonia Gandhi, had drawn the two closer together.

On their way home from New Delhi, Babuji and Sampat speculated about whether the meeting with Sonia Gandhi would lead to her being offered a ticket to run as a Congress Party candidate in the 2012 Uttar Pradesh elections for the state Legislative Assembly. The truth was that the party needed people like Sampat – a budding social leader with a growing, grassroots support base – to join their ranks in Uttar Pradesh, the weightiest electoral state in the country. Uttar Pradesh accounted for 80 out of 545 seats in the lower house of the parliament; the second-largest state in terms of parliamentary constituencies, Maharashtra, home to the finance capital Mumbai, trailed behind with 48. The Congress Party had not been an important player in Uttar Pradesh since 1988, when it was last voted into power in the state. Since then, the party had made winning back Uttar Pradesh a top electoral priority. In the 2007 elections to the Legislative Assembly of Uttar Pradesh, the Congress Party, which had ruled the country for most of India's post-independence history, was able to win only 22 out of 403 seats. Indian newspapers described the outcome as 'abject' and 'a complete humiliation'.

Babuji was not keen on the idea. 'I don't want us to be merged,' he told Sampat, concerned that the Pink Gang identity would be lost if she entered party politics. Sampat paid no heed to Babuji's reservations and told him that if Sonia Gandhi asked her to run, she would.

IF SAMPAT WERE to enter politics, then one of her biggest challenges would be maintaining unity within the gang. Despite Sampat's many years of instilling solidarity among gang members, discord has crept beyond her and Babuji and into the sisterhood. One of the worst ruptures within the Pink Gang had been between Sampat and the district commander of the Pink Gang in Mahoba, a woman called Suman Singh.

Suman was the first district commander Sampat ever appointed, and Sampat maintains that Suman's motivations for joining were insincere from the start. According to Sampat, Suman had thrown out her daughter-in-law three months before joining the Pink Gang, but she had failed to inform Sampat about this. 'She wanted to join the Pink Gang so that her daughter-in-law's father would not file a case against her. She thought that if she became a member of the Pink Gang, her daughter-in-law's father won't dare to attack her. That's why she came. I only found this out later,' Sampat says.

Soon after Suman became a member, Sampat suspected that Suman looked down on members of the Dalit caste, which was below the Chauhans, her subcaste, which fell under the umbrella Kshatriya caste. This was a problem as Sampat strictly forbids discrimination within the gang. Suman had once accompanied Sampat to the house of a Dalit woman, whose case the Pink Gang was handling, and had refused to accept tea and snacks that their hosts had offered them. 'I asked her why she was not eating, and she said, "I'm fasting today,"' Sampat remembers. But when they returned to Suman's house, one of the first things she did was to eat something. 'I thought you were fasting today!' Sampat exclaimed when she watched her dig into her meal. 'Oh! I completely forgot!' Suman replied sheepishly, but Sampat was convinced she was lying.

Later, Sampat caught Suman in a considerably more serious crime. Sampat had gone to the bank to withdraw some money, and when she met the bank manager at the branch, he expressed surprise at seeing her there. 'You just threatened me, and now you come in as if nothing happened?' he exclaimed. 'I never threatened you!' Sampat replied in disbelief. 'You did, just half an hour ago you threatened me on the phone!' the angered manager replied. Sampat asked him to dial the number he had received the threatening call from and to switch his mobile phone to loudspeaker.

'This is Sampat Pal, commander in chief of the Pink Gang,' replied the woman on the other line. Sampat could not believe her ears.

'That can't be! I am sitting here with Sampat Pal and she wants to speak to you,' the bank manager replied. It turned out that the imposter was Suman.

Suman begged Sampat for forgiveness, explaining that she had been desperate to help her brother, who had taken out a loan of 150,000 rupees – approximately £1,600 – and could not pay the interest. When the bank threatened action against him, Suman called the manager and, pretending to be Sampat, said that the Pink Gang would 'raid the bank'. Sampat was furious. 'I told her that that was not the right thing to do. She was threatening someone in my name! Now I do not know how many times she has used my name in the wrong way. . . . After that I told her she was not in my organisation anymore,' Sampat says. She did end up taking Suman back, however, as she worried that kicking her out would risk the breakup of the gang. 'If I throw out everyone who makes a mistake, there would be no one left in the gang,' she adds.

So far, the only district commander permanently expelled from the gang was a woman called Gyanmatti, whom Suman had recruited. Gyanmatti, a social worker, was very keen to move up the ranks within the gang as soon as she joined. Shortly after becoming a member she asked Sampat whether she could be made the district commander of Mahoba, despite the fact that Suman already occupied the position. When making her case to Sampat, Gyanmatti claimed that she would do a better job than Suman at managing her district, and that Suman was 'not giving her enough respect'. Against her better judgement, Sampat acquiesced by giving Gyanmatti another district, Hamirpur, to run. The appointment proved to be a disaster. 'Gyanmatti never made any members. She just went around with a board saying, "I am a district commander,"' Sampat complains. When reports came in that Gyanmatti was using her power as a local gang leader to demand protection money from people, Sampat stripped her of her title and membership, but that did nothing to stop her. Gyanmatti continued to claim she was a district commander, forcing Sampat to call the local police stations and newspapers to inform them that her former gang member had gone rogue and that the Pink Gang was not liable for anything she did.

SHORTLY BEFORE SHEELU'S ARREST, even Geeta, who otherwise got on with everyone in the gang, had locked horns
with Mitu Devi, the district commander from Banda, over
a case involving members from their respective districts who
were fighting.

Guriya, a gang member of Geeta's, accused her mother-
in-law, who was in Mitu's gang, of beating her and refusing
to accept her into the family after she eloped with her son.
What made this case even more urgent was that Guriya, who
was in her early twenties, was pregnant at the time. 'Her
mother-in-law would whip her with the rubber tube used
for the gas cylinder,' Geeta recounts.

In order to help Guriya, who had recently joined the
gang out of desperation, Geeta collected a group of women
from Chitrakoot to have a word with Guriya's mother-in-
law. That is when Geeta learned that the mother-in-law had
become a member of Mitu's group and therefore had the
protection of Mitu, who referred to herself as the 'Lion of
Banda'. This created an awkward situation between the two
district commanders, as both defended their own members
and accused the other party of distorting the facts.

In the end, Geeta had to call Sampat to resolve the dispute. '*Didi* made Guriya and her mother-in-law come to an
understanding. Mitu had to agree with *didi*. . . . Mitu's position was bad, I told her that. She didn't say anything. She
went away. She still keeps anger in her mind against me. I
said its okay. I have to live in Chitrakoot, not Banda. If she
wants me for any work, she can call me and I will come. . . .
I am not scared of her.'

Apart from these incidents, Sampat maintains that the majority of her gang members get along. 'They are like sisters. Had they not shared a feeling of friendship, then why would they have joined the group? If someone works for money, then it is not friendship, but here the women do not even demand any money. They are not forced to help each other – they do so out of friendship.'

'AT THE *VIDHAYAK'S* PLACE ATROCITIES WERE COMMITTED: SHEELU' – this is the headline that ran on the front page of the *Hindustan* the day after Sheelu's court appearance. Every other local newspaper covered the story, writing multiple articles for their morning editions. 'POLICE HAS CLOSED EYES, EARS AND MOUTH', declared the newspaper *Amar Ujala*. '*VIDHAYAK-JI*, IS SHEELU YOUR DAUGHTER OR MAID-SERVANT?' demanded the headline of another article in *Amar Ujala*, referring to contradicting statements made by the legislator and his family about his relationship to Sheelu.

Dwivedi would later tell journalists that it was because of his relationship with Achchhe, who he said was a friend and fellow BSP member, that he allowed Sheelu to stay at his house. The legislator said the reason Achchhe made this unusual request in the first place was that Sheelu felt she had lost her honour and dared not return to Shahbajpur after having been retrieved in Pathara. 'This girl said that she has no courage to go to the village and show her face there,' Dwivedi recalled.

He also hinted that she was a troubled girl who needed to be reformed. 'She has a big history,' he said vaguely, adding, 'I felt that this girl will maybe change for the good . . . if I allow her to live at my house.' He touched on her alleged waywardness again when speaking about her imprisonment. Dwivedi mused that while he thought jail was not 'the right place for her', it might 'make a change in her for the good', and that 'whenever she comes out of jail, her father must make the effort to change her'.

He also categorically denied the accusations of mistreatment that Sheelu was making. 'I gave her respect like a daughter and kept her with my family,' he said, before blaming Sheelu's accusations on his political opponents. 'You can see the Congress Party and Samajwadi Party are against me because I was standing in elections. . . . I will prove that everything that they are blaming on me is wrong.'

Up until the moment Sheelu made her claims about abuse public, some papers had been timid in their coverage of her arrest. They might have been paid not to write about it, which was known to happen in places like Bundelkhand – newspaper endorsements during elections there allegedly came with a price tag – or they could have censored themselves because they feared backlash from the politician. 'That legislator was very mighty. Even journalists were afraid of him. They didn't publish anything against him. Only Amit did,' Sampat says. Amit, Sampat's friend from the *Hindustan*, had been doggedly uncovering details and keeping the case on the top of his agenda with numerous follow-up stories and scoops. However, given the phenomenal number of people who had shown up for Sheelu's appearance at the court – 'I've never in my life seen so many people in court,' says one lawyer who was there – the newspapers could no longer afford not to write about a case that had captured the interest of the public.

With newfound confidence, the newspapers attacked the

police and the politician. 'Whose job are they doing? Whose rules and laws are they following?' *Amar Ujala* asked about the jailers, who had not yet performed a medical examination on Sheelu, despite the fact that she had claimed the legislator attacked her.

That day, all the papers ran the dramatic photo of Sampat and Sheelu's tender encounter. In the picture, Sampat is shown stroking the hair of the troubled young girl, who clutches Sampat's shoulder as she leans out of the police vehicle. One caption simply reads, 'Helplessness'. Another newspaper wrote an article to accompany the photo; the headline was 'HUGGING SAMPAT SHEELU SAYS: "*DIDI* HELP ME"'.

'The scene was filled with a lot of emotion,' one journalist for *Amar Ujala* wrote. In the same article the journalist emphasised the fact that Sheelu called Sampat '*didi*'. In a quote she gave to the paper, Sampat declared, 'Sheelu has called Sampat Pal sister, so I will be a sister towards her. Like an elder sister I will do my duties. If need be, I'll come out on the roads and fight for Sheelu's justice.' Now, the girl who had been described as a 'motherless child' in the *Hindustan* had an ally.

AS PUBLIC OUTCRY over Sheelu's arrest grew, those wanting to protect the legislator stepped up their pressure on Sampat. After Dwivedi's bribery attempt, the legislator's people visited Lakhan numerous times. Often, they came looking for Sampat. 'The legislator's uncle came to ask where Sampat was and when she was coming back. He told me that the legislator was innocent,' Lakhan recalls. The visits from the legislator's uncle occurred daily, but Sampat avoided bumping into him. 'I told her not to come to her office for a few days. I was worried that Dwivedi's men would take her away and threaten her,' Lakhan remembers.

Radhe Shyam Shukla, the feared subinspector who had allegedly framed Lakhan in a murder case, also paid him a visit. Instead of threatening Lakhan, he tried to reason with him. 'Why don't you change Sampat's mind? You're a Brahmin, I'm Brahmin, and so is the legislator. We are all brothers. Sampat should not be agitating like this – the legislator is innocent,' Shukla allegedly told him. Lakhan, not looking for trouble, said he would do what he could.

Apart from the numerous house calls by Dwivedi's family members and his friends in the police force, other rough-looking men who Lakhan had never seen before also came enquiring about Sampat's whereabouts. When Lakhan said she was out, they would sometimes sit in their car, parked across from the house, and wait for hours before driving off.

Having been burned once in the past owing to Sampat's meddling in political affairs, Lakhan grew increasingly nervous that this case could potentially lead to even greater trouble, and he urged her to be cautious.

CHAPTER SIX

THE EXORCIST OF SHAHBAJPUR

YOU'RE GOOD AT REMOVING GHOSTS,
AND YET YOU'RE SCARED OF A MAN?

—Sampat

EVER SINCE SHEELU WENT MISSING ON THAT DREADED DECEMBER morning, Achchhe had been living in fear of reprisals from the legislator's men. When Sheelu appeared at court on 24 December, Achchhe did not dare to go to see his own daughter, worried that he might run into Dwivedi's people. Lying low turned out not to be a good enough strategy, however.

The night following Sheelu's court appearance, two of Dwivedi's brothers, Chota and Raja, joined by a few armed men working for the legislator, allegedly terrorised the isolated hamlet of Shahbajpur. Before they could find him, Achchhe escaped into the forest, leaving his two youngest children in the care of Santoo, his teenage son.

Dwivedi's men allegedly barged into his home and intimidated Achchhe's terrified children, threatening, according to Achchhe, to 'wipe out' his whole family if Sheelu didn't change her statement. Some of Shahbajpur's villagers told journalists that the armed men had come up to them and demanded to know where Achchhe was, claiming that they would 'take him away' when he returned.

After Sheelu's arrest, Achchhe had frequently gone underground, leaving everyone to guess at his whereabouts. The media reported with concern and much speculation about his disappearance. 'ACHCHHE LAL HAS BECOME A REBEL', ran one headline in the *Hindustan*, feeding into Bundelkhand's long-standing narrative of ordinary men who, when denied justice, take up arms and go to live in the 'ravines', the hideout for bandits and revenge-seeking outlaws.

Another article in the *Hindustan* focused on the failure of the police to protect Achchhe. 'Achchhe Lal and Santoo are being stopped from meeting Sheelu. Not only this, they are unable to approach the police and tell their side of the story,' the paper reported after Sheelu's court appearance. 'Why are the police not taking action against these men? They are just sitting with their hands tied. Why aren't they getting in touch with Achchhe Lal?' the *Hindustan* demanded.

Sampat had the same concerns, and so she made it her priority to find Achchhe and support him.

DWIVEDI'S MEN INTIMIDATED Sampat too, but she made sure not to tell her family about the threats. Sampat reasoned that, as with so many other instances of danger she had successfully navigated on her own, it was best that her family remained in the dark.

After Sampat declared that the Pink Gang would 'start a movement' for Sheelu's justice, a journalist called Jagpath from *Dainik Jagran* rang Sampat one evening to give her a warning. 'He told me to lock the door because people were asking about me, and to stay alert,' Sampat remembers. 'Maybe he's just scaring me? I don't know,' Sampat thought at the time. It turned out that Jagpath was telling the truth.

The next morning, Sampat approached the man who ran a late-night stall opposite her house, and enquired nonchalantly about whether anyone had stopped by the house looking for her at night. He told her that the legislator's men had been around in big cars. 'They stayed for some time outside your door, and then left,' he said. 'Are they behind you now?' he asked with concern. 'Even if they are, so what?' Sampat replied defiantly. 'Are they gods, that we should be afraid? No, they're just men. That's all.'

Sampat had already decided that she would not let the politician intimidate her, even if he were to step up his pressure on her. 'I didn't think about what was going to happen to me. If that were inside me, how could I fight? In this world, at least *one* person has to fight. All over the world, someone comes forward who has courage. What would be the use if everyone were scared? This is India. There have been so many battles here. You have to forget your life and not be scared. That's how the country will go ahead,' Sampat says. She was, however, aware of the risks. 'Here, people can bump you off in a crowd, or in a market. How do you shout or call for help? How do you know who did it?'

Sampat has what she considers to be an unnatural level of courage. It forms part of the great parcel of talents that she received at birth and whose origins perplex her. Given her self-sufficiency, she rarely feels the need to confide in others and has no close friends, Babuji being the only exception. When those around her are incredulous of her bravery, not believing that she doesn't have moments of weakness, she retorts, 'Look, I don't get scared. I don't think about what's going to happen to me. If that were inside me, how could I fight? Tell me!' Her only weakness is her family. 'If they start worrying, that weakens me, so I don't tell them everything. I only tell Babuji and the Pink Gang everything,' she says.

The kind of conversations she has with her *gharwali* – literally 'house people' – has to do with 'household things'. 'Why should I tell them that this one gave me respect today, or that one gave me threats?' she questions. They rarely ask anyway. As for her husband, she purposefully hides information from him. 'Am I working for myself or for him? If I tell him these things, will he not start shouting or make obstacles?'

The truth was that Sampat had been in far greater danger without her family having any idea. None of Sampat's family members, not even her husband, knew the true reason why they suddenly had to uproot from Gadarian Purva and move to Badausa over a decade ago. Her children had only vague notions of why they had been wrenched away from their childhood home with but a few moments' notice.

'Mummy said people in the village were doing black magic on us,' says Nisha, adding that she and Munna suffered from persistent and mysterious illnesses in the run-up to their move. Champa knew a different version. 'We had family arguments – that's why we came.' Neither knew that

Sampat had packed up her life in her in-laws' village and fled to Badausa with the taste of death in her mouth.

ON AN OVERCAST, humid monsoon day in 1990, Sampat was sitting on a *charpoy* under the clay and bamboo stick awning of the mud hut belonging to Gulab, the man who had admired her speech at the meeting in the Rauli school. Gulab's house faced the whitewashed western wall of the school premises, which could be seen from where Sampat was sitting.

The two had become friends in the years since they first met, and Sampat had subsequently helped Gulab to become the village chief – the first Dalit to hold the post in living memory. 'It was a revolution in our village. Before there was a dictatorship,' Gulab remembers. The upper-caste Brahmins in Rauli were used to winning all village chief elections. Even when the seat was reserved for a member of a lower caste, they would put forward one of their land labourers as a proxy and 'control from behind', as Gulab says.

Sampat was visiting Gulab that stormy day to ask him to sign documents that would allow a friend of hers to apply for work at the school. Sampat often came by to meet Gulab for official matters. 'Many people told me, "Sampat-ji, please speak to Gulab about this matter, or that matter." Everyone knew I was close to him,' Sampat remembers. Jutting her thumb into her chest, she proclaims, 'It was thanks to *me* that he became the chief. *I* was the strength of women to him. *I* told all women to vote for him.'

When Sampat arrived at Gulab's house, she found her brother-in-law, Ramkesh, sitting there under the awning with Gulab. 'He must have come with something to discuss with him,' Sampat reasons. Sampat, being inquisitive, would normally have struck up a conversation with someone visiting the village chief, but she and Ramkesh were not on speaking terms.

'*Arre*, that one has a bad character, understand what I mean? He always made bad comments to us,' Sampat says with an irritated frown. Ramkesh, who was the only one of Munni's brothers to have gone to school, mocked Sampat's husband for being illiterate, while he, Ramkesh, bragged about his own academic credentials. 'Sister-in-law, your husband is not educated, but we are educated,' Ramkesh once told her when they were alone.

'Your wife must be lucky to have you, then?' Sampat snapped, adding, 'Our husband is also lucky. That's why he got me.' Ramkesh did not like the way in which Sampat talked back to him, she thinks. 'His wife was very simple, not much of a speaking person. So he was jealous.'

At Gulab's house that day, Sampat recalls clearly that the village chief's mother, an elderly woman, offered Sampat water flavoured with jaggery, a coarse brown sugar made from the sap of palm trees. Out of respect for the rules dictated by India's caste system, which placed Sampat a minor notch above Gulab, she should not have accepted the refreshment, but instead should have pressed her hands together politely and said, 'No thank you, sister', or 'Today I am fasting'. Those who lacked shame might have gone as far as to say, 'No, no! I can't. I get a bad stomach if I have food from a Charmar.' Gulab's mother would have understood. Since Gulab had won the village elections, members of a higher caste had been at pains not to sit on the same *charpoy* as him, or to accept food or drink at his house. Many in India continue to believe the lower castes are 'unclean' and that sharing food, drink or eating utensils with them can 'pollute' higher castes. Sampat, however, took the metal tumbler when Gulab's mother handed it to her.

'They are all fools who believe in caste. I think that I was born in some foreign country in my previous birth. That's why I don't believe in all these things,' Sampat says, with a chuckle and clap of the hand. One can imagine Sampat boldly swallowing the drink in one go.

Ramkesh had been outraged by what Sampat had done, and so after his meeting with Gulab he went straight to Gadarian Purva to tell his family what he had seen. 'He was annoyed with me and spread in the village that "*Kairiwalli* has drank water from the hands of Gulab."' (People in Gadarian Purva referred to Sampat as *kairiwalli*, which means 'the one from Kairi'.)

According to Sampat, Ramkesh went to her parents-in-law and told them that she was a 'rogue woman' who 'eats and drinks with anyone' and even 'sleeps with anyone'. 'He told bad words about me. . . . In the interiors and villages these stupid ideas about caste are still controlling people's minds. People don't eat from the plates of the Dalits; they don't drink water from them. It is too much here,' Sampat says, slapping her forehead in exasperation. 'My drinking water at Gulab's has made history!'

To punish Sampat for her flouting of social laws, Ramkesh and his friends ('He called Phandua, Bhola, and Babbu . . . they were all jealous of me') convened a village assembly, called *panchayat*, to be held late at night in the fields that surround Gadarian Purva. No women were invited, but one of

Sampat's oldest friends in the village, a woman called Sumintra, happened to overhear parts of the meeting. Sumintra had gone out to relieve herself under the moonlit sky, and on her way back home, she managed to listen to what was said by hiding behind her neighbour's mud hut.

Worried for Sampat, Sumintra went to her house first thing the next morning to tell her what had been decided. '*Didi*,' she warned. 'They're going to be making big problems for you.'

IN GADARIAN PURVA, one of the most effective ways to ostracise a member of one's own caste was to treat them like a person who is 'polluted'.

'Don't let *kairiwalli* touch your water pitcher. Avoid her in every possible way, even her food and water. Don't let her use the well,' Sumintra had heard the men at the *panchayat* decree in their midnight meeting.

'I thought in my mind that if what Sumintra was saying was true, I would know about it when I reached the well,' Sampat remembers.

The well, which was located in front of Sampat's front door, was the only place in Gadarian Purva where villagers could draw water for cooking, bathing and washing clothes – it formed the heart of communal life. The first thing that Sampat did the next day was to position herself by the door and watch the well for any activity. Before long, three elderly women, Rajrani, Jagiya and Ramdaiyya, came to wash themselves.

As soon as the women sat down around the well, Sampat marched over to them.

'Stop there! Don't come up to the well. Let us take a bath first,' Rajrani cried.

Sampat demanded to know what the problem was, but the elderly woman demurred. 'Don't you take a bath! Let us fill our pots with water first,' she repeated.

Sumintra was right – she was officially a pariah. 'I felt like laughing, so I did,' Sampat remembers. Sampat was not angry at the women – 'They were like my distant mother-in-law. . . . They were old and dying,' Sampat later said, adding, 'These women were scolded by the men who called the village meeting. They must have been told, "Do this!" and "Don't do that." They had to obey that order. Things like this happen in villages. Men scold women.'

'They were staring at me. I sat there coolly, like this,' Sampat says, acting out how she feigned indifference. 'I took out water and started cleaning and scrubbing my arms with soap. They got angry and left, without bathing.'

For the next month, Sampat raced towards the well and started drawing water from it every time someone approached it to bathe. Not allowed to wash in her presence, lest they too become 'unclean', the villagers retreated from the well. 'They got so troubled that they started pouring water at night, quietly-quietly. I never let them get water during the daytime!' Sampat guffaws, doubling over with laughter. 'What a bunch of idiots,' she says with amusement.

Sampat relished watching the lengths the villagers would go to keep themselves pure. Apart from bathing at night, they smashed dozens of earthen pots, used to draw water from the well, after Sampat touched them. 'For thirty days, I ruined all their earthen pots. I gave them a lot of trouble! They deserved it,' Sampat says.

Sampat's husband failed to convince Sampat to coexist peacefully with the other villagers. 'Let them take water first. When they are annoyed, why are you making them more annoyed?' he complained. Sampat stood her ground. 'What is different about a Charmar? They are also humans! If people here don't have any brains, what can I do?' she demanded.

A FEW WEEKS LATER, at the end of August, the village celebrated a festival called Raksha Bandhan, in which women tie red threads, called *rakhis*, onto the wrists of their brothers as a token of the bond between them.

That day, all of the women in Gadarian Purva had come together to pray for their sons and to make offerings of *kusa* (or lovegrass), a plant used in some Hindu rites. When Sampat arrived and lowered herself onto the ground where the women had congregated, those nearest to her stood up and moved away from her, as if her very presence were offensive. Sampat stood up and tried to approach the moving congregation, but every step she took in their direction was met with one step back, like a comical, slightly absurd, game of cat-and-mouse.

'You worship alone! Don't come near us,' one of the elderly women, Jagiya, finally ordered.

'Gods and goddesses are the same for everyone. Why should I go away?' Sampat barked, and then in a fit of anger, she uprooted the holy *kusa* plants, tearing them out of the soil and throwing them to the ground. Still furious, she upturned all of the steel offering plates carrying fried wheat seeds, rice, a fruit called *mahua* and curd, which the women were holding in their hands. 'I abused them fiercely that day and said if anyone says another word, I'll beat them up,' Sampat recalls.

Sampat walked home and locked herself in the house. 'That day I knew it would be very difficult for me to stay in that village. I started crying at night in deep sorrow, thinking how unjust this village is! A dog pisses here and there, and people don't care! Dogs piss on their idols, but they collect dust from there and put it on their foreheads! What sin have I done by drinking water from a Charmar? Why has this become so big! Human beings have no value at all!'

She was right on that last count, for after her iconoclastic behaviour at the festival, Sampat's enemies started plotting her death.

SAMPAT'S HUSBAND WAS out of the house when the visitors from out of town arrived. 'He was giving fodder to our cows and buffaloes; he was not there. Our animals were kept a little far from our house.'

Only one of the five men at the door, Chun Buddha, her aunt's sister-in-law's son, was familiar to her. 'I had never seen the other men before.' Sampat had at one time been on good terms with the wild youth. Chun Buddha always 'talked with respect' to her whenever they met at weddings or other celebrations that brought their families together. 'I had met him a thousand times. His family used to invite us, and we visited them. He treated me like his elder sister.'

But more recently, Chun Buddha, a 'physically strong', reckless man who had 'big eyes' and whose face was scarred by small pox, had gained a reputation as a loose cannon. 'Even from childhood he used to beat the other children. He

was a nice person, but then he started going to the bad side,'
Sampat recalls. Chun Buddha had once tied up his own aunt
and stolen gold from her that was intended for a dowry. 'He
was young when that happened. Must have been eighteen or
nineteen years old. My paternal aunt's daughter's wedding
ceremony was going on. There was jewellery all over. He tied
my paternal aunt's hands and set her clothes on fire. He did
not notice that there was a bucket of water lying there, so she
was saved. He was wearing a mask, but our aunt recognised
him. She did not tell anyone that it was Chun Buddha; otherwise people would have killed him. After that, he started
stealing other people's stuff as well and became a real thief.'

After the theft, Sampat's family saw less of Chun Buddha,
but the two had never fallen out. When Sampat saw Chun
Buddha at the door that day, she assumed he was in the area
and had stopped by to say hello. She welcomed the men into
the house, not knowing that they had been hired as assassins
to end her life.

Sampat remembers making tea for all of them and sending
one of her children to get some sweetmeat, made of stewed
pumpkin, from a stall in the village for the visitors. Sampat
dragged out a *charpoy* for the men to sit on, and while the *chai*
was brewing on the fire, she gave them water.

The men appeared tense and slightly awkward towards
Sampat. 'They were all looking at me. We were exchanging
normal words. I asked him, "Who are these men with you?
What village are they from?"' Sampat remembers.

Chun Buddah answered Sampat's questions. One man
was from Merajpur; another was from Badegaon. They told
Sampat the castes to which they belonged. 'They were from
different castes. One was a Kewat,' Sampat recalls.

Finally, Chun Buddha, after drinking the tea Sampat had offered him, asked her, 'Where does the wife of Munni Lal live?'

It was an unusual question, not least because Sampat was the wife of Munni Lal; this was a fact that Chun Buddha evidently did not know, as he had run away to become a bandit before she married.

'Why do you ask about her?' Sampat asked cautiously.

'She's a bad woman. She is getting into fights with everyone here. . . . Isn't that so?' he replied.

Sampat was silent.

'So why have you come for her?' Sampat asked, fearing what she would hear.

Chun Buddha leaned over and whispered into Sampat's ear. 'We have been paid ten thousand rupees to do away with her,' he whispered.

'But brother, that's me!' Sampat cried, jumping to her feet.

Chun Buddha and his men all darted their eyes towards Sampat in disbelief.

'Daughter, was there a fight between you and the village? Everyone is using bad language about you and is threatening you!' Chun Buddha exclaimed. He then stood up and, grabbing hold of Sampat's arm, led her off to one side. 'You be careful,' he whispered into her ear. 'We are your aunt's son; they can call someone else next time and kill you. Living here is not safe. If it were someone else, then you would have been murdered today.'

Sampat begged Chun Buddha not to tell her husband. 'I thought, he is a man, he might have worries in him, then it can lead to man-to-man enmity. I asked him to make sure nothing wrong should reach his ears. Men are more prone to revenge. They didn't tell him anything, but they cautioned me, saying that I should not live here,' Sampat says.

Chun Buddha was apoplectic that he had been contracted to kill Sampat. 'Those dogs wanted me to kill my own sister,' he shouted. 'Bring those bastards here!' Chun Buddha barked at his men, who went out to look for the men who had hired him.

'They must have thought that because of the enmity between my aunt and Chun Buddha, he must be hating me too,' Sampat reasons.

Chun Buddha and his men set out to confront the men who had hired them; they were the same men who were part of the late-night *panchayat* that had been called against Sampat in the fields.

'They abused them. There was a big fight when they had gone back. Chun Buddha said a lot of things and also told them, "We will kill you for asking us to do this bad job."' After the heated argument with their clients, Chun Buddha and his fellow assassins left the village, urging Sampat again to flee.

'Without wasting a single minute, I threw my few belongings into a bundle of cloth, gathered my children and boarded the first bus out of Gadarian Purva,' she recalls.

'This story has stayed in my heart. I never told anyone. I never shared my sorrow with anyone. I thought, Why should I tell my story to my husband? I have as many limbs as he does. If I told him, it was possible that he might have asked me to leave the house. . . . Or maybe he would have decided to do something drastic. That's why I never told my husband anything. I used to do whatever I felt like, and I thought that I would die the day I have to die. There are no worries in my mind.'

Sampat visited a friend of hers called Bhola Dwivedi, not related to the politician, who worked as a lawyer at the Atarra District Jail. 'When we asked the lawyer what should be done about Sheelu, he said, first of all, find the whereabouts of Achchhe Lal. Unless her father comes, the court will not hear you,' Sampat recalls.

'We thought, If we don't find him, what will we do? Our main worry was that as we were fighting against the legislator, Achchhe would refuse to come due to fear,' Sampat recalls. If the legislator managed to silence Sheelu's family and prevent them from testifying in the courts, then Sheelu stood less of a chance of being freed. Like the time when she ran against Thokia Patel's mother, Sampat realised that her biggest challenge would be giving people the courage and strength to stand up against a powerful opponent.

Despite Sampat's village network, it proved difficult to locate Achchhe: 'We enquired with a lot of people, but Achchhe Lal couldn't be located.' Sampat tried many sources, including Shiv Baran, who ran a small mobile phone store in Badausa. 'I asked him because he had a mobile shop. People buy SIM cards from his shop. Their names are registered with him.' The search came up empty.

Then Sampat contacted a man called Kallu Nishad who, like Achchhe, was from the Kewat caste. 'I thought, he is a boatman and they have relatives at many places. Maybe he is aware of where he is?' But when she spoke to Kallu, he told her that he was not related to Achchhe Lal, but that a man called Durjodhan would be able to help.

Durjodhan, a construction-site labourer, was one of the men who had helped build Sampat's house in Badausa. Sampat went to the construction site where he was working, but Durjodhan clammed up when she asked about Achchhe's current whereabouts. He whispered to her that he didn't want to discuss the matter in front of others and that she should come to his house the next day. 'He thought that if the legislator found out that he informed us about Achchhe's address, the legislator would pressure him,' she says.

Sampat had agreed to meet Durjodhan at his house, but when she arrived there the next day, the construction worker wasn't home; he had gone to a village called Baria. 'It's the place where cucumber and watermelon are grown,' Sampat says, adding, 'He had sown watermelon and went there to have a look.' Sampat was running from pillar to post, trying to find someone who knew where Achchhe was, to no avail. Then, the morning that Sampat returned empty-handed from Dujodhan's house, the information she was chasing fell into her lap.

SINCE SEPTEMBER, SAMPAT'S studious youngest child, eighteen-year-old Nisha, an earnest, acne-scarred woman, had been waking up before dawn every day of the week to bike to Badausa's Station Road, where she religiously attended an extracurricular chemistry class between six and seven o'clock.

When Nisha graduates from university, she will be the

first woman in her extended family with a higher-education degree. Perhaps because of her advanced schooling, Nisha is the only one of Sampat's daughters who has contributed to her work, albeit in a small way: she is the unofficial archiver of Pink Gang press cuttings. Every morning, her job is to go through all of the newspapers and see if there are any articles about the Pink Gang or her mother. In the local papers, Sampat often gets mentioned on a daily basis, so Nisha cuts out those stories and neatly pastes them into an A4-size school notebook for future reference. There are dozens of these fraying notebooks, stacked away in the metal *almirah*, or cabinet, at home that Sampat used to store her few precious documents.

Most of the articles are written in Devanagari, the Hindi script with the line running along the top from which the curled letters hang. The articles written in English are mostly from the Anglophone Indian press, though some are from Western papers, brought by visiting journalists who want to show Sampat just how far-flung her admirers are. Almost all of the articles feature a picture of Sampat, usually armed with a raised stick, her mouth open in a mid-protest shout, and with a large sea of women in pink behind her. In her careful script, Nisha writes the date and publication below the article. This job was initially Babuji's, but 'he keeps things here and there, not knowing where they are,' says Sampat with exasperation.

The archiving job is a source of bickering between Sampat and Nisha, who often get on each other's nerves. 'Does anyone want to take care of the clippings or not?' Sampat barks, when she sees the newspapers in a disorderly pile.

'You don't bring us a notebook, nor do you bother to give

us a penny to buy one! Where am I meant to put all these then?' Nisha snaps back at her.

That morning, Nisha would be of help to Sampat, but not in the usual way. Nisha's tutoring sessions took place in the one-room flat of Sanjay Gupta, a chemistry teacher who had been recommended to her by a friend who was a first-year student. That morning, when Nisha arrived at her tutor's spartan home, she saw a man she had never seen before, asleep on a large cot at the back of the room. Around ten minutes after the lesson started, Nisha watched the man wake up, wipe his eyes and make his way to the sink to wash his face. After he had freshened up, the man bid Sanjay Gupta farewell and slipped out the door.

After class, Nisha, a curious, astute young woman, asked Sanjay Gupta who the sleeping man was.

'That is Achchhe Lal. You must have heard of him – his daughter is the one that has run away from the *vidhayak's* house,' he replied.

Nisha's eyes widened, for she knew that her mother had been trying for days to find Achchhe Lal.

'What was he doing *here*?' Nisha asked, perplexed.

'Vishnu's sister had an evil spirit in her, and Achchhe Lal had come to get it out,' the chemistry tutor explained. For the scientist, it was not contradictory to think that medical problems might have supernatural causes.

Vishnu was a good friend of Sampat's son, Munna. His brothers also attended classes at Mr Gupta's house. Vishnu's mother had come to see Mr Gupta the other week to discuss the progress her boys were making and also to ask whether the teacher might know a good exorcist to rid her daughter, Uma, of the spirits she believed were plaguing her daughter with ill health. The chemistry tutor recommended Achchhe, well known across the district for his persuasive way with evil spirits and his mastering of *jhar-phuk*, the technique by which these spirits are 'swept away' with a special broom typically made of feathers. Achchhe may have taken the job because Mr Gupta's house was a safe place to sleep for the night, away from the dangers in Shahbajpur, as well as for some extra money.

Noticing Nisha's curiosity, the tutor asked, 'Do you have any spirit problems too?'

'No, no, *sir*! But if I do, I'll definitely tell you!' she blurted out.

In the Indian countryside, people turned to *jhar-phuk* when families faced prolonged periods of illness or misfortune. Nisha, who believed in the spirit world, was sceptical of those who claimed to wield influence over it.

The year before, Nisha had fallen ill with a fever. Her father told her, 'Maybe you've got a spirit problem – your fever comes and goes so quickly.' He put her on the back of his bicycle and pedalled all the way to a village called Hura, where many spirit healers practised.

'Please, see my daughter, something is wrong with her,' Munni had told a healer there, but he kept them waiting for over an hour.

A girl who had arrived much later than Nisha cut in the queue, after telling the priest that a mysterious affliction had befallen her. 'My heart keeps beating faster and faster!' she exclaimed, panicking.

'Well, you must be a thief then, if your heart is pounding so fast!' snapped Nisha, angry that the healer was seeing the girl before her. Turning to her father, she said, 'Let's go. I'm tired of all this nonsense!' Nisha took after her mother when she was irritated.

When Sampat found out about the episode, she was furious with Munni. 'She has a fever, nothing else!' she barked. 'In this May heat, you took her all the way to that village? You'll make her even more sick like that!' she said, cursing him. Sampat then took Nisha for a blood test in Atarra, where the true causes of her fever – malaria and typhoid – were detected.

'I SAW ACHCHHE LAL TODAY!' Nisha announced as soon as Sampat returned home. Sampat couldn't believe her luck when she heard how Nisha stumbled across Achchhe at her tutoring session. Nisha swiftly called Mr Gupta and asked for Achchhe's number so that Sampat could get in touch with him. 'I hope Sampat Pal can help that poor man. He is very afraid,' Mr Gupta said.

Nisha, who used to be teased when she was younger because of her mother's getting involved in every fight, has always been proud of Sampat and defended her whenever friends made negative comments. Now, she doesn't have to explain her mother's behaviour to anyone – most people want Sampat Pal on their side when they are seeking justice.

Sampat called Achchhe immediately.

'Hello, Achchhe Lal. Have you heard the name Sampat Pal before? I am the Pink Gang commander,' Sampat told Achchhe.

Achchhe sounded scared on the phone.

'I have seen in the newspaper that you are fighting for our Sheelu,' Achchhe responded.

When Sampat asked Achchhe where he was living these days, he responded that he was at home, but that it was dangerous for him to stay there.

'People come at night, and they want to kill me,' he confessed.

Achchhe cried over the phone as he narrated the threats to his life; he was not sure he had the courage to speak up against the legislator's intimidation.

'I told him, You're good at removing ghosts and yet you're scared of a man?' Sampat says. She then told him not to fear, that she was coming to meet him.

WHEN SAMPAT ARRIVED in Shahbajpur, she knocked on the doors of the mud huts that were congregated around the 'village square' – a stony strip of ground lined by a school on one side and huts on the other, with a large banyan tree in the middle under which villagers would gather when they had something to discuss. She asked the villagers where she could find Achchhe.

'They told me, "We know you, sister, from the time you ran during the elections. You got ninety votes out here from us. We were your supporters,"' she recalls the villagers telling her.

The residents of Shahbajpur had advice for Sampat. 'If you are here because of his daughter, don't get involved, *didi*. That girl has a loose character,' one said. 'She ran away with her lover,' said another, disapprovingly.

'Who cares about that right now! The girl is in trouble – where does her father live?' she asked, exasperated. The villagers pointed her in the direction of Achchhe's house.

Sampat walked down a narrow path that led between two of the huts that girded one corner of the village square. She passed tethered cows and goats and hillocks of cow dung cakes used for fuel, and went down a dirt track flanked by lentil fields.

Achchhe lived on the far edge of the village. If you looked closely at the cracked, flaking surface of his ochre-coloured clay hut, you could see impressions of smooth, uneven hand strokes formed by his application of layer after layer of mud, clay and dung. The roof, with eaves of bamboo sticks that jutted out over the front of the hut, was gently sloping and composed of a blanket of twigs and sticks, on top of which lay flat flakes of red brick. The door, made of solid planks of wood, was bolted shut. Sampat knocked, then pounded on the door, but no one came to open it for her.

Sampat walked back to the village square, where the people she had spoken to were waiting to see how her mission had gone.

'He's too afraid to see anyone – he's been in hiding on and off for days,' one villager told her.

'And what are you all doing about this? Shouldn't you be helping him?' Sampat demanded.

'It has nothing to do with us! Why should we risk getting killed by the legislator's men?' they asked.

Sampat asked the villagers to call everyone to the square for a meeting; she wanted to address them on the matter of Sheelu. Since the days when Babuji and Sampat had travelled from village to village recruiting women for their self-help groups, Sampat had developed her ability to gather together absolute strangers to listen to what she had to say, even if it was not what they wanted to hear.

That day, as she stood before the villagers of Shahbajpur, Sampat exhorted them to change their attitude. 'You say that Sheelu has misbehaved and you don't want her in the village, but don't you realise that if you let one girl fall to the fate that Sheelu has, then all of your daughters could be next? If the bandits, thugs and criminals find out that Shahbajpur is a place where no one stands up for their neighbour, then don't you think they will come back? What's to stop them from taking advantage of all of the women?' Sampat asked.

As she often did, Sampat sang the villagers a song to illustrate her argument. The lyrics, which she had composed herself, went '*Social oppression and injustice have to be removed, brothers and sisters. Together let us become united. For today I am oppressed, but tomorrow it is your turn.*' Sampat often repeats a song one or two times, until the lyrics have sunk in, and then, without waiting for applause, she jumps back into her speech without missing a beat.

'I know you are scared, but listen to what I have to say. If the legislator or his men come here again threatening Achchhe, pick up a *laathi* and beat them. Do you hear me? Together, you can beat them – not alone,' she exhorted. 'If the whole village stands together, then they will have no power over you.'

'Stand with Achchhe Lal – support him. If he falls, if he is defeated, then you all will fall with him, do you hear?' she continued.

After Sampat concluded her speech, the villagers offered to help Sampat speak to Achchhe. They all walked back to his hut and pounded on his door, telling him that 'Sampat Pal is here' and that it was 'safe to come out'.

After a long pause, the door opened a crack.

———

THE SQUARE OUTSIDE the district court in Banda is dusty and unkempt, reflecting well the neglect suffered by the law within the weathered court building. Sampat brought Achchhe there because the judicial magistrate in Atarra was on leave, and she believed it would be speedier to go through the district court. The atmosphere outside the court is one of quiet assiduity; the square is lined by dozens of lawyers who sit cross-legged on benches and chairs under tin roofs, typing up statements, complaints and affidavits on mechanical typewriters in exchange for a nominal fee. Court documents, agitated by whirring desk fans connected to a nearby power line, flutter under paperweights. Lawyers in black, British-style robes make their way to and from the court, unfazed by the honking of passing cars, the exhaust fumes, the barking of stray dogs and the vegetable hawkers shouting the list of their produce with well-trained lungs.

Sampat had brought Achchhe to the square outside the Banda District Court to meet with Jai Karan Bhai, who worked in a hole-in-the-wall lawyer's office tucked neatly under a great, bulbous banyan tree at the far end of the square. An affable middle-aged man with pink vitiligo patches on his skin, Jai Karan Bhai is one of many unofficial Pink Gang lawyers. From his small shed, he has helped Sampat fight countless battles on a pro bono basis.

JAI KARAN BHAI WAS the only child of labourers who had put all of their money into getting him educated. After passing an exam held by the police department, he was meant to be a subinspector in the force, but at the last minute he decided against it – he did not want to become corrupt like most of the other police officers he knew.

Normally a calm, quiet man, Jai Karan Bhai became a different person when he took to the podium. Once, when asked to speak about human rights on the birth anniversary of lower-caste political icon and author of the Indian constitution Ambedkar, Jai Karan Bhai delivered a heated speech that earned him the reputation of a firebrand. 'You have to snatch your rights. You can't keep asking for them for ever,' Jai Karan Bhai remembers exhorting his audience that day. 'If a crime is committed against you and you don't speak up, you are an even bigger criminal,' he had told the crowd.

Just two years after he started practising law, Jai Karan Bhai represented a family of Dalits the local police in Atarra were torturing and intimidating. The policemen had gang-raped one of the daughters at the Atarra station, and when the family tried to get justice, the police illegally detained and abused them. After Jai Karan Bhai decided to represent them, the policemen came to his house at night warning him to drop the case. He continued despite the threats to his life and eventually succeeded in getting the guilty officers thrown into jail. This earned him much praise and solidified his reputation as a warrior for justice.

Despite being radical in his beliefs as a former member of the Communist Party of India, Jai Karan Bhai did not consider vigilante tactics legitimate or effective in the long run. The Pink Gang, to his relief, almost always turned to the law first for justice. Sampat made it a point to accompany women, and sometimes men, to meet with lawyers for legal aid, negotiating hard on their behalf to get the legal fees down, as most people who came to the Pink Gang for help lived below the poverty line. If the beneficiaries still could not pay the fees, then the local Pink Gang members often pooled together money to help.

When Sampat brought Achchhe to Jai Karan Bhai that day, the lawyer greeted them both warmly. Whatever he was doing, Jai Karan Bhai always found time to meet with Sampat, whom he considered a friend. Sampat told Jai Karan Bhai that the Pink Gang was taking on Sheelu's case.

Jai Karan Bhai asked Achchhe about his daughter and was taken aback by the spiteful way in which he spoke of her. Achchhe was torn between blaming himself and blaming Sheelu for the mess that they found themselves in. He called her a whore one minute, and was beating his chest with regret and weeping bitterly the next.

Sampat and Jai Karan Bhai, seeing the turmoil within Achchhe, asked him if he was sure he wanted to get his daughter out of jail and whether he would co-operate with them. It would be devastating if, halfway through fighting her case, Achchhe were to turn around and work against them. He assured them that he did want Sheelu out of jail. While he was angry at her, his rage was not so blind that he wanted to see his daughter remain in one of Uttar Pradesh's notorious prisons.

During their meeting, Achchhe behaved like an awkward teenager who didn't know what to do with his long limbs or how to respond to authority. He flashed nervous, approval-seeking smiles, even when on the verge of tears, and when he sat, he folded himself up, bringing his knees defensively to his chest and clasping his shoulders with crossed forearms.

While speaking, he bit apprehensively at his lip, and when the pressure on him was too great, he pursed his lips and breathed out forcefully.

Jai Karan Bhai told Achchhe and Sampat that the next course of action would be to get Sheelu bail and to file a complaint against Dwivedi's men for threatening Achchhe. He asked Achchhe if the Pink Gang should submit the bail application on his behalf, and he consented.

'Are you going to get my daughter out of jail?' he asked. Sampat promised they would.

After Jai Karan Bhai gave them legal advice, Sampat and Achchhe, accompanied by a driver who came with the car she had rented for the day, drove to the Atarra District Court to meet Bhola Dwivedi, the Pink Gang lawyer who had first advised Sampat to find Achchhe. This was because, despite the judicial magistrate's leave, Sheelu's case would continue to be processed in Atarra court, not the Banda one in which Jai Karan Bhai worked. Together with Bhola and Sampat, Achchhe drafted a letter in which he gave Sampat the right to ask for bail for Sheelu on his behalf and also to make a formal complaint about the threats he had been receiving. After it was written, Sampat helped Achchhe to convene a small press conference.

Standing in front of the court that day, Achchhe told the assembled journalists about the threats to his life. He then rolled up his trouser leg, pointing to an injury he claimed the legislator's men had inflicted on him. 'See they have hit me here. . . . They have hit me very hard. They hit me on the back and also the head,' he said, pointing to the places on his body that had been injured.

He then took out the letter, and, not knowing how to read, he held it before the journalists. The television cameras zoomed in on it. It read:

To: The Police Superintendent, Banda
SIR,

The plaintiff from village Shahbajpur, police station Naraini, District Banda, requests you to note that on 24/12/2010, approximately midnight, Purushottam Naresh Dwivedi (MLA) and his brothers, Raja and Chotta and their friend, Urmaliya of village Pukari and two unknown persons, searched for the plaintiff with guns in their hands. The plaintiff left his house to hide in another place before they arrived. A lot of villagers saw these persons enter forcefully and beat up women and children and heard them as they kept asking 'Where is he?'

Due to this the family fears for their life because the plaintiff's daughter, Sheelu, is in jail. They want her to change the statements given by her. The plaintiff is also being threatened, he is told he should also change his statements against the legislator; otherwise the whole family will be wiped out. Prior to this incident, the plaintiff was beaten up very badly and a threat was given. They said: 'If you say anything against us you will be killed.' The plaintiff has been harassed for the past five days continuously. If they catch me they will definitely kill me. The plaintiff is not getting any security.

Getting support from Sampat Pal has given me

courage due to which the plaintiff is requesting bail for Sheelu. The plaintiff, to get his daughter released from jail, has agreed to ask Sampat Pal for help. I have full faith that with her help I will get justice.

Therefore, I request you to provide me with security and that legal action should be taken against the above mentioned persons and that they should be punished.

Applicant: Achchhe Lal, Son of Ramdin (Nishad)

THE BANDA BUREAU of the *Hindustan* is on the ground floor of a building located on a side street off one of the main thoroughfares in the town. The entrance to the office is at the top of a steep, ridged ramp made of cement. There are no doors or windows, just an iron shutter that is pulled up during working hours to let in daylight.

The inside of the bureau resembles a small car park; its cement floor has white markings on it, and two dominant, rectangular cement pillars occupy the centre of the room, which is lit by fluorescent tubes. The walls are bare except for posters advertising lottery cash prizes, a religious calendar with a picture of Hindu goddess Sita and a yellowed map of the district of Banda, annotated in Hindi script and hanging with dust-laden, stringy cobwebs. A dank puddle sits under a dripping plastic water cooler and next to a wire-sprouting inverter – a large back-up battery that activates during the regular power outages.

This was where Amit reigned.

Along the edges of the wall, in front of bulky desktop

computers, sit the six staff journalists who report to their twenty-eight-year-old boss, one of the youngest in the all-male bureau. Even amid the spartan decor, there are hints of Amit's diligence and careful management. All of the desk chairs have white pieces of paper stuck to them on which are written the names of their respective owners. Before Amit took over the bureau, desk chairs were regularly breaking, due to the way the restless journalists were for ever swinging and leaning into them as they wrote. Now, with Amit's system, everyone is responsible for his own chair. If it breaks, he has to pay. 'Now everyone sits dead-straight!' he says, laughing as he imitates someone in rigor mortis.

Amit, a baby-faced, pot-bellied man who always wears a smile, joined the bureau in July 2010. After finishing the last round of interviews in Lucknow, the capital of Uttar Pradesh where all the regional hiring for the newspaper takes place, the managing editor asked him where he wanted to be posted. Amit responded by saying that he was ready to live anywhere. The editor rattled out a list of the most conflict-prone regions in the country, including Kashmir, and Amit nodded enthusiastically to each of them. 'Could you even live in bandit-plagued Bundelkhand?' the editor probed. 'Not a problem,' Amit retorted, adding, 'I'm not fighting them after all, just writing about them!' Calling his bluff, the editor sent him to Banda. 'I heard that people don't eat in Bundelkhand. I thought, How will I manage?' he remembers, rubbing his stomach.

When Amit arrived, he quickly distinguished himself from his fellow journalists by deliberately seeking out the human story behind the news. 'My stories are different. I try to include new ideas and different views. When we talk about price rises, I don't just put stats. I speak to ordinary people and see how it affects them.' He says that in the early days, 'I did forty per cent of my work by the time the other journalists were trickling into work.' Other journalists he knew rarely left their desks, often basing their news stories on press releases, which poured in over the course of the day via barefoot delivery boys. When he went to the local press club, some fellow journalists would say, 'We've heard a lot about you. You can do twelve thousand characters in an hour,' Amit remembers proudly, adding, 'I'm a very fast typer.'

For those who knew Amit, it came as little surprise that he had got the scoop on Sheelu's suspicious arrest. Amit worked until midnight and rose every day at four in the morning so that he could exercise for two hours before going to work. 'I sleep six hours on Sunday to catch up,' he says nonchalantly.

Amit could be living a more comfortable life than the one offered by Banda. When he left a well-paying job as a public relations officer for a multinational accounting firm in India's financial capital, Mumbai, to become a journalist, in lawless, undeveloped Bundelkhand, it was not the money he was after. 'What I like about being a journalist is that I can help. The salary isn't much, just eighteen thousand a month' – about two hundred pounds. Another reason, he adds, using an English word, is that 'there is a certain *glamour* attached to working in media'.

WHEN AMIT FIRST BEGAN covering the Pink Gang in 2010, he was one of the few journalists in Banda who wanted to write about Sampat at the time. 'She was taking credit for everything. She didn't acknowledge the media.' Sampat's falling-out with the media had happened shortly before Amit's arrival. 'One day, at the court, she said publicly, What I did, I did on my own. The media has nothing to do with it. The way she insults the police? That's the way she insulted the media. All were angry about what she had said,' Amit recounts.

Arun Dixit, the bureau chief of Sahara Samay TV, who had been following the gang since its early days, was particularly disillusioned with the Pink Gang and personally offended as a result of Sampat's outburst. 'She takes credit for everything – she never acknowledges us,' he complains. Arun, who saw his media outlet as a 'partner' of the Pink Gang, got in touch with Sampat back in the beginning of 2006, after her road protest. Arun's poorly lit bureau was located on a little lane that led off from the Banda train station. Every week, aggrieved people – often farmers who had few others to turn to for support – would come to Arun's office and tell him about problems that their communities were going through in the hope that he might cover them: prolonged power outages, water cuts and teachers not turning up for class. Arun found it challenging to do stories on these social issues because the people who were affected by these problems did not come across well on camera. 'No one knows how to speak well in Atarra – whenever I'd ask someone for sound bites, they'd just run away,' he remembers. When the Pink Gang emerged, Arun was grateful because Sampat was good at speaking to the media. He started sending people to her, which benefited both of them: Arun would get an engaging news item, and Sampat would receive coverage for cases she was fighting.

'Media is a business. We need good stories, that's how news sells,' he explains.

The first of such 'collaborations' happened in 2006, when the Pink Gang stormed an electrical utility company that had been withholding power in exchange for bribes and sexual favours from the community. Arun 'passed on the case' to Sampat, telling her that 'if you do the protest, we'll cover it'. Sampat organised a group of women from nearby villages, including Uraiya Purva and Gokul Purva, and together they confronted the officials in the electrical utility office. When the civil servants refused to turn the power back on, Sampat bolted their office shut from the outside and locked them in with a padlock. 'The electrical utility office story sold really well – the general public liked what she was doing.'

Soon, citizens started going directly to the Pink Gang, in which case Sampat would call the media to alert them to scheduled protests. In the summer of 2010, however, Sampat started getting closer to the Indian National Congress party, which culminated in her highly publicised meeting with Sonia Gandhi in New Delhi in August. Some, like Arun, felt that her political ambitions were interfering with her grass-roots work. 'Now she's into politics. She goes out of town, meets Sonia Gandhi – she's left what she started,' Arun sighs. The TV journalist was also disappointed that Sampat had become less responsive to cases that he sent her way: 'She's too busy now. Her status has increased. She is often away.' He cites a case in the town of Fatehganj in which a young couple's parents were not allowing them to marry because they were from a different caste. 'Sampat has been working on love marriage for many years, yet when we gave her the case she just ignored us!' Arun complains. The bureau chief, who had once flocked to Sampat along with the other local TV journalists because 'we needed someone who was good in front of the camera', was now abandoning her. 'No one writes about her anymore, just a few people. You see, what Sampat was before, she is no more.'

Sampat pays little heed to her detractors. 'They criticise if some women are very famous. Let me tell you, everyone criticises others in the world, but if we are not wrong from within, then we will not get affected by criticism. I don't care who criticises me. Many people criticise me and many praise me. But I know that I am good from the inside. I don't need to worry about that. If I worry, I won't be able to do anything,' Sampat says.

She also snorts at the idea that the media played any role in the success of the Pink Gang. 'They sometimes say that Sampat-ji's success is due to them. I ask them how? If I don't work, what would you write? And if because of your writing I have got all the success, then you better write about your family members!' she says, laughing heartily.

She acknowledges, however, that journalists did help the Pink Gang in their struggles. 'Media is the medium to express our ideas worldwide,' she says, adding, 'I do good work, and they never write anything wrong about me. And where would they find it? If they write something wrong, I would not spare them then, but nobody has.'

AFTER ACHCHHE'S PRESS CONFERENCE, Sampat and Achchhe arrived at Amit's office in the afternoon, carrying Achchhe Lal's statement against the legislator. Achchhe's public declaration that he was being threatened would make it easier for the media to put more pressure on Dwivedi, but they would still have to treat the situation with care. 'Amit told me that, Sampat-ji, this is a difficult matter. Police is involved with the legislator,' Sampat remembers, adding, 'Amit told us to maintain the pressure and that he would keep writing about the case.'

When Sampat confided in Amit about the veiled threat passed on to her by Jagpath the journalist, she learned that Amit too was being threatened.

'One man walked up to me and said, "Aha, you're that guy from the *Hindustan!*" and started swearing. A lot of threats came through. People stood outside the office with guns. They glared and then left. I decided that if I'm shot dead, I'll say fine, at least I will have died for something. My family and office really supported me. I told my friends, if anything happens, please inform my family. At night, these thoughts came to my mind: "If something happens, at least I'm writing the truth and working for justice,"' Amit remembers.

During that time, Amit and Sampat had each other's back. 'We used to encourage each other, not to be afraid of anything,' Sampat says proudly. In the face of such danger, it was vital to have allies one could count on.

AFTER MEETING AMIT, Sampat made the two-hour trip to drop Achchhe back at Shahbajpur, as she had promised. She had hired a driver for the day especially for that purpose. It was pitch black by the time Sampat and the driver started back to Atarra. The journey to Achchhe's village had taken longer than expected, and now she was uneasy about travelling so late at night. Shahbajpur had been connected to a main road only for the past ten years and remained one of the most undeveloped and dangerous corners of Bundelkhand.

Leaving Shahbajpur behind, Sampat's car travelled down a lonely road on either side of which stood white-painted adobe huts that gleamed eerily in the moonlight. No street-lights lined the road, nor was there any candlelight perceivable in the houses, for they had no windows. There were no people to be seen outside either, for they usually went to sleep shortly after nightfall. Even if the residents here wanted to have a nocturnal social life, there would be nothing to do in the silent, dark streets, utterly devoid as they were of late-night eateries.

When the last of the adobe houses disappeared from view, the road widened slightly as it approached a bridge that crossed a silver-speckled, shallow tributary flanked on either side by wide sloping riverbanks. Before the bridge was built, a few years back, villagers had to rely exclusively on a small wooden raft to ferry them across the water when they wanted to sell their ropes and baskets in nearby towns. Years of physical isolation had made the Duaba, the local name for the area around Shahbajpur, with its uneven terrain, winding tributary and large boulders, a perfect place for bandits to go into hiding. Villagers, suspicious of the outside world and unco-operative with law enforcement agencies, were known to harbour these villains, making the region unsafe.

After the bridge, the road snaked round the swells and knolls that bulged out of the ground at every turn. Few farmers were able to till this unruly land; it was covered in a carpet of wild grass and weeds, punctuated by large rocks seemingly cast down to the earth arbitrarily. It was only when Sampat

and her driver neared the main road, which connected Naraini to Atarra, that another settlement appeared. Although it
too was dotted with adobe huts and had no electricity, the
economy of this hamlet appeared to be more advanced than
that of Shahbajpur. Its cluster of houses boasted shops, which,
judging by the advertisements hand-painted on the metal
shutters, sold a variety of products, including Coca-Cola.

Just as Sampat and the driver left this village and headed
towards the main road, she saw a car parked on the side with
its headlights on. Her driver continued on, and after he took
the right turn onto the main road, she noticed the lights of the
car they had just passed, which was coming around the bend.
The headlights, on full beam, shone brightly in the rearview
mirror of Sampat's car, blinding her and the driver. The two
cars were the only vehicles in sight, and beyond the silvery
birches that lined the road were only desolate rice paddies.

A tight, uncomfortable knot formed in Sampat's stomach.
Someone was following her. What did her pursuers want
from her? Looking back at the car through the rearview mirror, she could not make out the face of the person behind the
wheel. Every time she tried, her eyes squinted with the glare
of the headlights.

Confirming her worst fears, the car overtook hers in the
blink of an eye and then slowed down suddenly, the red
brake lights bathing her hands and face in an alarming scar-
let hue. Sampat's driver, who had not betrayed his fear until
that moment, responded with a start.

'What is all this, Sampat-ji?' He tried to overtake the car
from the right but could not. Just as they tried to pass it, the
other car sped up and then switched lanes, so that Sampat's
car was directly behind it again. Then, having succeeded at

keeping Sampat trapped behind it, the car slowed down once more, forcing Sampat's driver to do the same.

In a place as isolated as this, anything could happen, Sampat thought, looking nervously out the window. They had not passed a village, or even a solitary house, for that matter, since they turned onto the main road. If the people in the other car wanted to drive them into the ditch on the side of the road, they would succeed sooner or later. Even worse, if they wanted to shoot them, no one would ever know who had done it or why. Sampat was determined to avoid this.

'Sampat-ji, I'm leaving you here and I am going back,' the driver said in a panicky voice.

'What are you saying? How can you leave me on my own in the middle of nowhere?'

'It's dangerous for me. . . . I won't go further and I – '

'You're a man! You're getting this scared? They're *my* enemies, not yours. I'm here, now don't be scared!' she exhorted.

Sampat, a quick thinker, took off the *dupatta* that was wound around her neck and placed three apples, which she had brought with her that day, in the centre of the cloth. 'I'll scare them into thinking I have a bomb with me,' she thought, and was prepared to roll down the window and threaten to throw it at them.

Just before she proceeded with this last-ditch attempt to lose her pursuers, Sampat shouted an order to the driver. 'Try again!' The driver hesitated. 'Go!' Sampat shouted. The driver yanked the wheel decisively to the side, sending the car lurching out of its lane. Before he could accelerate, the car ahead dove forward and slammed on the brakes. Sampat's car skidded to a halt. Then the mysterious car sped off, leaving a cloud of red-lit dust in its wake.

CHAPTER SEVEN

THE SOUND OF THE BUGLE

FROM STREET TO STREET IT IS HEARD,
THAT THE NARAINI LEGISLATOR IS A THIEF!

—The Pink Gang

ON 28 DECEMBER, RAJJU PATEL, WHO WAS ALTERNATELY REFERRED to in the newspapers as Sheelu's rapist, kidnapper and 'lover-husband', appeared in front of the press for the first time since Sheelu's arrest. To the surprise of many, Dwivedi accompanied him.

A gangly youth with wavy hair, Rajju wore a shiny, grape-coloured shirt under a mint-green tank top and a white shawl. He was calm and composed as he declared that, contrary to what had been reported, Sheelu was actually his wife. That day, Rajju had attempted to visit Sheelu, but the jailer denied him permission. Rajju was reportedly carrying a love letter he wanted to give to her. At the press conference, Rajju offered his version of his relationship with Sheelu: 'When there were elections, I got to know

Sheelu. We fell in love, and then after that I took her from there and I lived with her at my place for around one and a half months.'

'She told her father that she did not want to go back to him. She said, "No, I want to stay here." After that she was taken by the legislator's men and kept in Atarra. I was not at home at that time. She called me and said she was not feeling good without me, and I told her to get out of there somehow,' he said, referring to Dwivedi's house. Rajju then said, 'I want to marry Sheelu. I want to make her my life partner.'

Sheelu believes that Rajju had agreed to appear beside Dwivedi because he was paid off. Why else would Rajju share the stage with the man who had allegedly assaulted his father and abused the woman he claimed was his wife? Dwivedi could only benefit from Rajju's declaration that he and Sheelu had eloped. After all, this would solidify her reputation as a transgressive, 'loose' woman and therefore diminish the value of her testimony in court.

Referring to what it called a 'game-changer', the *Hindustan* reported on Rajju's curious press conference and posed a series of questions to its readers: 'If Sheelu loved him, why didn't she disclose this to her father?' 'Where was Rajju in all these days?' 'If he married Sheelu then why did he keep her in confinement?' – the latter question assuming that he had, in fact, kept Sheelu in Pathara against her will.

No one knew the answers to these questions, and the police never sought to arrest Rajju, despite the serious allegations being made against him. Nor was any serious enquiry made into whether Sheelu and Rajju were actually married, as some newspapers, like the *Hindustan* reported.

If the press conference really was devised to mar Sheelu's public image, it was nothing compared to the vicious attack on her dignity that would take place the following day.

THERE ARE MANY WAYS in which corrupt officials might attempt to crush the spirit of a young woman accusing a powerful politician of rape. One of the cruellest forms of humiliation at their disposal was not even forbidden by the law. In fact, references to it find their way into Indian court-rooms on a daily basis.

When a woman in India claims that she has been raped, it is very common for her to be subjected to a demeaning, unscientific test called the 'finger test', designed to under-mine her reputation, character and perceived reliability. To perform this test, a doctor inserts two fingers into the vagina of a rape victim to determine whether it is 'narrow', 'roomy', 'lax' and so forth. From these 'conditions', the doctor is then required, according to Indian Medical Association protocol, to draw conclusions about the sexual habits of the woman, which can then be used against her in court.

Needless to say, the entire test is subjective in its meth-odology. 'Vagina admitted one finger with difficulty' and 'Vagina admitted two fingers tightly' are the types of com-ments that doctors write in their reports. The overwhelming majority of doctors performing these tests have little to no training in gathering forensic evidence. Nor are they trained in how to deal sensitively with rape victims. According to a Human Rights Watch report, in some hospitals it is common to keep women who have come to the hospital directly after an assault waiting for hours before giving them any medical attention. It is also common for hospital staff to refer to those women openly, and in front of other patients, as 'rape cases'.

In numerous High Court and Supreme Court judgements in recent years, doctors have used phrases like 'habitual sexual intercourse', 'accustomed to sexual intercourse', 'used to sex', 'frequent coitus', and 'sexually active' to describe the conclusions they reached after examining the results of finger tests. Once a woman has been labelled sexually active, or 'habitual', her character is questioned publicly in the courts. In a 2009 court case, the Supreme Court stated that a woman who was claiming to have been raped appeared to be 'a lady used to sexual intercourse and a dissolute lady', adding that 'she had no objection in mixing up and having free movement with any of her known person [*sic*], for enjoyment. Thus, she appeared to be a woman of easy virtues'. In 2008, the High Court in Bihar placed great weight on one doctor's opinion that a rape survivor was 'habituated to sex': 'Though the girl was aged 20 to 23 years and was unmarried but she was found to be "habituated to intercourse". This makes her to be of doubtful character.'

Although Indian law states that rapists can be successfully prosecuted on the basis of the victim's testimony alone, once reports from 'finger tests' are admitted into the court, they could jeopardise a strong case by weakening the morale of the victim and causing others to question her credibility and character – this was, no doubt, what any attacker of Sheelu was hoping for.

ON THE NEXT DAY, 29 December, two female doctors from the district hospital, Dr Vimla Sharma and Dr Mary Singh, conducted a medical examination on Sheelu in jail. Sheelu claims she knew right from the start that the doctors had the legislator's welfare in mind, not her own.

Sheelu had already had one negative experience with a government doctor. She had been brought to the Banda District Hospital on 20 December for a medical examination, after suffering from what newspaper reports called 'internal pains'. Dr Bhavna Sharma, a different doctor, allegedly dismissed her with the wave of a hand. 'She said I don't have time for her *doctory-voktory*,' Sheelu recounts. (When questioned by the press, the doctor defended herself by claiming she needed a court order to examine the girl and that she had not received one.)

Sheelu claims that when the doctors saw her in the jail on 29 December, they pressured Sheelu into dropping her accusations of rape against the legislator. 'Sheelu, don't say that it was such a big incident and calm down. *Vidhayak* will be put in jail for nothing,' she remembers Dr Vimla Sharma telling her. The doctor then allegedly tried to force Sheelu to sign an empty piece of paper, but she refused. 'I told myself, Even if they kill me, I will not sign.' It was after the doctors 'got angry' at her for not signing that they examined her. 'They didn't use gloves,' Sheelu said about the examination.

One cannot know what it feels like to have your insides probed and explored by seemingly malicious physicians who conspire to find within you 'evidence' that could be used against you. If Sheelu had been raped, then the invasive examination must have caused her to relive the trauma. Refusing examination would not have been a viable option; doctors sometimes label victims who do so as 'unco-operative', which defence counsels then use to suggest that the victims have 'something to hide'.

Sheelu closed her eyes and tried to think of other things while the doctors performed a roughshod examination within her.

ON THE SAME DAY that the two doctors visited the jail, Sheelu claims to have been subjected to five hours of interrogation by Radhe Shyam Shukla, the circle officer of Banda, and Anil Das, the police superintendent of Banda.

During the interrogation, the officers allegedly attempted to pressure her into signing a blank piece of paper and tried to bribe her with six hundred thousand rupees, approximately £6,600. According to Sheelu, she and Anil Das had the following conversation.

'You take this money and change your statement, we will get you justice,' he said, referring to the claims she was making to the police that she had been raped.

'If I take the money, how will I get justice?' she demanded.

When Sheelu insisted that all she was seeking was for Dwivedi to be punished, Anil Das allegedly replied, 'Don't trap *Vidhayak-ji* into this. He is not that sort of person.'

This back and forth continued for hours until someone within the jail tipped off Vivek Singh, the Congress Party legislator for Banda, about the suspect interrogation. When Vivek Singh arrived, he noticed that Anil Das had not entered his name into the logbook, the book that recorded the names of all visitors to the jail, as was required. This was a serious breach of the rules and suggested that Das had wanted to keep his meeting with Sheelu confidential. Singh then entered into the book the time the guards said Das had arrived, and below that entry, he wrote, 'Under whose permission was he there for five hours?' Singh also photocopied the logbook so that it could be sent to journalists.

After correcting the logbook, Vivek Singh stormed into the room where Sheelu was being interrogated. The legislator 'shouted like crazy at the SP', says Sheelu, referring to the superintendent. Singh accused the police of a 'cover-up' and ordered that no further visitors be allowed to meet Sheelu unless he signed off on them personally.

ON 1 JANUARY 2011, just a few days after Vivek Singh clashed with the superintendent about his alleged misconduct, the police publicly acknowledged for the first time that Sheelu had accused the legislator of rape. The headline on the front page of the *Hindustan* was succinct:

LEGISLATOR NAMED IN SHEELU RAPE CASE

The article argued that Sheelu's allegation was 'getting suppressed, hidden and stuck in political corridors', but that it had finally come out after Anil Das and Radhe Shyam Shukla had gone to interrogate Sheelu. Given that Sheelu had refused to retract her claims that Dwivedi had raped her, the police hoped that the results of the 'forensic examination' would discredit her.

The same article reported on the results of Sheelu's medical examination, which were released for the first time. The key finding, according to the chief medical officer, was that Sheelu was a *'habitual sex addict'*. Reporting the news that day, the *Hindustan* suggested that the doctors had devised the medical result in order to 'save the legislator'.

Unable to ignore the news, the chief minister of the state of Uttar Pradesh, Kumari Mayawati, ordered that day that a probe by the Crime Branch–Crime Investigation Department, or CB-CID, a state-level investigating unit of the police, be launched. The investigators arrived from the state capital, Lucknow, a day later and began looking into Sheelu's allegations.

On the following day, 2 January, Dwivedi was suspended from the legislature while investigations were ongoing. He told journalists at a press conference in Banda that 'the charges of sexual assault are politically motivated'. He also claimed to have proof that the rape allegation was baseless. He alleged he was impotent, adding, 'I am ready to be examined by any medical expert across the country to confirm what I am saying.'

Dwivedi's wife, Asha, later gave a statement to the media in which she echoed his defence, insisting that Dwivedi does not have the physical strength to rape anyone because of his alleged high blood pressure, diabetes and kidney problems. In addition to demanding a medical examination for her husband, she also told journalists, 'My house has two rooms. One is occupied by my son and daughter-in-law. How can a man rape a girl in front of his wife, son and daughter-in-law?' Like her husband, Asha blamed the accusations on a 'political vendetta'.

AFTER SHEELU'S RAPE CLAIM was made public, Santoo, the eldest child after Sheelu, found himself catapulted into the limelight. In the absence of Achchhe, who was appearing and disappearing with every new wave of threats from the legislator's men, Santoo assumed the responsibility of head of the family.

Like his father, Santoo has a shy nature, though he is no pushover. Santoo had inherited his father's features – high cheekbones, strong jaw and prominent eyebrows – but his appearance is less harsh than Achchhe's. A youth of simple pleasures, Santoo liked to while away his time by waiting for the weather to cool down and then walking towards the village for a 'roam around' until evening, when he would return home to eat and sleep. Other times, he and his friends would race each other, on foot, down a nearby road.

Santoo always tried to be back before sunset, however, when the lack of streetlights and electricity plunged Shahbaj-pur into a dense, heavy darkness. Late at night, he often saw torches flashing in the distance and was convinced that they belonged to the bandits, referred to as *badmash*, known to inhabit the nearby areas. 'They quietly roam outside. In the day they run far away. In the night they return again outside our village – it has to be the *badmash*, who roams at night,' Santoo ventures. None of the *badmash* men had threatened anyone in Shahbajpur, as far as Santoo could remember, but he was always alert to the threat they posed. 'Those who don't have food to eat, they steal from people, kill people, take money from the bank.' That those frightful, unruly men who prowled in the dark night might ever harm his sister – that was one of his biggest fears.

Santoo idolised Sheelu, with whom he spent hours playing as a child. She always seemed to win, regardless of whether they played catch or raced up a tree where the topmost branch represented the finish line ('Sheelu won more often than me'). Then, when their mother died and Sheelu dropped out of school to look after her brothers, Santoo's bond with her deepened. As the only woman in their family, she became a second mother to them. 'Our sister would grow roots and feed us. We had a buffalo, which gave milk. She would cut grass to feed the cow,' Santoo remembers of her contributions to the family.

Being the eldest brother, Santoo was perhaps more aware than his brothers of the sacrifice Sheelu had made, and so he tried to find ways of giving her something in return. It was Santoo who had secretly taught his sister how to ride on a relative's scooter, feeding her free-spirited nature. 'She had seen girls in the town riding *scooties* and wanted to learn too, so I said, Okay, I'll teach you.' He never ratted on Sheelu when she took the scooter and drove it around the village without permission.

Santoo had immortalised his love and devotion to Sheelu by tattooing her name on his forearm, underneath a heart. It was shortly after Santoo got the tattoo that Sheelu started spending more and more time away from home, living with relatives in other villages. Like Sheelu before him, Santoo was called to sacrifice his studies to make up for the absence of a working family member. His father pulled him out of school and sent him to New Delhi to earn money, where he worked long hours in a factory owned by Bata, the multinational shoemaker. 'The shoes are packed in boxes. I put the covers on boxes; prices are put on top,' he says laconically of his responsibilities at the factory. In between the long work hours, life in Delhi was not without its diversions. 'There are nice buildings, nice roads, nice gardens, nice parks. I like roaming there, feels nice. Not very dirty. There is no filth coming from the *nullahs*,' he recalls with a smile, referring to the sewage drains.

Whenever Santoo would call home, he would ask about his sister. He hoped that she was safe and well; she was often on his mind when he was away. It was during one of his trips back from New Delhi that the 'incident' with Sheelu happened. It was the biggest blow he had received since the death of his mother.

SOON AFTER SHEELU'S imprisonment became a top news item, Santoo met with a man called Vishambhar Prasad Nishad, a legislator for the Tindwari constituency belonging to the Samajwadi Party – the same party that had governed Uttar Pradesh during the time of the Goonda Raj.

Why would Santoo seek help from a politician belonging to a party with a reputation of being thugs, or any politician, in fact, after what had happened to his sister? Nishad was, like Santoo, a Kewat, a member of the boatman caste. Because they belonged to the same community, Santoo believed that Nishad would do his best to help his sister. Such thinking was not uncommon – caste allegiances play an important role, especially in politics. Many voters believed that politicians from their community would serve their needs better, hence the saying that 'in India you don't cast your vote, you vote your caste'. Nishad told Santoo that he would ensure that the whole party would get behind him and Sheelu. Nishad and the party, of course, knew that they would likely benefit politically if they were seen helping Sheelu, whose plight was now being hotly discussed by the media and the public.

'He said, Don't worry. We will help you all we can. We will take this fight from here to Delhi. What has happened with your sister is wrong,' Santoo recalls. Nishad told Santoo that he, not Sampat, should put forward a bail application for his sister, and that the Samajwadi Party would arrange for a lawyer from their same caste to represent her. The bail application would compete with the one made by Sampat on behalf of Achchhe; it would be up to Sheelu to decide which one she wanted to go for. Though her decision would be irrelevant in the eyes of the courts, it would reveal where her allegiances lay.

Santoo went to meet his sister in jail, and there, among many things, they discussed the question of bail. Nishad was able to offer Sheelu more than just the bail if she allied herself with him. 'He had said that he would arrange for us to get a place in Kanshiram Colony,' Santoo remembers, referring to a government housing project. Given how few such government houses are available to the public, and the length of the waiting lists, offers by politicians to use their influence to selectively award certain families with accommodation can be hard to turn down.

ON 4 JANUARY, Sheelu appeared at court and declared that she wanted to accept the bail put forward by her own caste, the Nishads, if the court decided to grant her bail. Sampat and one of her Pink Gang lawyers, Bhola Dwivedi, were at the courts that day expecting that their bail offer would be accepted. Now, Sampat looked like a fool – a busybody Samaritan from whom no one had asked for help. Sampat had wanted to avoid this situation by asking Achchhe for his con-

sent on her bail application; she did not want to be accused
of getting involved in a matter that was not her business. She
had not expected that Sheelu's brother would go against his
father. What irritated her more than her humiliation, however, was the blatant opportunism of the Samajwadi Party,
which was elbowing her out of the way for its own gain.

To Sampat, Vishambhar Prasad Nishad was nothing but
a thug, with a criminal sheet that lived up to the notorious reputation of the Samajwadi Party. Nishad had, in fact,
numerous charges pending against him, including punishment for rioting; rioting armed with a deadly weapon; and
wrongful restraint. Sampat also knew from past experience
that Nishad was not usually this responsive to injustice. Had
she not come to him when Sonam, whose small hut had
been burned down by goons, had needed help? Sonam was
from his very constituency, but despite promising to look
into the matter, he never did. It was ludicrous to Sampat that
a politician with such a long sheet of alleged crimes should
purport to have Sheelu's best interests at heart.

FOLLOWING SHEELU'S ACCEPTANCE of his bail application,
Nishad gave a press conference outside the courts, surrounded by some of his party men, when Sampat barged into
the crowd and shouted, 'One politician has already raped her.
Now you want to use her like a puppet? We're not going to let
that happen. You're a *vidhayak*, just like Dwivedi, don't forget
that. Don't think you can buy Sheelu with your money.'

'Sheelu is from my same caste – ,' Nishad started.

'There are so many people from your caste, do you help
them all?' Sampat demanded.

Nishad wrapped up his press conference and left, turning the media focus on Sampat. 'Sampat, this girl does not respect her father, and she does not respect you. So what are you going to do?' one of the journalists had asked her. 'Are you disappointed?' another demanded. Sampat replied in her short-fuse way, brushing away their questions with a sweep of the hand. 'I don't care whose bail she takes. When Sheelu comes out, I don't need her to pat me on the back, you know. Unlike others, I am not doing this to get anything – all I want is for her to be released. I'm a woman and I want to help her, as another woman. That's my duty.'

'When the injustice was done to Sheelu, no one came forward from her clan. It was after *I* jumped in that everyone else followed. Santoo is a minor, but the politicians are still using him for their own benefit. Is this right?' she demanded.

Sampat paused and then added, 'Anyway, I've decided to release her without paying bail – why should she pay to get out as if she were a criminal?' What Sampat wanted was for all charges against Sheelu to be dropped. Sampat would go ahead with the protest she had planned for the next day, 5 January, and emphasised that she would 'start a movement' that would not die until Sheelu was freed.

AROUND THE TIME that Sheelu's story was unfolding dramatically before the public's eye, Geeta was working on other cases within her own district that needed her urgent attention. She had recently received a disturbing phone call from Geeta Kori and her husband, Bhulwa, who told her that an elderly man in their neighbourhood had raped their daughter, a mute girl aged eleven. When the Koris, who live below the poverty line, called the police for help, they allegedly failed to take the case seriously. The Koris were too poor to pay the police a bribe to investigate the crime; Geeta Kori is a daily-wage labourer and her husband, whose limbs are gradually being eaten away by leprosy, cannot work. Not knowing whom to turn to, the parents went to the Karvi bureau of the Sahara Samay TV station, which is located a short distance from Chitrakoot, where they live. Desperate citizens often seek the help of journalists, who have a reputation for being socially conscious and educated enough to give people advice on what to do. The ultimate hope for many is that their plight might make it into the news: that is often perceived as being the best hope for attaining justice. The TV channel did not end up running a story on the alleged rape, but the journalists did recommend that the couple contact the Pink Gang and gave them Geeta's number.

'She started crying and asked for help,' Geeta recalls from their initial conversation. The parents then came to visit Geeta in her home with their daughter, who was still bleeding at the time. After Geeta heard the whole story, including the fact that the older man had allegedly abused other women in the community and was rumoured to have paid the police a bribe of thirty thousand rupees not to interfere, she called the local police station and demanded to know why they had not made any progress in arresting the rapist. The officers allegedly told Geeta that it was a 'small case', and they would get around to solving it soon. 'Get that guy arrested or your uniform will be decorating the walls on a clothes peg,' Geeta snapped, threatening to have them fired. Geeta then went with the family to the district hospital, but the nurses did not provide the injured and traumatised girl

swift medical attention. 'I said if you don't treat her immediately, I'll come back with the whole gang,' Geeta recalls,
threatening the nurses, who then attended to the girl the
next minute. Geeta covered the cost of treatment, five hundred rupees, out of her own pocket. 'I paid for it as they were
very poor,' she explains.

At the Koris' request, Geeta let the girl stay at her house
for the night, in case she needed to go to the hospital again,
which was close by. They also were concerned about bringing her back home when her rapist was still on the loose. The
next day, however, he was placed behind bars. All it took was
for Geeta to visit the police station in person and threaten
Pink Gang action for the local inspectors to finally arrest the
man. 'They are very scared of us,' Geeta says with a smirk,
adding, 'They only do their job when they are threatened.'

WHEN SAMPAT CALLED Geeta on the afternoon of 4 January,
confirming that the protest for Sheelu was to take place the
next day, the district commander from Chitrakoot was in
the town of Atarra, where Geeta's in-laws lived. By the time
Geeta got back to Chitrakoot, it was dusk. Across most of
rural India, the lack of streetlights means that people have to
rely on torches and the faint glow from backlit mobile phones
to make their way around on moonless nights. Despite the
fact that it was late, Geeta needed to get the message out to
her members that they were required for a protest the next
morning.

Given that many of Geeta's members do not own mobile
phones, or don't always have electricity to charge them, she
has a simple and effective method of communicating with

them. All Geeta has to do is contact five of her core members, each of whom in turn spreads the word to another five women, until everyone has received the message. Of her core of committed, loyal members, the closest and most reliable is Maya Goswami. It is Maya who Geeta turns to for 'special assignments', such as accompanying her on after-dark trips to contact gang members when it is unsafe to travel alone.

Maya, a victim of horrific domestic violence, joined the gang a month after Geeta became the local district commander. She was one of Geeta's first recruits. The two women first met at a police station, after word came to Geeta that Maya, badly beaten by her in-laws, was requesting the help of the Pink Gang. Geeta and another gang member, Pinki, travelled together to the station by bicycle. 'When we arrived, Maya was there alone sitting on a bench. I took biscuits, tea and painkillers for her. She was beaten with broken glass and badly bruised. I stroked her hair and told her not to worry. I said from today onwards we are good friends and I am here for you,' Geeta recalls.

By the time they met, the mother of four had already gone through domestic agony for years without anyone to help her. Maya's troubles started when her first husband, an elephant minder, or *mahoot*, was trampled to death by one of the tusked beasts under his care. The typical fears harboured by widows in India – such as increased abuse by in-laws or even forced eviction from the in-laws' home – were temporarily allayed when the brother of her late husband offered to marry her. It was only later that Maya realised the proposal had been her mother-in-law's scheme to get back the small parcel of land that her late husband had left Maya. The land was swiftly transferred over to her second husband after the marriage, and following the loss of her only property, Maya was kicked out onto the street. Maya's mother-in-law allegedly threatened to attack her with skin-corroding acid – a common threat made on women in the subcontinent – if she returned.

Concern for retrieving the inheritance bequeathed to Maya was also the reason why, prior to her eviction, her mother-in-law allegedly had forced her to take abortifacients when Maya discovered she was pregnant with her second husband's child: Maya's mother-in-law did not want an heir to have any claim to the land. It was after one of her many violent confrontations with her in-laws that Maya, badly injured, sought the help of the gang.

'I thought that there would be many good things in store for my life, but it's all full of problems now,' Maya said with tears, but Geeta told her not to worry. The next day the district commander called together all of the members of her nascent gang. Armed with bamboo *laathis* and dressed in their pink sari uniforms, the angry, shouting women surrounded the house of Maya's mother-in-law. Backed by gang members, Geeta threatened to knock down the property and come with thousands of other women from across the region if Maya's mother-in-law did not welcome Maya back into her home and let her live in peace. The elderly woman, seeing that she was outnumbered, agreed and apologised to her daughter-in-law in front of the gathered crowd. She promised to never again threaten Maya, and under the expectant gaze of the Pink Gang, she embraced her crying daughter-in-law.

Since then, Maya has always been at Geeta's disposal, no matter the hour. The Pink Gang has given Maya a renewed faith in her own capacity to survive and overcome struggle. 'God gave me two arms and legs. I don't need to suffer any-more. I can look after myself,' she now says.

ON THE NIGHT of 4 January, Geeta and Maya rode together on a bicycle to get the word out to the other women about the scheduled protest for Sheelu. The exact number of women who go to any given protest depends on the amount of funds available, as costs for travel and food for the Pink Gang are shouldered by local members and district commanders. On average, bringing approximately one hundred women to and from a protest costs five hundred rupees. 'If we don't have enough money, then fewer women go,' Geeta says about the economics of the Pink Gang protests. When the Pink Gang is fortunate, supporters lend them vehicles for their larger protests – there have been occasions on which the Pink Gang travelled to protest sites in the backs of tractors, in disused ambulances and on decommissioned school buses.

While auto-rickshaws from villages to the train stations and back cost money, the Pink Gang often gets away with not paying train fares when they are in a large group. 'The conductors don't ask for our tickets. They are too afraid,' Geeta says with a torrent of giggles. It was Sampat who had taught her this trick. 'When we have to go fight for a woman, we have to catch a bus. We make ten women stand on the road. We stop the bus and travel without paying. If they don't take us, then we block the road,' she says, adding that the bus drivers don't mind. 'They say, "You are Sampat Pal from the Pink Gang? Okay, fine, fine." Then they take us. We have got so much strength that wherever there are a hundred women, the bus driver is never able to stop us. They say, "Hop on, where is the Pink Gang going today?" Earlier it used to be very difficult. Today, if any woman is standing on the road in a pink sari, they ask, "Madam, where do you want to go?" See, we are social workers. We are doing good deeds,' Sampat says.

Geeta and Maya informed the other members that they had to assemble at six in the morning at the bus station in Chitrakoot. From there, they would be shuttled in an auto-rickshaw to the train station, from where they would take a train to Banda. Although it is common in India to arrive late for appointments, the Pink Gang members are always punctual when duty calls. 'The women are *never* late for rallies. In fact, more often than not, they arrive early,' Geeta says with pride.

IN ADDITION TO GEETA and her women from Chitrakoot, seven other district commanders and their local members were travelling from across the region to attend the day of protests in Banda on 5 January. The journey was, like most Pink Gang trips, a loud affair. When the gang takes trains, passengers in the carriage often crane their necks to get a look at Bundelkhand's most recognisable celebrities. 'Look, it's the Pink Gang,' people will inevitably whisper to each other. Those with camera phones take pictures. India's trains often have entertainment on board. Sufi mystics are known to put on *qawwali* (devotional music) performances with portable harmoniums and vocals that unwind from the depths of their bellies. Eunuchs ask for money, threatening to lift their skirts if they are not paid. When the Pink Gang is on board, however, they are the ones who provide travel-weary passengers with something to marvel at.

As they sat in the cramped carriage, some Pink Gang members started warming up their vocals for what was going to be a long day of shouting. District commanders led their members in a set of call-and-response chants, which had been adapted to the culprit of the day. '*Gully gully mein shor hai, Naraini Vidhayak chor hai!*' – From street to street it is heard, the Naraini legislator is a thief! '*Gulabi Gang Zindabad! (Zindabad! Zindabad!)*' – Long live the Pink Gang! (Long live! Long Live!) '*Dwivedi Vidhayak Murdabad! (Murdabad! Murdabad!)*' – Down with Dwivedi! (Down! Down!)

When they got off the train, the Pink Gang members met other divisions that were coming from nearby districts. With the women streaming through them, the train doors looked like open wounds, bleeding bright pink. Many of the women carried their sticks, which they had painted pink. Some balanced food on their heads.

Sampat was on the platform, awaiting them; she looked at the women with pride. When all of them were assembled, the station was flooded in pink, and the walls of the railway hall echoed their shouts. 'There was a sea of women at the railway station. So many women were gathered in Banda that officers were amazed. The Pink Gang became the talk of the town,' she says. Sampat had slept at the station that night, with Babuji and the women from the town of Orai, who had arrived late the night before. 'It was extremely cold. Everyone brought blankets and food along with them. They also brought one water bottle with them. One brought *sabzi poori*, vegetables with a deep-fried flatbread, another brought *lai*. They had reserves for two days. They didn't care how long the battle would take,' Sampat recalls.

The plan had been for the women from Orai to stay in a cheap guesthouse near the station, but as Sampat explains, 'Because of the legislator's terror, I wasn't welcome in anybody's house.' Babuji had gone to the Jain Dharamshala guesthouse to enquire about rooms. 'He asked about the Pink Gang. We informed him that we were going to hold a protest and that we needed a place to stay for those women. But he said that there was no vacant room available. We know he was lying,' Sampat says, referring to the owner of the guesthouse.

On the first day of protests, the Pink Gang marched through the streets. Sampat was at the helm of the march, and by her side were her district commanders. Babuji, who was not permitted by Sampat to be conspicuous during protests, hovered somewhere in the back of the group. Even now, she is still concerned that male supporters of the gang are vulnerable to police brutality if they are seen to be leading the women. It was cold that day, and it had rained that morning so the ground was muddy. Several women slipped and fell, dirtying their saris. Embarrassed, one of the women who had fallen tried to make light of her misstep. 'I'm not half as muddied as Dwivedi's conscience!' she fired, once she had wiped herself off.

The women stopped at Ashok Lad, a small enclosed space designated for protests near the district court. In the centre of Ashok Lad is the Ashok Lion capital, a column painted in the colours of the Indian flag with four lion sculptures, the national emblem, perched atop it. Under the emblem, carved in stone, is a memorial plaque recognising those who fought for Indian independence.

On either side of Ashok Lad are large concrete pillars sprouting iron rods that will support an overpass one day. Vegetable vendors huddle together on the edge of the road, competing for space with the bicycle rickshaws, pedestrians, cyclists, wandering cows, stray dogs, cars and motorbikes. Pyramid-shaped piles of baby aubergine, tomatoes, and cucumbers look like they might be knocked down at any moment in the rush of traffic that seems to come from all sides.

At Ashok Lad, Sampat turned to the women and shouted at them to sit down on the adjacent road to block the traffic. As the asphalt was still wet from the rain, the women squatted on their haunches, the elderly women lowering themselves slowly with the help of their friends. When they were all settled, they started singing a freedom song that Sampat had taught them.

A moment later, the drivers of the motorbikes and cars, having done their fair share of honking before the sit-in had even begun, now kept their hands on the horn. At least twenty vehicles contributed to the deafening blast. '*Chalo! Chalo!*' shouted some of the impatient motorcyclists up front. 'Let's get moving, women!' Sampat and the women did not budge. They lifted their heads in defiance at the angry drivers and, raising their sticks, shouted, '*Shee-lu Zin-da-bad!*' – Long live Sheelu! '*Gu-la-bi Gang Zin-da-bad!*' – Long live the Pink Gang!

The road they had blocked was completely choked with vehicles for as far as they could see. They had managed to attract a large crowd of people who were curious to see what all the commotion was about. 'Do not allow an innocent daughter to stay in jail!' they exhorted the multitude of people. 'Free Sheelu!' cried Sampat. 'Free Sheelu!' her Pink Gang responded vigorously.

The women then got up and continued their march towards the jail where Sheelu was being held. As the women marched, trying to stay upbeat despite the cold, Geeta asked Sampat if they could stop at the Hanuman temple to make an offering. Many of the Pink Gang members were devotees of the monkey deity and hoped that the god would bless their protest and grant them success. Given that the temple was on the way and they were not pressed for time, Sampat agreed.

The Hanuman temple was painted in a dusty-pink hue, and the entrance was composed of a large arch, on top of which sat a crowned and garlanded Hanuman, who lifted his right hand in greeting to passersby. Inside the courtyard of the temple complex hung posters featuring politicians pressing their palms together in a respectful gesture towards the deity.

As the temple was fairly small, most of the women stayed outside while Sampat and a handful of other women went in to make an offering of incense and *laddu* on their behalf. The Pink Gang members gave the offering to the priest, or *pujari*, who laid it at the feet of the idol. Some of the offering, now considered blessed by Hanuman, was then returned back to the women, each of whom ate a small portion.

Feeling fortified by their spiritual sustenance, the women marched on towards the jail. When they arrived, there were already several journalists present, waiting to cover the Pink Gang protest. The Pink Gang stopped at the gates leading towards the jail, which were closed and protected by two arms-bearing guards.

Sampat walked up to one of the guards and informed him that she had come to see Sheelu. The guard did not let her pass, and the jailer, V. K. Singh, was called to deal with the women. 'These are our demands!' Sampat told him. 'The *vidhayak* should be investigated. Sheelu's case should be squashed. She should be freed immediately and given ten *lakh* rupees' – a million rupees – 'as compensation,' Sampat said, handing a printed copy of the Pink Gang's demands to the jailer and sticking leaflets with the demands on the jail gates.

The next stop was to meet Mr Tripathi, the deputy inspector general (DIG) of police. Sampat had been going to the DIG's office regularly since Sheelu's arrest, pressurising him to look into Sheelu's allegations. The DIG would grant Sampat an audience and politely listen to her requests, but after he promised one too many times that he would do something about Sheelu's imprisonment, Sampat finally lost her patience with him.

Sampat told the women that their next stop would include a '*thoo-thoo* rally', which was the onomatopoeic name for a protest involving spitting. 'The police are useless. They would not listen to us. If we resort to violence we would be in trouble. So, I decided to embarrass them. We announced that we would not say anything to these officers but that we would just spit on their walls,' Sampat says with a crackling laugh. Babuji had also designed flyers to humiliate the local head of police. 'We used to stick bills on the walls that said, You are not a DIG, you don't deserve this post, you are not a man.'

Sampat frequently employed humiliating tactics in her quest for social justice. In 2006, she organised a dog rally in which she and her newly formed gang gathered dozens of dogs and marched with them down Bisanda Road towards the Atarra police station, where they proclaimed that since the police were corrupt and useless, they should be replaced by the 'dog police', who would be 'better than the police we have now'. On another occasion she organised a big *puja*, a Hindu prayer ceremony, asking the gods to restore sanity to the director general of police, Vikram Singh, who had accused Sampat of being a Naxalite, a member of an Indian militant group adhering to Maoist beliefs.

Soon after the women began their spitting protest, the DIG insisted that the women come inside to settle their disagreements. Sampat brought all the district commanders into the office, despite the DIG's orders that only two people could enter. Sampat demanded answers on a series of questions, from why Sheelu's medical examination had not been performed immediately to why she had been jailed at night, which contravened protocol. Sampat claims the DIG 'admitted that injustice was done with Sheelu', but said that he could not take a stand against 'rogue politicians'. Sampat was not impressed with that excuse. 'We said tomorrow somebody else's government will be there. Are you serving the law or the government?' Sampat recalls.

The DIG allegedly requested that Sampat stop spitting and sticking up posters that criticised him, and said that if she continued her fight, well, 'he too would be in better position to take action'.

THE GOVERNMENT HOSPITAL in Banda was a one-storey concrete building, painted in faded peach. On the asphalt pavement out front sat people hoping to be admitted for treatment. In front of them, in an empty car park, packs of stray dogs roamed around barking while others slept lazily under disused ambulances.

This air of despair pervaded the dim, poorly ventilated hospital foyer. Here relatives waited on plastic chairs, holding handkerchiefs over their mouths and noses; the sick were spread out listlessly on mats on the floor, waiting for medical attention.

It was into this lethargic, grim space that several-dozen Pink Gang members barged demanding to know where Dr Bhavna Sharma, the woman who had refused to perform the medical examination on Sheelu, was. The narrow, dark foyer was suddenly swelling with people. Confusion thick in the air, the women behind Sampat awaited instructions, gripping their sticks in anticipation. Sampat was not sure where she needed to go to find the offending doctor.

There is never any strategy session before the Pink Gang embarks on these missions. Sampat does not huddle together to form a game plan with her district commanders; she does not look them in the eye and tell them, 'Mitu, I need you to lead the women from the rear with chants', or 'Geeta, you make sure so-and-so doesn't escape through the backdoor'. Sampat throws herself in and then takes things from there, and the gang, following her blindly, takes her commands as they come.

During a momentary lull in the hospital foyer, Sampat turned to the women to fire them up. 'Long live the Pink Gang!' she cheered. 'Down with the Dr Bhavna!' she cried, raising a fist. 'Down with her, down with her!' the women rallied in unison.

Far from complaining about the noise, the crowd of

patients and their relatives were either apathetic or contributing supportive gestures and comments. 'Sister, I have also been wronged,' one woman said, coming up to Sampat. 'We haven't received any help for days. The doctors don't care about us here. They treat us like dogs,' she lamented. Other patients nodded in agreement.

'All government doctors sell off medicines! They are meant for the poor, but do any of you receive them?' Sampat asked, looking around at the neglected, sickly crowd. 'No, sister,' someone replied. 'That's right! You don't receive them! Tell me, why are they sold?' Sampat asked again, pressing her listeners for an answer, but she beat them to it. 'Because they are greedy, not happy with what they earn!' she said, with the zeal of a preacher in the heat of a sermon.

Sampat's ability to rouse the spirits of those around her sometimes backfires. She once went to a hospital in the city of Fatehpur to protest against doctors who had turned away a seriously ill rickshaw driver. One doctor had tried, unsuccessfully, to bribe the Pink Gang members not to protest about it. 'If we don't do anything, he'll die, Sampat-ji,' the district commander of Fatehpur, Sushila, told Sampat in a panicky phone call. When Sampat arrived at the hospital, other patients who had also been mistreated became angry. One woman, a relative of someone who had been turned away by the hospital, lashed out at and assaulted a doctor who was present during the protest, getting Sampat into trouble. The rickshaw driver, however, was given the treatment he needed. 'That man was an orphan and now he says I've become like a mother to him,' Sampat says proudly.

Finally, after the brief talk with the crowd, someone came

to Sampat with directions to Dr Bhavna's office. 'Let's go, then! Let's hear her side of the story. Maybe she had a reason for her behaviour?' Sampat added, only half serious. When they reached the door, it was bolted from the inside. 'Dr Bhavna? Are you inside there?' Sampat asked, knocking at the door. 'What are you so afraid of? You haven't done anything you are ashamed of, have you? If not, why are you hiding?'

'We're just here to talk. I want to hear what you have to say,' Sampat continued. Still, there was no response.

'We're not leaving, so you come out when you're ready. We're staying here. Aren't we?' she asked in a raised voice, turning to the women behind her.

'We're not going anywhere!' shouted the women.

'Have some mercy on me!' issued a female voice from behind the door.

'Come out, stop hiding!' Sampat responded.

The doctor came out, crossing her arms defensively.

'Why was no medical exam done on Sheelu earlier?' Sampat thundered.

'It's not my fault,' the doctor replied.

'Oh, I see. Maybe it's my fault then?' Sampat snapped, provoking sniggers from the onlookers.

'I don't know anything! What do you want me to do?' the doctor asked, raising her voice.

'I want you to do your work properly. With honesty, you hear? See these people? They are all complaining about you and all the other doctors here. Have you no shame, treating people the way you do?' Sampat went on.

Before the doctor could answer, Sampat herded her

women out of the hospital with a wave of the hand. 'We're done here. She understands now, don't you?' Sampat asked, with a threatening air.

'Yes, yes, . . . definitely, sister,' the doctor said, slamming her door on the crowds that still lingered expectantly.

CHAPTER EIGHT

THE SCRAMBLE FOR SHEELU

SHEELU'S STORY HAS TURNED
INTO A POLITICAL GAME.

—HINDUSTAN, *5 January 2011*

THE 15TH OF JANUARY 2011 SHOULD HAVE BEEN THE BEST DAY of the year for Mayawati, the chief minister of Uttar Pradesh. It was her fifty-fifth birthday, and befitting this politician who had built countless statues in the state capital of Lucknow glorifying herself, she had, 'in the interest of the people', declared the day to be 'Human Welfare Day', to be celebrated with gusto and the unveiling of six hundred government projects.

As part of the festivities, she planned to inaugurate government initiatives totalling 40 billion rupees – 552 million pounds – which she had dedicated 'to the poor and downtrodden'. These included more financial aid to struggling families, improved medical facilities in rural areas and the release of elderly or sick prisoners from jail. Several government agencies, including the Lucknow Development

Authority, the Lucknow Municipal Corporation and the Uttar Pradesh Public Works Department, had been tasked with preparing the city for the occasion. Firms from New Delhi had been contracted to illuminate memorials, gardens and crossings, and 'expert hands' had been hired to decorate statues of Dalit leaders, including those of Mayawati herself, with flowers. Two cakes, each weighing fifty-five kilograms (121 pounds) – one kilogram for each year – had reportedly been made especially for the politician, and large sections of the city, particularly streets named after lower-caste political icons, were lit up and festooned with flowers and ribbons. A group of Buddhist monks had even been called in to bless her on her special day. It felt like a royal celebration, but, then again, Mayawati's supporters did see her as the 'Queen of the Dalits'.

Just how much this fanfare was costing was unclear. In the past, party members had organised massive donation drives across the state to contribute to Mayawati's birthday celebrations, but the practice was curtailed significantly after one of her legislators from the constituency of Auraiya, Shekhar Tiwari, was arrested and later given a life sentence for the torture and murder of an engineer after he 'refused to pay donations for the Chief Minister's birthday celebrations in December 2008'. After Tiwari's arrest, Mayawati announced that 'the practice of fund collection on my birthday is being done away with and there should be no raising of funds from my next birthday'.

On 15 January 2011, however, a shadow that had nothing to do with the provenance of the birthday funding was being cast over the fanfare. The results of the preliminary inquiry by the CB-CID into Sheelu's allegations had been

published just five days before, on 10 January. After recording the statements of over a dozen people, the investigators
concluded that Dwivedi had raped Sheelu and that he had
framed her in a false theft case. They also accused the Banda
police of misconduct. The court ordered Dwivedi's arrest on
12 January. As officers escorted him to the police station the
next day, the legislator smiled and calmly told reporters that
he would 'take the revenge' on the ones who 'got him stuck'
in this mess.

With Dwivedi's arrest having taken place just a few days
before Mayawati's spectacular celebration, the national news
channels, news anchors and talking heads covering the event
repeatedly discussed the ongoing case live on air. 'Mayawati's
birthday expenditure has always drawn attention, she is used
to the criticism. What has made the mood gloomy is this, her
MLA' – member of the Legislative Assembly – 'of Banda has
been accused of raping a minor Dalit girl,' reported NDTV,
India's main news channel. The same channel chose the sub-
title 'Birthday Blues' for their coverage, a reference to the
colour of her party, in which she had lit up the entire city.

To dampen the birthday spirit even further, the Alla-
habad High Court made a surprise announcement in the
middle of the elaborate birthday celebration: the justices
were ordering the immediate release of Sheelu, who was still
imprisoned despite the bail applications made on her behalf.
Within minutes of the court verdict, while Mayawati was
busy inaugurating a new sewage treatment plant, her cabinet
secretary Shashank Shekhar Singh called an impromptu press
conference. There he announced that Mayawati had ordered
Sheelu's release. In a separate statement about the legislator
that day, Mayawati stated, 'No one will be allowed to take

law into his hand under BSP government. Strict action will be initiated against all those, whosoever they are, who take law into their hands.'

Some noted wryly that despite Mayawati's statement coming *after* the court ruling, it still 'claimed that the poor girl's release was a part of the chief minister's benevolent gesture on the occasion of her birthday', as one journalist put it. Mayawati would not be the only one to try to claim Sheelu's victory as her own. The battle over to whom Sheelu 'belonged' would grow even more fierce over the following days.

SAMPAT RECEIVED THE NEWS of Sheelu's release from Amit. 'You have succeeded in your fight – the government is scared of you, and they are going to release Sheelu. Sampat-ji, you have won because of your agitation,' he told her over the phone. It had been ten days since the Pink Gang began their protests in Banda. Sampat was especially pleased that Sheelu had not ended up being released on bail 'like a criminal', but that all charges against her were dropped.

'You have also helped Sheelu,' Sampat told her friend. 'You have published fair news and did not give in to pressure by the legislator. Look at all the other media. They were in the hands of the perpetrators. Some journalists even tried to intimidate us!' she added, remembering the veiled threats passed on through the journalist from *Dainik Jagran*. Sampat was not the only one who thought Amit had done a good job – he gained five hundred new readers after December, owing to his coverage of Sheelu's case.

Sampat felt proud of her contribution to freeing Sheelu. 'After we started fighting for Sheelu, then all the political parties started to protest. At the beginning no one else was there for her, just me. And those who were not happy with the *vidhayak* were very happy that Sampat Pal did a good job,' she said.

The local television stations that had limited their coverage of Sampat over the preceding months after their bureau chiefs, including Arun Dixit, had fallen out with her, were once again running stories on her protests and activism. They could hardly cover Sheelu's case without mentioning Sampat.

After speaking to Amit, Sampat contacted the district commanders who were in charge of organising their members for the 15 January protest: Mitu Devi, the district commander for Banda, and Suman Singh, the district commander for Mahoba. Over the past ten days, members across ten districts had been mobilised on a daily basis to pressure the government into releasing Sheelu, and in order not to overburden members, Sampat had organised a rotation so that district commanders and their members could take turns protesting.

On the day of Sheelu's release, around fifty Pink Gang women marched towards the yard in front of the jail, which was slowly filling up with protesting political parties, journalists and passersby. Sampat, in the front of the group, wore a burgundy sari – her pink one was in the wash – with a black cardigan draped over her shoulders. Her black hair was tied back in a ponytail, and her gold nose stud glinted in the afternoon light as her nostrils flared with each rallying cry. Suman Singh was on her right, wearing a pale-pink *salwar kameez*. Sampat let Suman, the district commander with whom she had a brittle relationship, lead the women in call-and-response protest chants. 'The officer who is just is our brother, the one who cannot respect women is useless! We want justice for Sheelu! We want the criminal punished!' Suman cried, her voice breaking with the strain. 'Punishment wanted! Punishment wanted!' the other gang members responded. Many of the women echoing her chant sounded like they had sore, hoarse throats, perhaps from the cold or from exhaustion.

Suman rubbed her throat in between chants, as did some of the others. The women had not eaten much during the past fortnight of protests. 'I didn't have dinner in those days. When I returned home, it was too late to eat; there was nothing left. During the day, I had food and juice. I didn't like to eat. I had pain within me because officials weren't listening and the poor weren't getting justice,' remembers Sampat.

When Sampat and the Pink Gang stopped at the gates of the jail, journalists and passersby formed a circle around them as Sampat launched into an impromptu press conference. Sampat expressed her outrage at Dwivedi for publicly threatening his enemies for cooking up the 'conspiracy' that had landed him in jail. 'He says, "I will take revenge on all the party people and every one who did this." What revenge will you take, hm? You change your habit – it will be much better for you! What reason is there for you to take revenge? You did a crime in the open!' she blasted to the journalists who surrounded her.

SAMPAT WAS NOT the only one attracting the attention of journalists. Nearby, other protesters were gathering in front of the jail. Most of them were led by politicians who had marched to the jail with their flag-waving, slogan-chanting supporters. What united all of them was the chant 'Down with Mayawati! Down with Naraini *Vidhayak*!' Members of the Samajwadi Party, headed by Vishambhar Nishad (the same politician who had submitted a bail application on Sheelu's behalf), waved their red-and-green flag with its bicycle party symbol in the centre. Nearby were the BJP, the Hindu conservatives, flying their lotus-symbol flags and working themselves into such a frenzy of clapping and impassioned chants of 'Down with Mayawati!' that at one point the woman leading the protest (that day all parties were pushing their women's wing leaders into the front) looked like she might faint. Near the BJP group, a handful of local Congress Party members gathered, waving their own flag – the Indian tricolour with the party's hand symbol in the centre – and trying not to be overshadowed by the other actors crowding the field. 'Congress people were with us – we were working hand in hand,' Sampat says. While she accused the other parties of opportunism, Sampat considered the Congress Party's concern for Sheelu to be genuine and only right, given that they were leading the ruling coalition in the central government.

Of all of the political parties gathered in front of the jail that day, Vishambhar Nishad's Samajwadi Party was the most decisive in claiming Sheelu's release as its own victory. When the Samajwadi Party crowd – around fifty men led in a barrage of anti-Mayawati chants by one token woman – arrived at the jail, Nishad gave a press conference to state his perspective on how Sheelu had been released. 'The Samajwadi Party protested in front of the jail and Achchhe Lal, Sheelu's father, wrote a letter to the minister. On the basis of that they announced that Sheelu was innocent and had been falsely blamed for robbery.' Nishad then directed a hit at the chief minister, saying, 'Sheelu has been in jail for a month, in spite of being innocent, and today Mayawati is celebrating her birthday and cutting cake.' He ended his press conference with a statement that caused Sampat's blood to boil. 'I thank the media and everyone else who supported Sheelu. *Samajwadi Party will take care of Sheelu's protection now.*'

Rumours had been circulating that Nishad had offered Sheelu government housing, via her brother Santoo, who later confirmed this. Sampat decided that she would not let Sheelu be exploited by the self-serving politicians – she would ensure that Sheelu went home with her father. Despite his shortcomings, Sampat thought that Achchhe would look after her better than the politicians.

HOURS PASSED, AND STILL there was no news of when Sheelu would be released. It was cold out, and as the sky darkened, Sampat suggested that the other gang members go home. 'They are thinking to release her after we leave. Because of this it is becoming too late,' Sampat surmised. 'But until they release her I will not go,' she told Mitu, Suman, and the other gang members. Babuji and Lakhan waited with Sampat – along with journalists, curious members of the public and the political party members, who had exhausted all of the chants and interviews they could perform in one day.

Now there was only one person, Rajju, who was missing from the picture. He was not among those standing at the jail gates to greet Sheelu upon her release. Since his request to meet her in jail was rejected, he never again tried to contact her. If there ever was love between them, it was surely killed the moment Rajju appeared alongside Dwivedi during his press conference, which Sheelu later claimed Rajju had agreed to do in exchange for money. On 24 January, Rajju would appear at a protest with Dwivedi's wife, Asha, and his son Mayank, who were proclaiming the legislator's innocence.

Around the darkened jail premises, yellow streetlights flickered to life, but the roads leading to the jail and the dirt yard directly in front of it were barely illuminated.

It was dark when Achchhe Lal arrived with Santoo.

There was some commotion when they emerged from the vehicle, which the crowds surrounded. Achchhe was let through the gates and onto the jail premises, but he did not enter the building; he was told to wait outside until Sheelu decided if she wanted to go home with her father.

Soon after his arrival, rumours circulated through the crowd that Achchhe was drunk, which would not be surprising given that he was known to have an alcohol problem. 'That was why he was not let into the jail. There are rules against intoxicated people entering,' Tirath, Sampat's son-in-law, would later clarify. In the dense atmosphere of mutual suspicion built up between the various parties gathered that day, some, including Sampat, speculated that the Samajwadi Party had plied Achchhe with alcohol to strengthen its case that Sheelu should be entrusted into its care. '[The party] gave him free drinks, so that he wouldn't say anything against anyone. And if he said something they wouldn't believe him because he was drunk,' she says, adding, 'If Sheelu's father drinks, it doesn't give anyone the right to take away someone's daughter. This doesn't give anyone the right to do wrong.'

Journalists stuck microphones through the bars of the jail compound gate towards a nervous Achchhe, and pelted him with a torrent of questions. 'What is Sheelu saying?' 'Why doesn't she want to go with you?' 'She is your daughter!' 'What is the lawyer saying?' 'What is she saying?' *'Why is the girl not willing to go home along with you?'*

Achchhe, holding his head and pacing back and forth, was in visible distress. He shouted at the journalists, but the meaning of his words was unclear. 'Do you want me to get stuck in the same direction again?' he yelled in an agitated, pleading voice. 'I want to go home,' he shouted at the journalists behind the gate, clutching his head with his wiry hands.

Sampat was concerned that Sheelu might in fact be lured into living with Vishambhar Nishad. She marched over to the police on duty to discuss the matter. 'Vishambhar Nishad of Samajwadi Party is trying to take her to his home! He is persuading his father and brother of this,' Sampat told them. 'Hand over Sheelu to her father – she doesn't need help from any *neta*,' she told them. They responded by telling her that the courts had ordered that 'no one except her parents could take her with them', and that the 'matter was over'. But, as Sampat would soon see, it was far from over.

INSIDE THE JAIL, preparations for Sheelu's release had been going on for hours. Additional police forces from across the district had reported to duty, in the expectation that much commotion would accompany Sheelu's walk through the jail gates. The police now stood idly outside the jail, in their khaki trousers and military-green shirts, joking among each other as they looked on at the protesters, who, like them, were growing cold in the night chill.

From his desk, Tirath had heard the growing chorus of protesters chanting outside of his window all day. Like everyone else, he could not recall the last time there was this much activity in and around the jail premises; the phone had been ringing non-stop, journalists were trying to get statements from his seniors, and everybody in the room was wondering what the fall-out of this Sheelu case was going to be. Ever since Dwivedi's arrest, everyone had been asking what would happen to the jail staff who had allegedly known about Sheelu's rape claims yet had failed to act on that knowledge. Now, with Sheelu's lawyers demanding that the Central Bureau of Investigation, the national criminal investigation agency, take over the investigations in the case, citing bias of the local Crime Branch towards the politician, this mess looked too large to sweep under the rug. It felt to Tirath, at least today, that the whole country was watching what was going on in there.

Investigations into the jail staff had already begun. On 8 January, it was reported that Tirath's friend Shahjehan Begum, the female jail officer who first told him about the rape, told the CB-CID investigators that she had been aware of Sheelu's rape claims from the day she arrived in jail. Begum and another member of the Banda jail staff, Rama Shankar Shukla, were criticised in the *Indian Express* for not bringing attention to Sheelu's claims earlier. Begum defended herself in an interview she gave on 17 January with *IBNLive*, saying that she had taken the matter to her superiors, but they ignored her. '[Sheelu] told me the legislator behaved with her in such and such way. She told me each and every word and I told those to the jailor. He didn't take those words seriously, just laughed and walked towards home,' she said. She also claimed that when she insisted that something be done to help Sheelu, her job and life were threatened. The callousness and corruption that had pervaded Sheelu's case would come out, like pus slowly being drained from a bulging abscess, in the following weeks as investigators and the media were informed of the extent of the negligence and malpractice in the jail.

Finally, Sheelu was brought to Tirath's desk; it was his responsibility to perform certain bureaucratic functions during the release of prisoners. For the first time, he got a good look at her from up close. 'Like everyone else, there was a lot of curiosity inside me to see her,' he remembers. That day, Sheelu wore a papaya-coloured *salwar kameez* with a russet embroidered shawl wrapped around her head. Her eyes beamed with joy.

The jail officials asked Sheelu whether she wanted to go home with her father, given that he appeared to be intoxicated. 'Many politicians are outside. They are all offering you a place,' one of them told her.

A part of Sheelu was tempted by the offer. Over a year ago, she had left home over differences with her father, and these had only grown in the past few weeks. Despite this, she decided that for the time being, she would return home.

Once the matter of her destination was cleared, Tirath got up and went to the metal *almirah*, where various stamps, stationery and forms are kept. He took out the stamp that is required for the occasion. On it is written, *'JAIL SE MUKT'* – FREE FROM JAIL.

Tirath pressed the stamp into an inkpad, and then, asking

for Sheelu's arm, he marked her flesh – once on her palm and a second time on her inner arm – with the sign of freedom.

'You need to get the stamp signed by two people, one by the jailer and one by the deputy jailer. Then you show it to the man at the gate,' Tirath explained. 'Then you're free.'

WHEN SHEELU FINALLY left the jail, it was eleven o'clock at night; despite the cold and the long wait, throngs of people – mostly journalists and political parties – were waiting at the gates to watch her release.

She emerged amid a scrum of policemen who congregated around her as last-minute preparations for her departure were discussed. A man with a large folder flicked through a few pages inside it, apparently checking that everything was in order. When he signalled that they could leave, Achchhe knelt down and touched the man's feet several times out of gratitude; he then slunk to the back of the group of policemen and administrators surrounding Sheelu. Achchhe and Sheelu didn't interact at all during her release. Rather, Santoo, wearing blue jeans and a suit jacket and carrying plastic bags full of her clothes, stood at his sister's side.

Someone garlanded Sheelu with marigolds, as if she were a politician being honoured by her followers, and then she walked towards the front gate, behind which stood a large, poorly lit mass of flag-waving, chanting, photo-flashing people. The shouts of the media drowned out everyone else. 'Sheelu, wave your hand,' 'Sheelu you are being released, tell us how are you feeling,' 'Hey, Sheelu come here a little forward,' 'Sir, let us talk to her!' – these were some of the commands and questions that flew at Sheelu from every direction. Sheelu flashed a dazzling, victorious smile and waved graciously as she walked towards her supporters; in that brief moment she did have the demeanour and air of a politician. Once she was escorted through the gate, however, her joyous expression vanished. The shouting crowd swallowed her up. Sheelu panicked. She grabbed hold of her brother; the clamour overwhelmed her.

Apart from the journalists, the political parties were also shouting for Sheelu's attention. 'When Sheelu was released, all the *netas* were outside. They were outside shouting at one another. One said, We will get her a house. Another said, No, *we* will get her a house. We said, No, we will not go to anyone's place, we will stay in our house. So we came home,' Santoo remembers. '*Netas* thought we will be talked about, become *vidhayak*, people will vote for us because of Sheelu. So we said that the help that you have given us is enough. We will live in our house,' he later remembers, adding, 'I said that we are still alive – her brother, father are still alive – so how can I let my sister go to any *vidhayak*'s house? She should live in our house. My sister was underage, she can't go with someone else and no one can take her. They,' Santoo says, referring to the courts, 'said that she should be handed over to the father as she was underage.'

Sheelu, Santoo and their father, Achchhe, were then loaded into a police van and driven to Shahbajpur.

TWO DAYS AFTER Sheelu's release, Sampat made her way to Shahbajpur to meet Sheelu. They had not spoken since the day outside the court when their picture was taken. Nisha, who rarely joined her mother on expeditions, asked if she could go with her this time. When Sampat asked her why, Nisha replied, 'The whole world is coming to see her. Why not me?'

Sampat carried with her a pink sari, which was neatly folded in a bag. She did not expect Sheelu to join the Pink Gang, but wanted to extend an invitation nonetheless and offer her any help she might need. Sampat did not bear Sheelu any ill will for not accepting her bail – 'She is just a girl,' she thought.

When Sampat arrived at Shahbajpur, she found Sheelu surrounded by media and several-dozen uniformed police-men, who had been assigned to protect her at all hours. The personal guards were deemed necessary given that on the night of his arrest Dwivedi went on camera swearing to take revenge on his enemies, and also because of Achchhe's formal complaint that his family was being threatened with death.

Two police checkpoints had been set up to control the flow of people to the village. Journalists were pouring in from local towns, such as Banda, and others had travelled all the way from Lucknow and even New Delhi. Large white vans with satellite dishes and large logos printed on their doors lined the narrow road leading to Sheelu's house. They had parked in the fields, in the school courtyard opposite Sheelu's house and in the little square in front of it.

That day, Sheelu was wearing a strawberry-coloured, faux-chenille cardigan and a white shawl.

She was excited to see Sampat. '*Didi!*' she cried out. 'How are you?' The two women talked for 'around half an hour', remembers Sampat. The Pink Gang leader enquired about Sheelu's health, about whether the police were doing a good job at protecting her, and what her hopes were for the future.

'You should study, that's important. You're still a young girl. It's not too late to get an education,' Sampat told her. 'How can I go to school now? My mind is occupied with my case. I'm only thinking about that. Also, how will I go with six guards into a classroom? That won't work,' Sheelu said grimly. She knew that she would still have to testify in court against Dwivedi, and that thanks to India's creaking justice system, it could be years before a verdict is reached.

'I will ask Sonia-ji for help. Maybe you can get a tutor? There will be a solution, don't worry,' Sampat said, referring to Sonia Gandhi.

Then, Sampat gave Sheelu some advice. 'Political parties are trying to complicate things. You should think about your future without falling into political wrangles. They are just taking advantage of an innocent girl's helplessness. If these political parties are trying to build political capital out of this, then how will you ever get justice? You must be careful. Don't get drawn into all of this. Don't let yourself be used,' she urged.

Sheelu nodded.

Sampat then took her bag and gave her the pink sari. 'This is the uniform of our Pink Gang,' she said, handing the dress to her. 'With us, you will get justice for yourself and you will help other women get justice too. It will be good for you to help others, but it is your decision. You take your time and think about it. We are here when you are ready,' Sampat said.

AFTER SAMPAT LEFT, Sheelu gave a string of interviews. In them, she painted herself as a willing heir to Phoolan Devi, India's famed Bandit Queen turned parliamentarian who avenged her gang-rape by allegedly slaughtering twenty-two upper-caste men she considered complicit.

Sheelu had been sequestered in jail for a month, during which time she had been allowed only a few meetings and opportunities to speak to the press. On 17 December, during one of Sheelu's first televised interviews, she still looked vulnerable. Her eyes were wide and looked imploringly at the journalists gathered around her. When they asked her about what had happened, she looked left and right, as if searching for a way out, and then, after a moment of hesitation, she spoke. Her voice was shaky and broke frequently, like a pubescent boy's. 'What will you do if you don't get justice?' one of the television journalists asked her.

'I will get justice myself, by turning into a bandit. I will become a Phoolan Devi,' Sheelu said, her voice cracking. 'The culprits should be hanged. . . . I feel like doing it myself,' she added after a pause. Sheelu might have looked scared, but she was also angry, and that anger was reflected in her words. 'Let them kill me, but I won't be silenced anymore. . . . I am ready to fight them until justice is given to me. And I will get justice only when the guilty are punished.'

It is likely that the defiant tone and the reference to Phoolan Devi was not a signal that Sheelu was preparing to become an outlaw, but rather, like Devi, a parliamentarian. Despite Sheelu's nemesis being a politician, politics was her surest ticket out of Shahbajpur. It was clear that she could not go back to her old life. Her best hope of progressing in life was to accept what had happened to her and to use it, as far as it was possible, to her advantage. 'I'm famous now,' Sheelu mused in an interview. 'Everyone will look at me and think, That's the girl who brought the *vidhayak* to jail.' A new and dangerous world of politics was opening up to her. Her phone rang constantly, and it was often local party leaders who wanted to help her. They made her feel wanted and important. Suddenly, her life after jail was filled with possibility and the promise of advancement and success. 'Maybe I can be a legislator one day . . . or even an MP,' she would later say.

THE FOLLOWING DAY, a tidal wave of Samajwadi Party members poured into Shahbajpur. They were so numerous that they clogged the road through the hamlet; they might have even outnumbered the villagers. Two-dozen female party members led the sea of people, which was composed almost entirely of men.

When the women met Sheelu, they surrounded her, wrapping their arms around her. For most of the visit, two women flanked Sheelu, each with an arm draped on Sheelu's shoulder.

Cameramen from local television stations covered the event.

All of the female party members tried to speak to Sheelu at once, offering her advice, consolation, hugs, and pats on the head. 'There is no need to cry. Don't cry, dear. We all are with you. Don't cry,' said one, wiping Sheelu's tears. 'Don't worry, we are with you,' said another. 'Sheelu must rest,' offered one. 'Sheelu, tell us your problem,' said yet another, and so it continued for a while.

Sheelu looked forlorn and miserable. 'They have moved me from one jail to another jail,' she said, referring not only to the police protection but, perhaps, also to the media camped outside her house.

Sheelu was steered towards a bench, where the women of the party installed themselves around her. In the back stood Vishambhar Nishad, the legislator who had offered to find a house for her. The most senior of the female party members, who wore a white sari, large glasses and her silver hair in a braid, turned to the politician, reaching out her hand. He gestured to her to wait. After a few moments, she turned around again, and one of the politician's men reached into the inner pocket of his coat and withdrew three thick wads of cash, which he handed to her.

The woman grabbed the newspaper that Sheelu held in her hand and wrapped the money in it.

'This is three *lakhs* [one hundred thousand] of rupees from the Samajwadi Party for the betterment of your life,' she declared, holding the hastily wrapped package in front of Sheelu. The woman sitting to Sheelu's left, who held her arm protectively around the girl, reached down and held the newspaper too. More hands reached over, around, and across to hold the package as it was being presented to Sheelu – some of the women even tried to take it so that they could give it to her themselves.

The villagers, the police, and all of the party members tightened the circle around this spectacle, craning their necks, jostling and pushing, as they tried to get a better look.

A large red sports bag was then produced from the same party man who had retrieved the wads of cash from his coat. It was passed overhead until it reached Sheelu. The bag lay at her feet, unopened.

'She must get minimum of fifty *lakhs*, a house, education and protection,' said the silver-haired woman who had handed Sheelu the money. 'We want the government to fulfil this, and if they don't do this, then the Samajwadi Party will strike for her. And she has to get a house either on rent and then later buy one, and the rent has to be given by the government or Mayawati or the *vidhayak*. If she doesn't get all this, then the Samajwadi Party will strike on the roads for her.' The woman from the Samajwadi Party then used the opportunity to take a swing at her political opponent. 'Mayawati must resign, because raping a minor is a shame on the government of UP [Uttar Pradesh]. Mayawati is a woman – what was she doing for fifteen days?' she asked, referring to the time that had elapsed from when Sheelu's rape allegations were made public to when her release was ordered. 'The government has to answer for this. What kind of society is this?' she continued.

After all of the gifts had been handed over and the speeches made, there was a final wave of fussy displays of affection and friendship – more hugs, more squeezing of arms, more patting of cheeks – and then the women, now smiling and self-content, led the horde of Samajwadi Party men out of the village.

In the absence left by the visitors, the cameramen from local television stations hung around to capture the village scene, now dominated by the police who had been ordered to protect Sheelu. At least eight police jeeps were parked in front of the school at Shahbajpur, and every corner of the village seemed to contain uniformed officers carrying *laathis* and some rifles, some wearing camouflage helmets and protective vests – as if prepared for a riot. They milled about aimlessly, this way and that, as the bewildered villagers shepherded their large buffaloes through the busy thoroughfare.

IT WAS ON 7 FEBRUARY that Sheelu met the most handsome man she had ever seen in her life. She was sitting in her house when her father came to tell her that Rahul Gandhi, son of Sonia Gandhi and heir to the Gandhi family dynasty, had arrived to meet her. She had heard the name before, but she could not bring a picture of him to mind. 'If my family were Congress supporters, then I would have known what he looks like,' she says. The Congress Party had very few supporters in Shahbajpur, let alone Uttar Pradesh. That was why Rahul Gandhi was there. More than any other member of his party, Mr Gandhi had made it his personal mission to win back Uttar Pradesh, and pundits looked at the upcoming election, which would take place in fifteen months, as an indicator of whether Mr Gandhi was prime-minister material. Such was his investment in the Uttar Pradesh elections that, as the Indian newspaper *Mint* put it, Mr Gandhi had 'staked his political future on reviving his party's fortunes in the populous northern state'.

Sheelu emerged from her house and set eyes on the tall man with creamy white skin, forest-green eyes and dimples when he smiled. The man had arrived in a convoy of large white jeeps that unsettled the dust on the only road in the hamlet of Shahbajpur, leaving ochre clouds in its wake. The man was gleaming in his starched white *kurta pajamas*.

He walked up to her and, taking her hand, asked, 'Are you Sheelu? I'm Rahul, from Delhi.' Sheelu swooned at the gentle nature and refined manners of the half-Italian. 'His hand is so soft, like dough when it is in water,' she later said. There was no big crowd that day, and no media – the entire area had been cordoned off, and access was restricted while the VIP visitor from the capital was in Shahbajpur. 'Don't worry, we'll help you,' Rahul said.

Sheelu, who had taken a seat beside her handsome guest on a *charpoy* underneath a tree opposite her house, worried that she was being rude for not inviting him inside. No one had trained her in the etiquette surrounding visiting dignitaries of his stature.

'Come to my house,' she offered.

Rahul looked at his personal assistant, who checked their schedule and told him, in English, that they had no time. Sheelu was disappointed.

'Please, what will people say if I don't give you something to eat?' she insisted.

'Next time I'll eat with you,' he promised.

'Okay then . . . ,' she said, 'Wait one minute.' She leapt up and rushed inside. When she emerged a few moments later, she was holding a steel tumbler and a metal canister containing milk. She poured a glass for him.

'At least have this!' she said, giving it to him.

Rahul accepted it graciously, and after he drank it all, Sheelu poured him another glass, which he downed.

'When I'm older, I want to join the Congress Party. They've supported me the most,' Sheelu told Rahul, referring to the two-hundred-thousand-rupee cheque given to her days earlier by Vivek Singh, the local Congress Party *vidhayak*. 'I'm a Dalit girl. Mayawati should have helped me!

She's running the state. She could have started an investigation straight away!' she complained.

'Here is my number,' Rahul said. 'Call me if you ever need help.'

EIGHT MONTHS AFTER Sheelu's release, Sampat got an offer that came right from the very top of the Indian National Congress party. Rahul Gandhi himself asked Sampat whether she would run for a seat in the Legislative Assembly next year as the Congress candidate.

Sampat had met Mr Gandhi for the first time in May 2011, when he accompanied Prime Minister Manmohan Singh on a visit to Bundelkhand to promote their development projects. By then, Sampat had already met Sonia Gandhi on three separate occasions, but she had never met her son. During Mr Gandhi's visit to Bundelkhand, Sampat was part of a brief meet-and-greet event with other social workers and active members of civil society, and the two did not get to speak much. The next day, however, Mr Gandhi's assistant contacted Sampat, saying that Mr Gandhi would like to meet her in New Delhi.

As with her meetings with Sonia Gandhi, Mr Gandhi's assistants were in touch with Sampat about travel arrangements for her and Babuji. Sampat was excited to meet the son of her biggest political idol and wore her best clothes to the rendezvous.

She arrived at the meeting carrying a photo album of her Pink Gang rallies, protests and festivals. Mr Gandhi leafed through the pages of the album with interest, asking her questions about her education and how the Pink Gang had been formed.

'Rahul-ji, you don't have time for me to explain the whole formation of Pink Gang. You will listen a little bit and will go away,' she told him cheekily. He laughed at her boldness and insisted that he would like to listen. 'He said he was aware of what I was doing and that it was nice.'

'You are a strong woman,' he said finally. 'We want you to run for elections.'

Sampat had prepared for this moment, but, having been so close before, she didn't want to get her hopes up. There were many emotions running through her. Apart from excitement, she also felt fear. 'I don't want to get into all this. I don't want to be their slave,' she had thought during the train ride to Delhi.

Sampat had never taken orders from anyone before, not her husband or her parents. Not even from the police if she felt they were wrong. She worried about being pressured and compromised by the world of politics. Babuji often spoke of politics as a world populated only by corrupt, selfish actors. Sampat agreed, but instead of steering clear of the murkiness of elected office, she felt all the more compelled to enter the race. 'Coming to politics is not bad,' she reasons. 'If a social worker like me gets into politics, it would be a direct advantage for people. It is very important for good people to enter into politics. Unless good people get into politics, they will distribute spoils among themselves and sell off the country,' she later says.

She thought about how it had taken her a long time to get to where she was today, and about all she had achieved in her life: leaving her mother-in-law's house; then escaping Gadarian Purva and starting a new life in Badausa; and founding an organisation known throughout the country for fighting injustice – all without any education. The Pink Gang had accomplished much too. It had helped women to participate in public life, made them confident about themselves, and taught them that they, too, could have power and a voice, even in Bundelkhand.

The gang has its weakness as well, she thought. 'The Pink Gang is very good, but we don't have the law with us. The Pink Gang is certainly big, but we only fight with sticks. If I had become a legislator, after contesting the elections honestly, then do you know how much good it would be for the girls of the Pink Gang?' she asks.

She played different scenarios in her mind. 'If Sonia Gandhi has called me, then I should do good work. If she asks me to do something wrong, then I won't be able to do it. I will only do the right thing. That greed is not inside me that I should listen to her even if she does something wrong. If they do anything wrong, then we won't listen to them. They might as well throw me out of the party, I don't care,' she thought with resolve. Taking her train of thought one station further, she maintained, 'Even if they remove me from the party, I will not join another party. I will do my own work. I don't want to do that kind of politics that will ruin my character.'

Sampat knew that, like the other political parties, the Congress Party also had its fair share of corrupt politicians. How would she feel to have those people as her colleagues? Wouldn't she have to tolerate their unlawful behaviour? 'If anybody is doing a wrong thing in Congress, I won't let them get away with it. I will scold them and ask, Why are you doing this? Right now, I consider only Rahul Gandhi and Sonia Gandhi my leaders. I don't consider the other traitors in the party. I oppose them. I will tell Rahul-ji that they are destroying his party.'

Sampat had faith in her own integrity; she thought her virtues would be able to safeguard her from falling into the same traps that everyone else had. 'As long as you are bound by greed, you won't be able to do anything for people. There is no greed in me,' she thought confidently.

Sampat considered all of the temptations she had faced in her life, all of the people who had tried to corrupt her along the way – the *vidhayak* being one of many to have tried and failed. 'I get many offers to do wrong things. But I am not wrong – that is why not everyone becomes a Sampat Pal. It is very difficult to become Sampat Pal.' Temptations exist for a vigilante leader as much as for a politician.

'If I become corrupted, it is in my hand, not their hand. It is my soul that has made me honest. And if my soul says that I should remain honest, then I will be. I will do what my will says.

'My master is my soul.'

EPILOGUE

THE YEAR FOLLOWING SHEELU'S RELEASE WAS AN EVENTFUL ONE. On 20 January 2011, the CB-CID filed a charge sheet against Dwivedi. He and four suspected accomplices, Suresh Neta, Rajen Shukla, Ram Naresh (alias Rawan), and Virendra Garg, were charged with rape, causing hurt, wrongful confinement and criminal intimidation.

Later in the year, in September, the Supreme Court of India ordered that the investigation into Sheelu's allegations against Dwivedi be moved from the hands of the state-level Criminal Investigation Department to the national Central Bureau of Investigation after Sheelu's lawyers claimed an impartial investigation would not be possible in Uttar Pradesh. The investigation is ongoing, and Dwivedi remains, at the time of writing, incarcerated in Banda. He continues to deny all charges.

FOR THE FIRST YEAR after Sheelu's release, the seventeen-year-old minor continued to live in Shahbajpur with her father and her six security guards, provided by the state for her protection while the case against Dwivedi was still ongoing. Santoo went back to being a migrant labourer, working in factories and at construction sites in Delhi, Mumbai and Surat.

In February 2012, more than twelve months after her release, Sheelu, after turning eighteen, accepted an offer from a local *pradhan* from the Nishad community to let her and Santoo live for free in his second house in Banda. Sheelu and Santoo shared the house with numerous other tenants, who lived in the other rooms.

The two siblings hoped to start a new life together there, away from their father and his drinking habits. They had never lived in a house like this before. They each had their own room with a bed, a built-in cupboard and electricity. The two-storey house also had a bathroom with a ceramic toilet, a sink, and running water – a far cry from the outdoor water hand-pump in Shahbajpur.

Sheelu's security guards, who were assigned to stay by her side twenty-four hours a day, also moved into the house. Within a month, however, there were problems with the arrangement. The wife of the *pradhan* had grown tired of having messy security guards in the house who spit jets of red-coloured saliva onto the walls while chewing tobacco *paan* and whose presence was rapidly speeding up the general wear-and-tear of the property.

In March, Sheelu and Santoo were asked to leave, just a month after they settled in. 'Where will I go now? How can I go back to Shahbajpur?' wondered Sheelu. She must have thought she had got rid of her father and country life once and for all when she left for Banda. 'Maybe I should eat poison and die? These worries are eating my head,' she said at the time.

The next month, Sheelu did attempt suicide by consuming hair dye. She was rushed to the hospital, where her stomach was pumped. The media, once again, leaped to cover the event, and Sheelu was once more in the limelight. There were fewer journalists than when she was released from jail, though, and they stayed for less time. Soon everything returned to how it was before.

After she recovered, Sheelu moved back to Shahbajpur. By then, the simple brick house her father had been constructing with the money given to her by the political parties was complete. Her father and siblings live in that house, which sits opposite the school where she was allowed to study for those few, short years in her childhood.

Sheelu lives on her own in the old mud hut where she grew up, on the other side of the hamlet. She spends most of her days sitting in the dark interiors of the hovel, making calls to new friends, often journalists and political people she has met over the past year. The mobile phone provides for all of her entertainment, for on it she also listens to devotional Hindi songs or watches televised dramatisations of the Hindu holy book Ramayana.

Despite the new house being only a short walk from her hut, she rarely goes there and almost never speaks to her father. When she does, it usually ends in an argument. 'If it wouldn't have been for him, none of this would have happened to me,' she says caustically.

THE SAME MONTH that Sheelu attempted suicide, Sampat contested elections in Manikpur, east of Chitrakoot, for the Legislative Assembly in Uttar Pradesh. The Congress Party had not given her an easy constituency to run in; it had been over twenty years since the party had won a victory there. Manikpur is plagued with bandits who control the lucrative tendu tree crops, from which popular cigarettes, called *bee-dis*, are made. It is an area known for both 'shoot-outs' and 'communal riots' fuelled by politicians, wrote one journalist in India's *Frontline* magazine.

The months of campaigning had been gruelling. Geeta, being the district commander nearest to Manikpur, mobilised her local Pink Gang members to canvass for Sampat and to accompany her on the countless visits she made to the small villages in the constituency. Geeta and her women did so willingly. 'If *didi* wins, it will be good for all of us,' Geeta said.

Not everyone in the gang was as enthusiastic, however. Sampat frequently fought with Babuji, who had been sceptical of her entry into politics since the beginning. He was also displeased by the involvement of Sampat's family, who sometimes accompanied her during election rallies. Among them was Tirath, who had been released on bail and now seemed to be out for good. 'Where were they before? They never supported us. So why are they coming forward now?' Babuji complains.

The campaign brought other old rivalries, long simmering, to the fore. Suman Singh, the district commander of Mahoba, accused Sampat of not doing enough to promote other senior gang members. Suman had asked Sampat to lobby the Congress Party to add her name to the ticket, and when the party did not come through, she blamed Sampat behind her back. 'No other woman asked for a ticket this time. Why did Suman? Because she has this greed within her,' Sampat says.

On the day the votes were counted, Sampat learned she had lost to a candidate from the BSP, Dwivedi's party. Sampat had come in fourth out of twenty-two candidates and had received 23,003 votes, more than any other Congress candidate in recent history.

Sampat cried that night on her terrace, as she sat under the starlight, surrounded by those who had spent the last few months canvassing with her. 'A good person will never win here,' she lamented, shaking her head. Much of Uttar Pradesh was gloomy when the election results were announced. Mayawati's party had taken a bad beating and was to be replaced by the Samajwadi Party, notorious for its links to bandits and gangsters.

The next day, *Headlines Today*, a popular Indian television show, asked the question that was on everyone's mind. 'The Return of Goonda Raj in Uttar Pradesh?' was the title of its news segment on the election results. Countless newspapers across the country ran similarly titled stories.

Disturbing things started happening from the first day that the Samajwadi Party came to power in Uttar Pradesh. Gun-toting supporters of the party staged large victory processions, blocking roads and causing locals, fearing violence, to stay in their homes. One seven-year-old was reportedly killed by a stray bullet when Samajwadi Party supporters fired celebratory shots into the air after their victory. Several men associated with the Goonda Raj flourished under the new rule. A man called Vijay Mishra, who had been jailed for a bomb attack on a political rival, became a legislator. Even more worrying was that Raghuraj Pratap Singh, also known as Raja Bhaiyya – a politician who had spent time in jail during the BSP rule – became the jail minister. Soon after assuming office he started to improve facilities for imprisoned politicians, which included providing them with telephones.

People braced themselves for new heights of lawlessness in a state already plagued by corrupt police and politicians. Perhaps that was one reason why some supporters of the Pink Gang, like Babuji, felt a slight relief that Sampat had not won. This way, she would be able to dedicate herself fully to policing Bundelkhand and holding elected officials accountable.

There is no doubt that a strong Pink Gang is needed now more than ever. The challenge criminal politicians pose is a national problem. Fuelled by the vast fortunes that can be made from the economic liberalisation of the 1990s, politicians are becoming more rapacious in their exploits.

This may be the main reason why life in India is steadily worsening for women, who suffer the most when the police and judiciary systems are corrupted. Rape is now the fastest-growing crime in the country. In the past four decades, the number of reported rapes has shot up by 792 per cent. Conviction rates, however, are dropping. A similar story is found in domestic violence, which has climbed by 30 per cent in the same time period. Across the board, crimes against women have been increasing.

The scale of the problem, which seems insurmountable, has made Sampat even more bent on social justice. She thinks she knows how it can be achieved. Drawing on the wisdom she learned when taking on powerful landlords as a mere child, she says, 'If the problem is big, we must become even bigger than it. In unity there is a lot of power, that is why politicians fear us,' she says.

Now, however, she is not hoping to simply reform wayward politicians. She wants to *replace* them.

'I will run again and next time, I will not lose. You'll see.'

NOTES

PROLOGUE: NOTHING CAN GO WRONG

1   At dawn on an otherwise quiet morning: Author's interview
    with Santoo Nishad in Banda, March 2012.

1   feared liquor don: It has been reported that Dwivedi has links to
    the liquor business: "When the World Came to Banda," *Indian
    Express*, January 23, 2011, http://www.indianexpress.com/news/
    when-the-world-came-to-banda/741030. Accessed January 31,
    2012. Dwivedi's reputation as a feared liquor don has been men-
    tioned in author's interviews with Lakhan Upadhyay in Atarra,
    March 2012, and Deepak Singh in Chitrakoot, March 2012.

2   'Wake up, bastard!': This and all other dialogue in the prologue is
    reconstructed based on the author's interviews with Achchhe Lal
    Nishad in Shahbajpur, May 2012, and Santoo Nishad in Banda,
    March 2012.

4   'I was not able to talk to the girl': Achchhe Lal Nishad's statement
    in a press conference held on December 12, 2010, in Banda. A
    video recording of Achchhe's statement was obtained from the
    Sahara Samay TV bureau in Banda.

4   Achchhe considered joining the bandits: Achchhe Lal Nishad
    was quoted saying, 'If the police does not provide justice for the
    atrocities committed on my daughter I will take up arms and go
    the ravines.' "Someone Get Me a Gun: I Want to Finish Off My
    Enemies," *Sri India*, December 17, 2010.

CHAPTER ONE: A ROSE IN THE BADLANDS

5   'EVEN GOD CAN'T CONTROL CRIME IN UTTAR PRADESH': Pankaj
    Shah, "Even God Can't Control Crime in Uttar Pradesh: Min-

ister," *Times of India*, March 9, 2012, http://articles.timesofindia
.indiatimes.com/2012-05-09/lucknow/31641061_1_sp-mla-sp-
regime-sp-members. Accessed January 31, 2013.

6   'She's stolen from the *vidhayak*'s house': Author's interview with
Geeta Singh in Chitrakoot, December 2011.

6   'None of this is true!': This and all other monologues in this scene
are reconstructed based on the author's interview with Sampat
Pal in Badausa, December 2011. Descriptions of Sampat's actions
in this scene are based on the author's interview with Sampat Pal
and observations (of her morning routine, bathing habits, etc.)
that the author made when living at the home of Sampat Pal in
August and December 2011.

7   Nineteen per cent had serious charges pending: Association for
Democratic Reforms (ADR), National Election Watch, *Analysis
of MLAs of Uttar Pradesh, Punjab, Uttarakhand, Goa and Mani-
pur (2007–2012)* (New Delhi: ADR, 2012), http://adrindia.org/
research-and-reports/combined-report/2012/analysis-mlas-
uttar-pradesh-punjab-uttarakhand-goa-and-manipur-2007-2012.
Accessed January 31, 2013.

9   entire villages are indebted to loan sharks: Author's interview
with Raja Bhaiyya, who works in Atarra for an NGO called
Vidya Dham Samiti, in Atarra, March 2012.

9   'See this road?': Author's interview with Lakhan Upadhyay in
Atarra, December 2011.

9   'This is a road, what?': Author's interview with Sampat Pal in
Badausa, July 2011.

9   'Yes, Sampat-ji': Author's interview with Sampat Pal in Badausa,
July 2011. This incident was described briefly in Anuj Chopra,
"Pink-Clad Women Fight for Justice in an Indian Village,"
National, January 19, 2009, http://www.thenational.ae/news/
world/south-asia/pink-clad-women-fight-for-justice-in-an-in-
dian-village. Accessed January 31, 2013.

9   twenty thousand members: Emine Saner, "Sampat Pal Devi,"
Guardian, March 8, 2011, http://www.guardian.co.uk/world/
2011/mar/08/sampat-pal-devi-100-women. Accessed January
31, 2013. Namita Kholi, "The Power of Pink," *Hindustan Times*,
January 19, 2008. Both articles provide this figure, as does Sampat Pal. However, it is hard to confirm how many Pink Gang
members there are because membership records are poorly
maintained by the gang. Twenty thousand would mean there are
an average of 1,500 members per district. District-level protests,

despite sometimes lasting days and being self-funded, can attract several hundred women. Turnout at any given time is assumed to be a fraction of the membership numbers, given the limited funds for transporting the women to the protests. More importantly, the precarious work situation of members, many of whom are daily-wage labourers, means that every day spent at a protest is a day less of pay. It is therefore assumed that only a minority is able to make this sacrifice regularly.

9   double the size of the Irish army: There are approximately 8,500 soldiers in the Irish Army, according to the Defence Forces Ireland website, www.military.ie/info-centre. Accessed November 6, 2012.

9   eight times larger than the estimated number of al-Qaeda operatives: There are between 2,500 and 3,000 al-Qaeda fighters in Afghanistan according to Ahmed Rashid, *Taliban: The Story of the Afghan Warlords* (London: Pan Books, 2001).

10   '*from zeero to heero*': Author's interview with Dr Khanna in Atarra, December 2011.

12   among the most 'backward' places: Rahul Gandhi is quoted as saying Bundelkhand is 'among India's most backward regions' at a rally. "PM, Rahul Attack Maya over 'Backward' Bundelkhand," *Rediff.com*, April 30, 2011, http://www.rediff.com/news/report/maya-govt-doing-nothing-for-bundelkhand-pm-rahul/20110430.htm. Accessed January 31, 2013.

12   'lawless': Sonia Gandhi was quoted saying, 'The state has become "*andher nagri*" (dark city), where there is no law and order. There is anarchy and lawlessness in UP.' "There Is Anarchy & Lawlessness in UP: Sonia," *Outlook*, May 19, 2011, http://news.outlookindia.com/items.aspx?artid=722470. Accessed January 31, 2013.

15   'I don't even trust my own brother!': Author's interview with Babuji in Chitrakoot, March 2012.

16   'He is the first to disappear': Author's interview with Lakhan Upadhyay in Atarra, March 2012.

17   'All have left': Author's interview with Kodia Dai in Uraiya Purva, July 2011.

17   initial government commission fee of two thousand rupees: Voluntary Operation in Community and Environment (VOICE), *A Report on the Success and Failure of SHG's in India – Impediments and Paradigm of Success*, Report submitted to Planning Commission, Government of India (New Delhi: VOICE, 2008), p. 13, http://

planningcommission.nic.in/reports/sereport/ser/ser_shg3006
.pdf. Accessed January 31, 2013.

19   'Just *who* are you?': Author's interview with Sampat Pal in Badausa, July 2011.

22   'Hope is a very big thing': Author's interview with Lungi Dai in Uraiya Purva, July 2011.

22   'A lot of women were joining': Author's interview with Kodia Dai in Uraiya Purva, July 2011.

24   'big fan': Author's interview with Lakhan Upadhyay in Atarra, March 2012.

24   'Who will believe such a thing will happen here?': Author's interview with Lakhan Upadhyay in Atarra, March 2012.

24   'Tsk! Brother, I already know about it!': Author's interview with Lakhan Upadhyay in Atarra, March 2012.

26   'HUNDREDS OF THOUSANDS OF RUPEES': Amit Tripathi, "Hundreds of Thousands of Rupees Have Been Stolen from a People's Representative's House – It Is Said That a Girl Living in the House Committed the Theft," *Hindustan*, December 14, 2012.

26   'wash cooking utensils': Ibid.

CHAPTER TWO: BANDITS ON BALLOTS

35   Uttar Pradesh police force is the largest: Uttar Pradesh Police website, http://uppolice.up.nic.in/. Accessed November 7, 2012.

35   'There is not a single lawless group': Supreme Court of India, *The State of Uttar Pradesh vs Mohammad Naim*, March 15, 1963, judic .nic.in/supremecourt/helddis.aspx. Accessed January 22, 2013.

35   'It has become obvious': Human Rights Watch, *Broken System: Dysfunction, Abuse, and Impunity in the Indian Police* (New York: Human Rights Watch, 2009), p. 37, http://www.hrw.org/reports/2009/08/04/broken-system-0. Accessed January 31, 2013.

36   'reasonable suspicion': Chapter 5 of the Code of Criminal Procedure, 1973, Section 41. Law Commission of India website, http://lawcommissionofindia.nic.in/reports/177rptp2.pdf. Accessed January 31, 2013.

36   There are virtually no remedies available: Law Commission of India, *One Hundred and Seventy Seventh Report on Law Relating to Arrest*, D.O. No. 6(3)(63)/99-L.C.(LS), December 14, 2001, p. 32, http://lawcommissionofindia.nic.in/reports/177rptp1.pdf. Accessed November 7, 2012.

36   It is a system in which police: Human Rights Watch, *Broken System: Dysfunction, Abuse, and Impunity in the Indian Police* (New York: Human Rights Watch, 2009), p. 58, http://www.hrw.org/reports/2009/08/04/broken-system-0. Accessed January 31, 2013.

37   'I go to the police station to meet him': Author's interview with Sampat Pal in New Delhi, June 2012.

37   In India, the majority of complaints: Ibid., p. 42.

37   One of the stories that recently: "Woman Gang-Raped in UP Police Station," *Times of India*, July 23, 2012, http://articles.timesofindia.indiatimes.com/2012-07-23/lucknow/32803426_1_police-station-woman-gang. Accessed January 31, 2013.

37   'Why are you keeping her husband?': This entire dialogue with Zameer Ul Hassan is based on author's interviews with Sampat Pal. Hassan has since been transferred to another station.

39   'For truth and justice our blood will always flown – The Pink Gang': We know this thanks to footage from Sahara Samay TV dated August 3, 2006. All descriptions and dialogues related to this event that are recounted in this book are based on this same footage and audio transcripts thereof, unless otherwise indicated.

45   'The Pink Gang has tied up the subinspector': Author's interview with Lakhan Upadhyay in Atarra, December 2011.

45   'I saw Sampat slap him': Ibid.

45   'He was saying, "Please, please! Stop!"': Ibid.

45   'Even the general public were shouting': Criminal Case no. 147/06 filed at Atarra Police Station on August 3, 2006, at 4:45 p.m. by Zamir Ul Hassan. This First Information Report (FIR) was obtained from Bhola Dwivedi, a Pink Gang lawyer based in Atarra.

45   case was registered against Sampat: Ibid.

46   Often fatal road accidents lead to: See, for example, "Mob Attacks Police after 3 Killed in Accident in UP, 5 Injured," *India Today*, June 4, 2012, http://indiatoday.intoday.in/story/mob-turns-violent-in-uttar-pradesh/1/199060.html. Accessed November 8, 2012.

46   On several occasions, disgruntled, overworked employees: In 2009 employees in the city of Coimbatore killed a human resources executive at Pricol, a car instruments manufacturer. Peter Wonacott, "Deadly Labor Wars Hinder India's Rise," *Wall Street Journal*, November 24, 2009, http://online.wsj.com/article/SB125858061728954325.html. Accessed January 31, 2013.

46   burned to death: In 2011, a steel-factory executive at Powmex Steels burned to death near Titilagarh, near Bhubaneshwar. "Four Held for Burning to Death Orissa Steel Plant Executive," *DNA*, March 4, 2011, http://www.dnaindia.com/india/report_4-held-for-burning-to-death-orissa-steel-plant-executive_1515330. Accessed January 31, 2013. More recently, in 2012, a human resources manager at a Maruti Suzuki plant burned to death in Manesar. Henry Foy and Anurag Kotoky, "Insight: Deadly India Car Factory Riot Sounds Alarm Bells for Industry," *Reuters*, August 6, 2012, http://in.reuters.com/article/2012/08/05/us-maruti-unrest-idUSBRE8740QM20120805. Accessed January 31, 2013.

46   beat the serial rapist and murderer Akku Yadav: Description of this event is based on an excellent article: Raekha Prasad, "Arrest Us All," *Guardian*, September 16, 2005, http://www.guardian.co.uk/world/2005/sep/16/india.gender. Accessed January 31, 2013.

47   'pivotal role in uplifting the status of women': "'Gulabi' Gang Shows Solidarity against Malpractices," *Hindustan Times*, August 11, 2006.

49   Yadav was a middle-aged, clean-shaven man: Physical description of Yadav is based on a stock photo obtained from the Sahara Samay TV bureau in Banda.

50   'What's this story': This and all other dialogues between Yadav and Sampat in this chapter are based on author's interviews with Sampat Pal.

51   data compiled by Bloomberg News: Mehul Srivastava and Andrew MacAskill, "Poor in India Starve as Politicians Steal $14.5 Billion of Food," *Bloomberg.com*, August 29, 2012, http://www.bloomberg.com/news/2012-08-28/poor-in-india-starve-as-politicians-steal-14-5-billion-of-food.html. Accessed November 8, 2012.

51   India runs the largest rationed food distribution system: Ibid.

52   greying officer, with a moustache: Physical description of Shukla is based on a stock photo obtained from the Sahara Samay TV bureau in Banda.

52   'I am busy – come another time': This dialogue with Shukla is based on the author's interviews with Sampat Pal.

53   'the average tenure of an SP': Revati Laul and Brijesh Pandey, "Maya Needs to Walk About," *Tehelka*, July 9, 2011, tehelka.com/maya-needs-to-walk-about/. Accessed January 22, 2013.

54 fire shots into the air: See, for example, "Child Killed in Samajwadi Party Victory Celebration," *India Today*, March 6, 2012, http://indiatoday.intoday.in/story/child-killed-in-samajwadi-party-victory-celebration/1/176714.html. Accessed January 31, 2013.

55 'As long as you work hard': "India Minister Shivpal Yadav: 'You Can Steal a Little,'" *BBC*, August 10, 2012, http://www.bbc.co.uk/news/world-asia-india-19204967. Accessed January 31, 2013. Though this comment was not made during the years of the Goonda Raj, it still reflects well the attitude of the Samajwadi Party.

55 One legislator, jailed for murdering his lover: "Jailed SP Leader Amarmani Tripathi Spends Leisurely Day at BRD Medical College," *India Today*, June 21, 2012, http://indiatoday.intoday.in/story/jailed-sp-leader-amarmani-tripathi-breaks-prison-rules/1/201733.html. Accessed January 31, 2013.

55 'Prison is where': "Prison Is Where UP Politicians Go for a Holiday," *Sunday Guardian*, June 24, 2012, www.sunday-guardian.com/news/prison-is-where-up-politicians-go-for-a-holiday. Accessed January 31, 2013.

57 147 criminal charges against him: "Notorious Dacoit Thokia Gunned Down," *Indian Express*, August 5, 2008, www.indianexpress.com/new/notorious-dacoit-thokia-gunned-down/344749. Accessed January 31, 2013.

57 'If you want to live in peace': Author's interview with Babuji in Atarra, December 2011.

61 One *pradhan* from Naugawan: Some in this village were supporters of Thokia. 'Thokia extracts tax from the government contractors, but doesn't disturb us. When we approach him, he is ready to help us,' Raju Prasad Verma, a resident, told the *Indian Express*. Darshan Desai, "Banda Villagers May Bank on Dacoit Rather Than a Neta," *Indian Express*, April 27, 2007, http://www.indianexpress.com/news/banda-villagers-may-bank-on-dacoit-rather-than-a-neta/29440/0. Accessed January 31, 2013.

CHAPTER THREE: THE RED ROOM

66 'You'll get hurt': Author's interview with Sheelu Nishad in Shahbajpur, July 2011.

66 She frequently argued with her father: "The Young Girl Who

Ran Away with the Legislator's Rifle Has Been Caught," *Hindustan*, December 15, 2010.

66   Sheelu had been absent: Achchhe Lal Nishad's statement in a press conference held on December 27, 2010, in Banda. A video recording of Achchhe's statement was obtained from the Sahara Samay TV bureau in Banda.

67   aunt Sheelu was staying with in Lacchapurva: "Now the Game Is Changing by Putting Rajju in the Front," *Hindustan*, December 30, 2010: 'Sheelu's father Achchhe Lal and her brother Santoo have accused Sheelu's aunt of selling her to Rajju Patel for 50,000 rupees.' The article falsely names Sheelu's aunt's village as Harnampur, when it is actually Lacchapurva.

67   who was feuding with Achchhe: Author's interview with Achchhe Lal Nishad in Shahbajpur, July 2011.

67   thought to have links to bandits: Sampat Pal claims that she saw Rajju Patel working for Thokia Patel during the 2007 elections, in which Sampat ran against Thokia's mother. Achchhe Lal Nishad too has accused him of being a criminal.

67   Sheelu had fallen in love with Rajju: "Why Were the Banda Police Hiding Sheelu?" *Hindustan*, December 16, 2010.

67   large proportion of kidnapping complaints: In an excellent article on the subject, Prem Chowdhry finds that 'in runaway cases, the registration of kidnapping charges is a must and many a time even advised by the police'. Chowdhry, "Private Lives, State Intervention: Cases of Runaway Marriage in Rural North India," *Modern Asian Studies*, vol. 38, no. 1, February 2004, pp. 55–84.

67   state government of Uttar Pradesh reportedly pressured: "Seasonal Elopement of Girls from East UP Baffles Cops," *Times of India*, July 26, 2012, http://articles.timesofindia.indiatimes.com/2012-07-26/varanasi/32868688_1_elopement-maximum-cases-case-studies. Accessed January 31, 2013.

69   'Don't go to the police': This and the entire dialogue that follows are based on the author's interviews with Achchhe Lal Nishad.

71   front door opens into a narrow entranceway: Description is based on how Sampat's family home looked in 2010. It has since been expanded.

72   four of her five children: Munna's legal name is Kamta Prasad, Prabha's full first name is Prabhawatti, and Champa's is Champawatti.

79   'This shameless girl won't listen!': This and all other dialogues in this chapter between Sampat and her mother-in-law are based on

the author's interview with Sampat Pal in Chitrakoot, December 2011.

79   'This one needs a slap to listen': Ibid.

82   'What do you know?': This and all other dialogues between Ram Milan and Sampat in this anecdote are based on author's interview with Sampat Pal in Badausa, March 2012.

84   at the thatched ceiling: Description of the ceiling is based on author's visit to Sampat's former home.

85   'Think you're better than me, do you?': Author's interview with Sampat Pal in Badausa, March 2011.

85   'Who did this?': Ibid.

85   'Your woman is very clever': Ibid.

86   'He will come and shout at me': Ibid.

89   Sampat's lament about injustice: Author's interview with Gulab in Rauli, July 2011.

90   'Find another husband': Author's interview with Sampat Pal in New Delhi, June 2012.

90   'Who are you?': Ibid.

92   large jeep arrived carrying Dwivedi's men: "Now the Game Is Changing by Putting Rajju in the Front," *Hindustan*, December 30, 2010.

92   'Sheelu's father said Sheelu was being kept forcefully': Author's interview with Nattu Lal Pal in Pathara, May 2012.

93   'They gave him several blows, kicks and slaps': Ibid.

93   'kicked him, punched him and tied him up': Author's interview with Sunaria Patel in Pathara, May 2012.

93   small outhouse belonging to Rajju's uncle: Author's interview with Nattu Lal Pal in Pathara, May 2012. The uncle is Beletu.

94   'What are you saying, Achchhe Lal?': This whole exchange is based on author's interview with Achchhe Lal Nishad in Shahbajpur, May 2012.

94   'You're my man, my disciple': Newspapers reported that the relationship between the two men was that of 'guru and disciple' based on their interviews with Achchhe Lal Nishad. Achchhe Lal Nishad repeated this in author's interviews with him in Shahbajpur, May 2012. "Sheelu's Father Achchhe Lal Becomes a Rebel," *Hindustan*, December 28, 2012.

95   'What place could you take': Author's interview with Achchhe Lal Nishad in Shahbajpur, May 2012.

98   'burned herself and died': Author's interview with Sheelu Nishad in Banda, March 2012.

99   she alleges that the politician: This exchange between Sheelu Nishad and Purushottam Naresh Dwivedi is based on author's interview with Sheelu Nishad in Banda, March 2012.

100   'Don't you agree to it': Author's interview with Sheelu Nishad in Banda, March 2012.

101   'And when you do': Ibid.

CHAPTER FOUR: LOVE IN BUNDELKHAND

102   14 December at 8:16 p.m.: "Why Were the Banda Police Hiding Sheelu?" *Hindustan*, December 16, 2012.

102   'dacoits murderers and cattle-thiefs': Edwin T. Atkinson, *Descriptive and Historical Account of the North-Western Provinces of India* (Bundelkhand: North-Western Provinces Government Press, 1874), vol. 1, p. 107.

102   around three in the morning: According to the bail application Achchhe Lal Nishad made for his daughter at the Ld. Judicial Magistrate, Atarra (Banda), in January 2011 (actual day is missing on original bail application). C. Cri. No.-379/10.

103   'He wanted to rape me again': Author's interview with Sheelu Nishad in Banda, March 2012.

103   Dwivedi's men sexually harassed: "Chargesheet against MLA, Three Aides," *Indian Express*, January 21, 2011. www.indianexpress.com/chargesheet-against-mla-three-aides/740330/0. Accessed February 8, 2013.

103   'Those people were drunk': Transcript of a press conference given by Santoo Nishad in which he reads out a written statement on behalf of his sister, recorded by Sahara Samay TV, January 3, 2011.

103   'What is the reason why Sheelu': "Why Were the Banda Police Hiding Sheelu?" *Hindustan*, December 16, 2010.

109   'Your mother-in-law is here': Author's interview with Tirath Pal in Badausa, March 2012.

110   'She'll come soon': Ibid.

111   long outdoor shed with a corrugated tin roof: Description of visiting area is based on author's interview with Tirath Pal in Badausa, March 2012.

113   'Sit down!': Author's interview with Tirath Pal in Badausa, March 2012.

113   'Stay on your side!': Ibid.

113   'Sampat-ji, if you want to meet Sheelu': Ibid.

118   it is sometimes rumoured: Author's interview with Lakhan Upadhyay in Chitrakoot, March 2012.

120   'Let us die': Author's interview with Geeta Singh in Chitrakoot, May 2012.

124   'shame on society': Barney Henderson, "UP Village Bans Love," *DNA*, July 14, 2012, http://www.dnaindia.com/india/report_up-village-bans-love-it-s-arranged-marriage-or-nothing_1714957. Accessed January 31, 2013.

124   To prevent romance: Ibid.

126   'the voluntary union of a maiden and her lover': I came across this description in Prem Chowdhry's article "Private Lives, State Intervention: Cases of Runaway Marriage in Rural North India," *Modern Asian Studies*, vol. 38, no. 1, February 2004, pp. 55–84. He borrows the quote from Thomas R. Trautman, *Dravidian Kinship* (Cambridge: Cambridge University Press, 1981), pp. 288–291.

126   Another, the Rakshasa, is described as: George Bühler, trans., *Sacred Books of the East*, vol. 25: *The Laws of Manu*, chap. 3, nos. 33 and 27, http://www.sacred-texts.com/hin/manu/manu03.htm.

128   'You told the truth, *bhai*!': Author's interview with Deepak Singh in Chitrakoot, March 2012.

138   'the consent of the guardians of the wife': Delhi Government Portal, Marriage Certificate and Registration, http://delhi.gov.in/wps/wcm/connect/DoIT/delhi+govt/community/marriage+certificate+and+registration. Accessed January 31, 2013.

138   parents often deliberately underreport: Prem Chowdhry, "Private Lives, State Intervention: Cases of Runaway Marriage in Rural North India," *Modern Asian Studies*, vol. 38, no. 1, February 2004, pp. 55–84.

CHAPTER FIVE: EVERYTHING WRONG HAS HAPPENED

140   'Will Sheelu be able to rise above this or will she break?': "Many People Gather at Sheelu's Court Hearing," *Hindustan*, December 25, 2010.

140   'The commander of the Pink Gang': Amit Tripathi, "Sampat Couldn't Meet Sheelu," *Hindustan*, December 20, 2010.

140   'The lady who fights for women's causes': Ibid.

142   'I'm Sheelu Devi': This dialogue and everything following it in this scene, including descriptions, are taken from a transcript of Sahara Samay TV footage dated December 25, 2010.

143   'He ripped it up': Author's interview with Amit Tripathi in Banda, July 2011.

145   'The legislator wants to talk to you': Author's interview with Lakhan Upadhyay in Chitrakoot, March 2012.

145   'What do you have to say on all this?': Transcript of Sahara Samay TV footage dated December 25, 2010.

145   'There's been a robbery': Transcript of this entire interview is taken from Sahara Samay TV footage dated December 25, 2010.

146   '*Bhen-ji*' – sister: The dialogue between Lakhan Upadhyay and Purushottam Naresh Dwivedi in this scene is based on author's interview with Lakhan Upadhyay in Chitrakoot, March 2012. The account of the phone call is corroborated in author's interview with Sampat Pal in Badausa, July 2011.

148   'I'm interested in fighting elections': Author's interview with Beenu Pal in Badausa, December 2011.

148   'If it's a woman's seat': Ibid.

152   twelfth most powerful person: "World's Most Powerful People: Sonia Gandhi," *Forbes*, www.forbes.com/profile/sonia-gandhi. Accessed November 7, 2012.

155   'Then she asked': This entire exchange is based on author's interviews with Sampat Pal in New Delhi, June 2012.

156   'abject' and 'a complete humiliation': Dhiraj Nayyar, "Why Congress and BJP Lost in Uttar Pradesh," *India Today*, March 7, 2012, http://indiatoday.intoday.in/story/uttar-pradesh-election-result-congress-bjp/1/176789.html. Accessed January 31, 2013.

158   'Oh! I completely forgot!': Author's interview with Sampat Pal in New Delhi, June 2012.

158   'You just threatened me': All dialogue in this scene is based on author's interview with Sampat Pal in New Delhi, June 2012.

159   'not giving her enough respect': Author's interview with Sampat Pal in Badausa, September 2010.

161   'AT THE *VIDHAYAK*'S PLACE ATROCITIES WERE COMMITTED: SHEELU': "At the *Vidhayak's* Place Atrocities Were Committed: Sheelu," *Hindustan*, December 25, 2012.

161   'POLICE HAS CLOSED EYES, EARS AND MOUTH': "Police Has Closed Eyes, Ears and Mouth," *Amar Ujala*, December 25, 2012.

161   '*VIDHAYAK-JI*, IS SHEELU YOUR DAUGHTER OR MAID-SERVANT?': "*Vidhayak-ji*, Is Sheelu Your Daughter or Maid-Servant?" *Amar Ujala*, December 25, 2012.

161   Dwivedi would later tell journalists: All quotes from Dwivedi in the following three paragraphs are from video footage of a

press conference dated December 27, 2010, and obtained from the Sahara Samay TV bureau in Banda.

162   'I've never in my life': Author's interview with Bhola Dwivedi in Atarra, December 2011.

163   'Whose job are they doing?': "How Insensitive," *Amar Ujala*, December 25, 2012.

163   'Helplessness': "Many People Gather at Sheelu's Court Hearing," *Hindustan*, December 25, 2012.

163   'HUGGING SAMPAT SHEELU SAYS: "*DIDI* HELP ME"': "Hugging Sampat Sheelu Says: '*Didi* Help Me,'" *Amar Ujala*, December 25, 2012.

163   'The scene was filled': Ibid.

163   'Sheelu has called Sampat Pal sister': Ibid.

163   'motherless child': "Many People Gather at Sheelu's Court Hearing," *Hindustan*, December 25, 2012.

164   'Why don't you change Sampat's mind?': Author's interviews with Lakhan Upadhyay in Chitrakoot, March 2012.

CHAPTER SIX: THE EXORCIST OF SHAHBAJPUR

165   Chota and Raja, joined by a few armed men: According to an official letter addressed to the police superintendent in Banda by Achchhe Lal Nishad, dated December 27, 2010, and obtained from Bhola Dwivedi.

166   'wipe out': Ibid.

166   'take him away': "On Being Threatened by Anti-Socials, Achchhe Lal Has Run Away," *Hindustan*, December 26, 2010.

166   'ACHCHHE LAL HAS BECOME A REBEL': "Achchhe Lal Has Become a Rebel," *Hindusthan*, December 28, 2010.

166   Another article in the *Hindustan*: "On Being Threatened by Anti-Socials, Acche Lal Has Run Away," *Hindustan*, December 26, 2010.

167   'They stayed for some time': Author's interview with Sampat Pal in Badausa, July 2011.

170   'Sister-in-law, your husband': Author's interview with Sampat Pal in New Delhi, June 2012.

170   'No, no! I can't': This was recounted to the author by Mehul Srivastava, a Bloomberg journalist, who heard a villager in Uttar Pradesh say this.

172   'Don't let *kairiwalli*': Author's interview with Sampat Pal in New Delhi, June 2012.

173 'Stop there!': Ibid.

173 'Don't you take a bath!': Ibid.

174 'Let them take water first': Ibid.

174 'You worship alone!': Ibid.

177 'Where does the wife of Munni Lal live?': The entire exchange between Chun Buddha and Sampat Pal is based on author's interview with Sampat Pal in New Delhi, June 2012.

183 'Do you have any spirit problems too?': Author's interview with Nisha Pal in Badausa, July 2011.

183 'My heart keeps beating faster and faster!': Ibid.

184 'She has a fever, nothing else!': Ibid.

184 'I hope Sampat Pal can help': Ibid.

184 'I have seen in the newspaper': The entire exchange between Sampat and Achchhe is based on author's interview with Sampat Pal in Badausa, July 2011, and confirmed by Achchhe Lal Nishad in an interview in Shahbajpur, July 2011.

185 'If you are here because of his daughter': Author's interview with Sampat Pal in Badausa, July 2011.

191 'Are you going to get my daughter out of jail?': Author's interview with Jai Karan Bhai in Banda, July 2011.

191 'See they have hit me here': Transcript of Sahara Samay TV footage dated December 27, 2010.

192 'To: The Police Superintendent, Banda': Reproduction of an official letter addressed to the police superintendent in Banda by Achchhe Lal Nishad, dated December 27, 2010, and obtained from Bhola Dwivedi.

194 'Could you even live': Author's interview with Amit Tripathi in Banda, December 2011.

201 'What is all this, Sampat-ji?': Author's interview with Sampat Pal in Banda, July 2011.

202 'Sampat-ji, I'm leaving': Ibid.

CHAPTER SEVEN: THE SOUND OF THE BUGLE

203 'When there were elections': Transcript of Sahara Samay TV footage dated December 28, 2010.

204 'She told her father': Transcript of Sahara Samay TV footage dated December 28, 2010.

204 'If Sheelu loved him': "Now the Game Is Changing by Putting Rajju in the Front," *Hindustan*, December 30, 2010.

205 very common for her to be subjected: Human Rights Watch,

Dignity on Trial: India's Need for Sound Standards for Conducting and Interpreting Forensic Examinations of Rape Survivors (New York: Human Rights Watch, 2010), p. 31, http://www.hrw.org/reports/2010/09/06/dignity-trial-0. Accessed January 31, 2013.

205   'narrow', 'roomy', 'lax': Ibid., p. 28.

205   'Vagina admitted one finger with difficulty': Ibid., p. 41.

205   'Vagina admitted two fingers tightly': Ibid.

206   'rape cases': Ibid., p. 17.

206   numerous High Court and Supreme Court judgements: Ibid.

206   In a 2009 court case: Ibid., p. 34.

206   In 2008, the High Court in Bihar: Ibid.

207   'internal pains': "When Will Sheelu's Story Come to an End?" *Hindustan*, December 22, 2010.

207   doctor defended herself: "After 6 Days They Remembered to Do Sheelu's Medical," *Hindustan*, December 22, 2010.

207   they pressured Sheelu: Sheelu repeated these claims to the *Times of India* saying, 'The lady doctors kept saying I was not raped and that I was lying.' "Senior Cops Threatening Me: Banda Woman Jail Warden," *Times of India*, January 17, 2011.

207   'unco-operative': Human Rights Watch, *Dignity on Trial: India's Need for Sound Standards for Conducting and Interpreting Forensic Examinations of Rape Survivors* (New York: Human Rights Watch, 2010), p. 44, http://www.hrw.org/reports/2010/09/06/dignity-trial-0. Accessed January 31, 2013.

208   'something to hide': Ibid., p. 31.

208   officers allegedly attempted to pressure: Author's interviews with Sheelu Nishad. The bribe claim was repeated in other media interviews: "Senior Cops Threatening Me: Banda Woman Jail Warden," *Times of India*, January 17, 2011; "Sheelu Did Not Meet Rajju, Met Her Brother," *Amar Ujala*, January 3, 2011.

208   'You take this money': Author's interview with Sheelu Nishad in Shahbajpur, May 2011.

208   'Don't trap *Vidhayak-ji*': Ibid.

208   When Vivek Singh arrived: Vivek Singh's inspection of the logbook and his editing of its entries were recounted to me by Tirath Pal, who saw the book in Badausa, March 2012, and *Hindustan* journalist Amit Tripathi in Banda, July 2011.

209   'cover-up': "Ritu Joshi Was Not Able to Meet Sheelu," *Hindustan*, December 31, 2010.

209   'LEGISLATOR NAMED IN SHEELU RAPE CASE': "Legislator Named in Sheelu Rape Case," *Hindustan*, January 1, 2011.

210   Unable to ignore the news: "Banda Rape: Maya Orders CB–CID Probe," *Indian Express*, January 2, 2011, http://www.indian express.com/news/banda-rape-maya-orders-cbcid-probe/732048. Accessed January 31, 2013.

210   'the charges of sexual assault': "Maya Fires MLA for Raping a Dalit Girl," *India Today*, January 2, 2011, http://indiatoday.in today.in/story/maya-fires-mla-for-raping-a-dalit-girl/1/125388 .html. Accessed November 14, 2012.

210   'I am ready to be examined': "Banda Rape: Now BSP MLA Says He's Impotent," *Rediff.com*, January 4, 2011, http://www .rediff.com/news/report/banda-rape-now-bsp-mla-says-hes-impotent/20110104.htm. Accessed November 14, 2012.

210   'My house has two rooms': "He Is Physically Incapable of Raping: Wife," *Indian Express*, January 21, 2011, http://www .indianexpress.com/election-news/he-is-physically-incapable-of-raping-wife/740325. Accessed November 14, 2012.

210   'political vendetta': Pervez Iqbal Siddiqui, "Banda Rape Case: Quite a Few Heads May Roll," *Times of India*, January 18, 2011, http://articles.timesofindia.indiatimes.com/2011-01-18/luck now/28371440_1_cb-cid-banda-burglary-case. Accessed January 31, 2013.

213   caste allegiances play an important role: For more on this, see Kanchan Chandra, *Why Ethnic Parties Succeed: Patronage and Ethnic Head Counts in India* (Cambridge: Cambridge University Press, 2004).

215   Nishad had, in fact, numerous charges pending: Based on affidavits published by the National Election Watch and the Association for Democratic Reforms: Vishambhar Prasad (Criminal & Asset Declaration), in "About 47% of the MLAs in Uttar Pradesh Assembly 2012 Have Self Declared Criminal Cases against Them," http://myneta.info/up2007/candidate.php?candidate_id= 595. Accessed November 2012.

215   'One politician has already raped': Author's interview with Sampat Pal in Chitrakoot, March 2012.

215   'Sheelu is from my same caste': Ibid.

216   'Sampat, this girl does not respect her father': Ibid.

216   'Are you disappointed?': Ibid.

216   'When the injustice was done to Sheelu': "Sheelu's Story Has Turned into a Political Game," *Hindustan*, January 5, 2011.

217   'small case': Author's interview with Geeta Singh in Chitrakoot, July 2011.

224 'I'm not half as muddied as Dwivedi's conscience!': Author's interview with Geeta Singh in Atarra, July 2011.

225 'Do not allow an innocent daughter': Author's interview with Mitu Devi, Pink Gang district commander for Banda, in Banda, March 2012.

230 'Sister, I have also been wronged': Author's interviews with Sampat Pal in Chitrakoot, April 2012, and Mitu Devi in Banda, April 2012.

231 'We're not going anywhere!': Ibid.

231 'Have some mercy on me!': Ibid.

231 'It's not my fault': Ibid.

CHAPTER EIGHT: THE SCRAMBLE FOR SHEELU

233 her fifty-fifth birthday: "Mayawati Doles Out Rs 4,000 Cr Projects on 55th Birthday," *Economic Times*, January 25, 2011, http://articles.economictimes.indiatimes.com/2011-01-15/news/28423934_1_dalits-pradesh-chief-minister-mayawati-birthday. Accessed January 31, 2013.

233 'in the interest of the people': Ibid.

233 'Human Welfare Day': Ibid.

233 'to the poor and downtrodden': Deepak Gidwani, "Court Order Spoils Mayawati's Birthday," *DNA*, January 16, 2011, http://www.dnaindia.com/india/report_court-order-spoils-mayawati-s-birthday_1495087. Accessed November 16, 2012.

233 Several government agencies: "For Maya's Birthday, Govt Agencies Work Overtime to Light Up Lucknow," *Indian Express*, January 10, 2011, http://www.indianexpress.com/news/for-mayas-birthday-govt-agencies-work-overtime-to-light-up-lucknow/735493/. Accessed November 16, 2011.

234 'refused to pay donations': "Maya Orders Stoppage to Collecting B'day Fund," *IBNLive*, August 29 2008, http://ibnlive.in.com/news/stop-collecting-birthday-fund-mayawati-tells-partymen/100133-37.html?from=rssfeed. Accessed January 31, 2013.

234 'the practice of fund collection': Ibid.

235 Dwivedi had raped Sheelu: "Preliminary Inquiry Finds BSP MLA Raped Banda Teenager," *Mid-Day*, January 11, 2011, http://www.mid-day.com/news/2011/jan/110111-preliminary-inquiry-BSP-MLA-Purushottam-Naresh-Dwivedi-raped-Banda-teenager.htm. Accessed November 16, 2012.

235 court ordered Dwivedi's arrest: "MLA Rape Case: HC, Not

Maya, Ordered Victim's Release," *Reddif.com*, January 15, 2011, http://www.rediff.com/news/report/mla-rape-case-hc-not-maya-ordered-victims-release/20110115.htm. Accessed January 31, 2013.

235 'take the revenge': Transcript from Sahara Samay TV footage dated January 13, 2011.

235 'got him stuck': Ibid.

235 'Mayawati's birthday expenditure': "Shadow over Mayawati's Birthday Celebrations," NDTV, January 15, 2011, http://www.ndtv.com/video/player/news/shadow-over-mayawatis-birthday-celebrations/187774. Accessed January 31, 2013.

235 he announced that Mayawati had ordered Sheelu's release: "MLA Rape Case: HC, Not Maya, Ordered Victim's Release," *Reddif.com*, January 15, 2011, http://www.rediff.com/news/report/mla-rape-case-hc-not-maya-ordered-victims-release/20110115.htm. Accessed January 31, 2013.

235 'No one will be allowed': "Mayawati Orders Release of Banda Rape Victim," *Outlook*, January 15, 2011, http://news.outlookindia.com/items.aspx?artid=708494. Accessed January 31, 2013.

236 'claimed that the poor girl's release': "MLA Rape Case: HC, Not Maya, Ordered Victim's Release," *Reddif.com*, January 15, 2011, http://www.rediff.com/news/report/mla-rape-case-hc-not-maya-ordered-victims-release/20110115.htm. Accessed January 31, 2013.

237 On the day of Sheelu's release: Descriptions of the day are based on footage obtained from Sahara Samay TV, dated January 15, 2011.

237 'The officer who is just is our brother': Footage obtained from Sahara Samay TV, dated January 15, 2011.

239 'The Samajwadi Party protested': Transcript of statement is from Sahara Samay TV footage dated January 15, 2011.

241 On 24 January, Rajju would appear: Deepak Gidwani, "Banda Rape Case: Minor's 'Husband' Surfaces," *DNA*, January 25, 2011, http://www.dnaindia.com/india/report_banda-rape-case-minor-s-husband-surfaces_1498770. Accessed January 31, 2013.

242 'What is Sheelu saying?': All quotations from journalists are taken from transcripts of Sahara Samay TV footage dated January 15, 2011.

243 it was reported: "Jail Staff Knew of Banda Rape," *Indian Express*, January 8, 2011, http://www.indianexpress.com/news/jail-staff-knew-of-banda-rape/734962. Accessed January 31, 2013.

243 Begum and another member: Manish Sahu, "Jail Staff Knew of

Banda Rape," *Indian Express*, January 8, 2011, http://www.indian express.com/news/jail-staff-knew-of-banda-rape/734962. Accessed January 31, 2013.

243   Begum defended herself in an interview: "UP Govt to Probe Jailor's Harassment Charges," *IBNLive*, January 17, 2011, http://ibnlive.in.com/news/up-govt-to-probe-jailors-harrassment-charges/140689-3.html. Accessed November 16, 2012.

245   'Sheelu, wave your hand': All quotations from journalists are taken from transcripts of Sahara Samay TV footage dated January 15, 2011.

247   '*Didi!*': Author's interviews with Sampat Pal.

247   'What will you do if you don't get justice?': All quotations from journalists are taken from transcripts of Sahara Samay TV footage dated January 17, 2011.

249   tidal wave of Samajwadi Party members: All quotations and descriptions in this scene are taken from transcripts of Sahara Samay TV footage dated January 18, 2011.

253   'staked his political future': "Rahul Gandhi's Charisma Fails in Uttar Pradesh," *Mint*, March 6, 2012, http://www.livemint.com/Politics/XCEeGGpp38J40eiiI6kinK/Rahul-Gandhi8217s-charisma-fails-in-Uttar-Pradesh.html. Accessed February 8, 2013.

253   'Are you Sheelu? I'm Rahul, from Delhi': Dialogue is based on author's interviews with Sheelu Nishad.

254   two-hundred-thousand-rupee cheque: Based on author's interview with Sheelu Nishad in Banda, March 2012.

256   'Rahul-ji, you don't have time for me to explain': Author's interview with Sampat Pal in New Delhi, June 2012.

EPILOGUE

259   Later in the year: "Rape Case: CBI Registers Case against BSP MLA," *Times of India*, September 22, 2011, http://articles.timesofindia.indiatimes.com/2011-09-22/india/30188660_1_cbi-registers-case-dalit-girl-banda. Accessed February 7, 2013.

261   The next month, Sheelu did attempt suicide: Sahara Samay TV footage dated April 6, 2012.

262   over twenty years since the party had won: The last Indian National Congress candidate to win Manikpur was Siya Dulari in 1989. "Manikpur," *IBNLive*, http://ibnlive.in.com/elections2012/constituency/uttar-pradesh/manikpur.html. Accessed November 21, 2012.

262 'shoot-outs': Aman Sethi, "Rule of the Outlaw," *Frontline*, vol. 22, no. 26, December 17–30, 2005, http://www.hindu.com/thehindu/thscrip/print.pl?file=20051230004301700.htm&date=fl2226/&prd=fline. Accessed February 13, 2013.

263 'The Return of Goonda Raj in Uttar Pradesh?': *Headlines Today*, July 23, 2012, http://headlinestoday.intoday.in/headlines_today/programme/goonda-raj-in-akhilesh-up-rape-police-station/1/209873.html. Accessed November 21, 2012.

263 One seven-year-old was reportedly killed: "Dear Akhilesh, Your Law and Order Problem Begins Now," *Firstpost.com*, March 6, 2012, http://www.firstpost.com/politics/dear-akhilesh-your-law-and-order-problem-begins-now-236650.html. Accessed November 21, 2012.

264 man called Vijay Mishra: "Prison Is Where UP Politicians Go for a Holiday," *Sunday Guardian*, June 24, 2012, http://www.sunday-guardian.com/news/prison-is-where-up-politicians-go-for-a-holiday. Accessed November 21, 2012.

264 Rape is now the fastest-growing crime: "Crime in India: Statistics," National Crime Records Bureau, Ministry of Home Affairs, 2011.

264 In the past four decades: Ibid.

264 Conviction rates, however, are dropping: Ibid.

264 similar story is found in domestic violence: Ibid.

264 Across the board, crimes against women have been increasing: Ibid.